Paul ~
For new *heights*
of inspiration. Merry
Christmas !
                I love you,
                    Lynne
                    1990

HIMALAYAS

Title page: *Ladakhis gazing at the granite mountains north of Leh.*

Endpapers: *The syllables of the traditional Sanskrit phrase pictured here carved into rock in Tibetan letters read "OM VAJRA SATTO SA-MAYA." They are directed at Vajra-sattava, one of the manifestations of the mystic Buddha, and invoke his power to forgive sins and edify the mind. This phrase is evidence of the practice of Mahayana Buddhism in the Himalayas.*

Dust jacket: *The Lingkor of the Sera monastery near Lhasa.*

Text:
Blanche Christine Olschak
Augusto Gansser
Andreas Gruschke
Concept and Design:
Emil M. Bührer

HIMALAYAS

GROWING MOUNTAINS, LIVING MYTHS, MIGRATING PEOPLES

Facts On File®

New York • Oxford

**Library of Congress Cataloging-
-in-Publication Data**

Olschak, Blanche Christine.
 [Himalaya. English]
 Himalayas / text by Blanche
Christine Olschak, Augusto Gansser,
Andreas Gruschke;
 designed by Emil M. Bührer.
 p. cm.
 Translation of: Himalaya.
 Bibliography: p.
 Includes index.
 ISBN 0-8160-1994-0
 1. Himalaya Mountains. I. Gansser.
 Augusto. 1910 –
II. Gruschke, Andreas. III. Title.
DS485.H604713 1988
954--dc19   88-7204 CIP

General direction:
Motovun (Switzerland) Co-Publishing
Company Ltd., Lucerne

Editorial advisors:
Ursula Markus-Gansser
Michael Henss
Tsenshab Rimpoche

Translation from German:
Katherine Badger
Jan. A. Deleay
Joseph Nykiel

© 1987 by
Motovun (Switzerland)
Co-Publishing Company Ltd.,
Lucerne

© 1987 for the English-language
edition by Facts On File Publications,
New York

Lithography:
Lanarepro, Lana / Meran
Printing and binding:
Rotolito Lombarda,
Pioltello / Milan
Typesetting:
F. X. Stückle, Ettenheim, Germany

Dust jacket:
Front picture: Augusto Gansser
Back side picture: Sepp Friedhuber
map. p. 24/25:
carta, Lüthi + Ramseier, Berne,
Switzerland

Printed in Italy

CONTENTS

The Himalayas p. 6

The Growing Mountains, Living Myths and Wandering People are introduced by B. C. Olschak and A. Gansser.

How the Himalayas came into Being p. 12

The Ice Ages and Their Lakes. Flora and Fauna in the Growing Mountains. The Birth of Mount Kailas. Map: Himalayas and Karakorum (p. 24/25). Geological Map (p. 30/31).*

The Great Rivers of the Kailas p. 38
The Yarlung Tsangpo p. 40

The Exploration of the Source. Lhasa. Through the Namche Barwa Gorge to Assam. The Eastern Himalayas. Sikkim. The Kingdom of Bhutan.*

The Indus p. 80

From the Sources to Ladakh and Zanskar. Along the Old Caravan Route past the Nanga Parbat toward the South.*

The Sutlej p. 122

The Cave Town on the Shib Chu. The Old Kingdom of Guge. The Missionaries of the 17th and 18th Centuries: Andrade and Desideri. The Legendary Sarasvati.*

Karnali and Ganges p. 134

The Little-Known West of Nepal. The Three Headwaters of the Holy Ganges: Alaknanda, Mandakini, Bhagirathi. The Exploration of the Ganges' Sources.*

*In Sanskrit, the ancient Indian language,
the word for snow is* hima *and the abode of a person who
lives there is called* alaya.
Thus, the Himalayas are the "Abode of Snow."

The Authors

*   *Augusto Gansser,*
**   *Blanche Christine Olschak,*
*** *Andreas Gruschke.*

*One part of the captions was
written by Michael Henss. We
thank him and Ursula Markus-
Gansser for their assistance with
the picture selection and completion of the book.*

Picture credit

*Aberham/IFA: 29, 37, 85, 90, 92 (1st row
2nd and 4th photographs; 2nd row, 2 photographs, 93 (left), 94/95, 96 (left), 97 (right),
98 (left), 100 (left), 101, 105, 166, 171 (top),
174 (1st row left), 177, 180 (far left), 197,
212 (left), 214, 234/235, 240, 261, 262, 263
(left), 269 (bottom), 270 (right), 271 (right),
276/277*
Victor Chan: 78/79
G. W. Essen: 58/59
Everts/IFA: 209, 215, 221
Fiedler/IFA: 92 (1st row, 3rd photograph), 198
*Sepp Friedhuber: 137, 138, 139, 140 (2), 141
(2), 144, 145, 146 (2), 147 (2), 148, 149, 255*
Johannes Frischknecht: 157 (bottom left)
*A. Gansser: 6/7, 9, 13, 16 (3), 28, 34, 35
(3), 36, 42, 44, 45, 46/47, 53, 54, 55, 56
(left), 57, 62/63, 68, 75, 76, 81, 99, 102,
103, 104, 106, 107, 110/111, 112, 113,
118, 119, 120/121, 172, 173, 174 (2nd row
left), 179 (bottom), 184, 187, 199, 201,
203, 204, 205, 207, 211, 212 (right), 220,
242 (2), 244, 249, 253, 263 (right), 270
(left) 271 (left). Maps: 14, 15, 38/39, 41,
69, 82, 86, 108, 124, 135, 224, 266.
Illustrations: 18, 19, 30/31, 118, 196, 210,
216, 217, 270, 271*
A. Gruschke: 264 (left)
Heinrich Harrer: 246 (bottom)
*Michael Henss: 2/3, 40, 49, 60 (top), 61, 64,
65, 66/67, 80, 87, 89, 96/97, 98 (right),
100 (right), 117, 122, 124, 128, 129, 131,
132/133, 134/135, 152/153, 156 (5), 157
(5), 164, 165, 168, 174 (2nd row right), 177
(top) 178, 180 (bottom right and far right),
185, 190/191, 192, 219, 247*
André Herold: 123, 126, 127, 130, 194, 195
Peter Herrle (Silva Verlag): 142/143
Marlis Isler: 158, 196 (top), 208 (left)
*Jugoslovenska Revija: 43, 50, 51, 52 (3), 56
(right), 60 (left), 70, 71, 72, 73, 74, 179 (2),
218 (2), 245, 260, 268/269*
Giovanni Kappenberger: 256/257
Janusz Kurczab (Silva Verlag): 109
*Lennart Lindquist: 92 (1st row, far left),
176 (left), 254*
*Ursula Markus: 8, 11, 17, 77, 116, 159,
160 (right), 161 (left), 162 (2), 163, 167,
169, 174 (1st row, center), 175 (right), 176
(right), 180 (4), 181, 182 (2), 183 (2), 202,
206, 213, 217, 241, 243, 258, 259, 264
(right), 267, endpapers*
Martinelli (Touring Club Italiano): 150/151
NASA: 20/21, 22/23, 48, 83, 86/87, 108, 125
NHK: 226
Romolo Nottaris: 32, 33
*B. C. Olschak: 84, 88, 129 (top), 134, 154,
160, 161, 188 (H. Hoffmann), 189, 200,
208, 222, 226, 246, 248, 250*
Schmidt/IFA: 251 (2), 252
*Thiele/IFA: 93 (right), 155, 174 (1st row
right), 175 (left), 272/273*
Herbert Tichy: 254 (right)
*Eric Valli/Diane Summers: 26/27, 170,
170/171, 186, 223, 225, 227, 228, 229,
230/231, 232, 233, 236 (2), 237, 238/239,
265, 269 (top), 274/275*
Edward H. Worcester: 193
Rudolf Wurzer: 114/115

Between Myth and Reality   p. 152

The Variety and Unity of Religious Traditions. The Rainbow Circle. Lightning in the Hands of the Gods. When the Waters Receded. The Ancient Indian Noah-Manu. The God and the Daughter of the Himalayas.**

Holy Mountains, Lakes and Rivers   p. 188

Journey around Sacred Mount Kailas.* The Unapproachable Mistress of the Mountain of the Gods. The Ancient Home of the Gods and Men.**

Variety of Himalayan Buildings   p. 208

Between Caste Walls and Religious Monuments.* The First Missionaries and Founders of the Stupas and Temples. The "Leonardo da Vinci" of the Himalayas.**

In the Gorges and the Heights   p. 222

Faces along the Karakorum Road.** On the Backs of the Sherpas: The Ascent of Chomolungma (Everest), Kanchenjunga, Machapuchare, Nanga Parbat.* The Saga of Yeti.*

The Blessing of Earth   p. 258

Farmlands and Meadows in the Highlands.* The Divine Monkey and the Heavenly Kings. Holy Grain, Alcohol and Butter Tea. Ancient Trade Goods and the Treasures of the Earth.**

Appendix   p. 278

Portraits of the Himalaya Countries: Bhutan, Nepal, Mustang, Tibet, the N.E.F.A., Sikkim, Indian Federal States and Areas of Pakistan, and Ladakh.*** Index.

THE HIMALAYAS

"In a hundred ages of the gods, I could not tell thee of the glories of the Himalaya." Thus does Indian tradition call down to us from the Puranas, the "Ancient Stories." These texts consist of myths, legends and stories passed down by word of mouth throughout the millennia and tell of the beginning of the universe, its being, passing away and rebirth; of the genealogies of the "gods," the *devas*, shining like stars; and of man. These words, not written down until about 2500 years ago, have preserved views of cosmic and earth history that we have lost, but that still survive in the countries of their origin and dissemination . . .

GROWING MOUNTAINS, LIVING MYTHS, MIGRATING PEOPLES

Modern science can explain how the Himalayas, the world's youngest mountains, were formed. We believe we have discovered evidence of the relative land movement between India and Eurasia and also of the collision, the mighty "crash" of the original continents that caused the formation of the young mountains. In an era out of the geological past, small primitive horses galloped and rhinos wandered over wide tropical river plains where now the Himalayas rise. The animals drifted from the south to the north and found refuge in low hills covered with primeval forests. Those hills were the Himalayas in that age . . . Confirmation can be found in the fossilized remains of both the rhinos and primitive horses buried in the same layers of rock. Today, they rest about 5000 meters [16,500 feet] above sea level in an area where wild rivers have eaten deep gorges into the layers, which are still horizontal. Here in the western Himalayas 1000 and more years ago was located the kingdom of Guge, whose inhabitants could only reach their palaces and monasteries via 5000-meter-high [16,500-foot-high] passes. They were surrounded by the wild glacier-covered peaks of the Himalayas, which grew from low hills to the highest mountains in the world over millions of years in the earth's history and, indeed, are still rising today.

Yet aren't these tales which were known long before the rational research of the present? Perhaps they are veiled in the great myths about the earth's origin – myths that by no means have all been interpreted, with their allusions to the Tethyan Ocean, which once separated the original continents and covered the Himalayan area. Or are they hidden in the sagas about a great flood?

The old texts in which we could seek these reminders were transmitted orally in an unbroken chain (a fact that must be emphasized) from generation to generation and even today are equally acknowledged in the Hindu

and pre-Buddhist Jain traditions. They were also adopted by the Buddhists; Western historians initially smiled condescendingly at them and dismissed them as fantastic exaggerations. Yet 100 years ago it was already known that these traditions were also maintained by the learned lamas in Tibet and that they still survived in folklore.

The British scholar L. A. Waddell thus thoughtfully observed in 1894 that "... many of these fantastic beliefs with their idolized heroes and worship of nature are in reality the fossilized remains of the archaic beliefs of our own Indo-European ancestors."

What was it, then, that seemed madness to scholars from the West at that time? It was the story of the origin of the universe, the earth and mankind, the counting in hundreds of thousands, millions and finally hundreds of millions of years, which appeared as strange to them as it seems so strangely correct to us now.

One ancient Indian eon, a *kalpa* (adopted into the Tibetan language from the Sanskrit), lasts 8,640,000,000 years. In mythological language this is one night and one day in the life of Brahma, the god of creation; we have now reached exactly the halfway point, i. e. 4,320,000,000 years. This concept can be found in the old texts. The classic reference works of Hindu

Nam Tso, or "Sky Lake," 4720 meters [15,576 feet], the highest and largest lake in the world at this altitude, is located north of the Nyenchen Tangla range. These mountains include peaks over 7,000 meters [23,100 feet] high that have not yet been climbed by man. A side arm of the Transhimalayas, the Nyenchen Tangla atypically stretches toward the northeast; the fault zones on its edges confirm the youthful age of the mountains.

mythology confirm that this system was already established at the time of the Great Epic, the Mahabharata (about 1500 B.C. according to Indian tradition), and even then was based on much more ancient sources. The origin of the world is also depicted graphically in the drawings of the "Cosmic Mandala," which illustrates the beginning of our world system, specifically designated as merely one among millions. Not only is the first creation dated precisely, but the world ages, the *yuga*, are also mentioned; four of them are listed and their durations apparently measured in "years of the gods." Each of these years corresponds to 360 human years. A *manayuga* lasts 4,320,000 years. It is also called *manuantara*, i.e., "period of a *manu*," or a "primordial ancestor." According to this tradition, we are now in the "Black Age," Kali Yuga, which is supposed to last 432,000 years, having begun about 3102 B.C.

This cosmology describing the continual cycle of becoming, being and

Serenity of the Mind

"Serenity of the Mind is a means by which to perceive the Truth, for to achieve this perception a Mind that has been agitated and confused must become pure and serene."
These words are taken from Buddha's Life *by Buston (1290 – 1364), the great Tibetan philosopher and historian of religion.*

"Serenity of the Mind" is reflected in the faces of the Himalayas' inhabitants. It shines from the countenance of the Bhutanese boy as well as in the features of the old man on the right, who has spent his entire life under severe natural conditions in one of the highest settlements on earth: Thanza, located in the far north of Bhutan at 4100 meters [13,530 feet].

disintegration leading to a new beginning is emphasized in all the old texts, as are the instability and transcience of all factors of existence which are void of absolute eternity. Buddhist writings on transcendental wisdom, in which one would hardly expect to encounter metaphysical ideas, also underscore the transcience and transformability of the tiniest particles, smaller even than the smallest grain of sand. In these writings the particles are described as miniature world systems, analogous to atoms yet also corresponding to the "Cosmic Mandala."

To discuss these views in detail would exceed the scope of this book. Nevertheless, after relating the extensive geological history of the Hima-

The Cosmic Mandala

In the ancient texts, our world system is explicitly designated as only one among millions. Void of color and shape in infinite space, the Spiral of Primary Movement forms like a wild circle of wind, the basis of the creation of matter. The movements are depicted by rings in rainbow colors. These rings progress in development to aggregate states (of the elements): yellow and square symbolize the solid earth; white or light blue, fluid and water; flaming red stands for changeability and fire; green for gaseousness and air; blue for formless ether. This is a microcosmic and macrocosmic pattern, repeated in stupa design, and its numerous variations always suggest the impermanence of all factors of existence and the lack of absolute eternity. The analogy between ancient writings and scientific findings about the earth's age (over 4 billion years) is quite curious.

Facing page: *This powerful work, which appeals to us as if it were a picture from our own atomic age, is the "Cosmic Mandala." It flanks the entrance gate to the main temple together with the wheel of life (here as a fresco in Paro Dzong in western Bhutan). It is not a meditation mandala but a flaming graphic means of explaining the origins of the universe.*

laya mountains and the "Roof of the World," we wish to show in word and picture how popular mythological tales of the Himalayan peoples strangely correspond to present knowledge obtained through research. We hope to convey the fascination of these parallels, starting with the ammonites (the index fossils of the geologic Middle Ages) that once populated the great Tethyan Ocean, which formed the deposits that make up the Himalayan rocks, and concluding with the origins of the landscape and mountains as they are mirrored in the vivid myths. They tell us of the divine genealogy of the first kings as well as the descent from an ape and the introduction of farming. We will also read of the Indian Noah, who tied his ark to a cliff in the Himalayas, and of the first wanderers, who carried material and spiritual goods from one side of the mountain range to the other, trading and preaching on their way. Most interesting of all is the discovery that the old myths have survived and are brought back to life in rites and mystery plays over and over again. This testifies to mankind's need to seek, know and ritually re-enact his very beginnings. We can now grasp this inner urge to know and understand the first beginning (an urge we also experience) through the most up-to-date studies and in the oldest traditions. As Mircea Eliade, an expert in the comparative history of religion, has said, "There are no sacred scripts, no mysteries or portrayals of the Most Holy, that are not also 'historical' in the broadest sense of the word as of the time of their first conception."

The first wanderers, also, gazed trembling with respect up to the glacier-covered peaks so near to the sky. Being convinced since the beginning of time that all good things came from heaven, they worshiped these mountains as paradises of the gods, as the homes of the "gods" who shone in the heavens, the devis and devas, who according to their name are "Brightly Shining Like Stars."

The mountains have remained holy to these peoples. Surrounded and protected by their peaks, the people have retained a "Serenity of the Mind" that is reflected in their faces. Whoever has been lucky enough to see the Himalayas will remember the words of Kalidasa, who "may be considered as the brightest star in the firmament of Hindu poetry": "In the northern part there is a mighty mountain, *Himalaya* by name – the abode of perpetual snow – fittingly called the Lord of Mountains, animated by Divinity as its soul and internal spirit, or, in other words, Divinity Incarnate. Spanning the wide land, from the scale of the earth sea, he stands as if it were, like the eastern to the eastern."

BLANCHE CHRISTINE OLSCHAK AND AUGUSTO GANSSER

10

This picture of the first origin of a world system is also appropriate for our atomic age. As a temple fresco, it reminds us of the becoming, being and vanishing of all worlds and of the impermanence of all existing things:

from the first movement, the cosmic Primary Sound (the spiral), which leads to being and from there on to an inevitable passing away, out of which, however, a new beginning arises.

How the Himalayas Came into Being

A famous English mountain climber was once asked, "Why do you want to climb Everest?" His laconic, and now equally famous, answer was, "Because it's there." Well, it's there all right, and so is the whole Himalayan range. But why it's there and why the range has the form that we see today are questions for geologists.

Legends surround the Himalayas; the highest mountain range on earth, which, with the Transhimalayas in the north and the Karakorum in the northwest, is not only the most impressive of all the mountain chains but also the youngest. As a range of the alpinotype, i.e., formed between two continents, the Himalayas differs from ranges of Andean formation (formed at the edge of a continent). The chain extends almost 3,000 kilometers (1,800 miles) from its eastern limit at the Mishmi-Naga and the Burmese chain and ends in the west in the north-south chain east of Kabul.

The mountains that so impress us today are, geologically speaking, very young. In fact their formation is not yet complete, as evidenced by the uplifting process that is still going on (measurable at about one centimeter [0.4 inch] per year, though this differs from time to time and place to place), and the lateral contraction that is still in process, producing earthquakes as it occurs. There is little doubt today that the Himalayas, Transhimalayas and Karakorum were formed as a result of a collision between the northward-moving Indian subcontinent and the very complicated southern edge of Eurasia.

According to geological research, India once belonged to the former continent called Gondwanaland and was separated from the Eurasian continent by a vast sea known as the Tethyan Ocean. Even today, opinions vary as to the extent and depth of the Tethyan Ocean. Geophysical measurements and geological findings are by no means easy to combine into a single conclusion.

What science is sure of today is that most of the oceans of the world are expanding, and that this expansion occurs along the oceanic ridges, where deep oceanic crust and mantle material comes up, spreads across the ocean floor and travels toward the continental shelves, at a rate varying between 1 (0.4) and 10 centimeters (4 inches) per year. Deep-sea sediment builds up on the ocean floor and moves, as if on a conveyor belt, also toward the continents. By means of borings it has been possible to determine the rate of movement and estimate the age of the oceans, which at a maximum of 180 million years is very young in comparison to the 4.6 billion years accepted as the age of the earth itself. Geology becomes complicated where the expanding ocean floor and its sediment meet the edge of a continent. The ocean floor and continents are also known as the oceanic and continental plates, and the relationship between these two plates is called plate tectonics. The term *"plate"* itself often leads to the supposition that we are dealing with rigid geological formations. On average the oceanic plate is 10 kilometers (6 miles) thick and the continental plate 35 kilometers (21 miles) thick. Compared to the lateral dimensions involved – often thousands of kilometers – these are in fact thin skins. The interplay of forces during the forcing up of a mountain range is still not very well understood. Under mountain ranges the crust is more massive; below the Himalayas, for example, the crust is up to 75 kilometers (45 miles) thick. Similar thicknesses have also been measured under Tibet.

Facing page: *Unknown, unnamed and unclimbed: a 7,000 meter (23,100 foot) peak in Bhutan. The extensive moraine marks the glacier's last advance, 150 years ago.*

Compared with the Atlantic and Pacific oceans, the Indian Ocean is much more complicated, containing the remains of old continental blocks, e.g., the Seychelles. Measurements of the spreading ridges are therefore inaccurate, and this results in inaccuracy in measuring the rate at which India is moving northward, which in turn is reflected in the phases of Himalayan buildup.

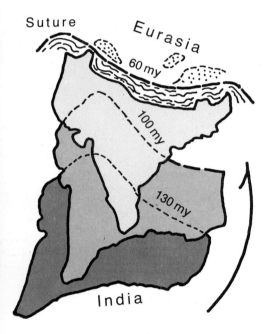

Sketch of the northward drift of India toward Eurasia up to the collision. The dates involved are still very much in dispute. (my = million years)

Where the two plates meet, the oceanic plate is often forced steeply down below the continent, in a process known as subduction. The oceanic material that is forced downward contains a considerable amount of water in its surface layers, which lowers its melting point; in the depths it is heated so much that it melts and rises again, mixed with continental crust, as huge granite masses (plutones) into the upper crust of the continental shelf. On the surface this process leads to the formation of volcanoes. Subduction is also responsible for mountain ranges that run parallel to the coastline, such as the Andes in South America, with its granite masses and volcanoes. It is known today that the Himalayas and their precursors, the Transhimalayas, went through a similar phase before the collision. Identical granite plutones and vulcanites of the same age are definite proof.

In 1851, the Geological Survey of India, a scientific society for research into that country and one of the earliest geologic surveys, was formed, and the golden age of Himalayan research began, largely through the activities of European geologists in the area. Even without the aid of modern forms of transport, such as jeeps and helicopters, these pioneers managed to study remote and inaccessible areas. In those days there was plenty of time for exploring, or so it seemed; but even during the 19th century some regions of the Himalayas were forbidden to foreigners, and geological research had to be carried out by trained natives (Pundits) or by Europeans dressed to look like natives. The results of these early geological investigations were mostly of a stratigraphical nature (studies of strata based on fossil findings). Recognition of the complicated structures involved came only much later, despite the fact that important overthrusts (nappes) were discovered in the Himalayas long before such phenomena were detected in the Alps.

It was not until 1936 that geologists became convinced of the large overthrusts in the Himalayas, as a result of the work of the geologists J. B. Auden, A. Heim and A. Gansser in the central Himalayas. Since there is no doubt that the collision of India with Eurasia played the central role in the development of the Himalayas, the Transhimalayas and the Karakorum, we should really speak of pre- and postcollision periods.

The precollision period began extremely early, in fact at the time when the oldest rocks of the northern Indian shield were formed, some 2 billion years ago. We know today that the oldest rock material in the Himalayas in the cores of the great crystalline thrust-sheets corresponds to that in the original mountains in the north of the Indian continent, with the same geological history that led to the formation of the striking north-south Aravalli chains of north India. One billion years ago these formed a high range similar to the Himalayas. After this phase a long period of sedimentation occurred, and then in the Cretaceous period, about 130 million years ago, the northward movement of India began, compressing the ocean basin more and more. The steep downward thrust (subduction) of the deep-sea ocean crust under the southern edge of the complicated Asian continent caused the crustal material to melt, and this was followed by the upthrust of granite into the already existing Transhimalayas. With the actual collision, at the beginning of the Tertiary period some 60 million years ago, the precollision phase came to an end.

The postcollision phase begins the actual formation of the Himalayas and, as already mentioned, this is still going on. As a result of the collision itself and the related contraction of the Tethyan Ocean, all the rocks of this area, from the mountains of north India to the oceanic crust, and the deep-sea sediment of Jurassic and Cretaceous ages joined in the formation of the Himalayas. During the collision, both oceanic crustal material and deep-sea sediment were forced upward (obduction). The corresponding types of rocks, ophiolites (magmatic and green volcanic composition), are characteristic of the important plate interface known as the Indus-Yarlung suture zone. The river Indus in the west and the Yarlung-Tsangpo (Brahmaputra) in the east follow this alignment.

After 60 million years the Indian and Asian plates became closely welded together, along the suture zone. The northward movement of India continued but at a slower rate (2 to 3 centimeters [0.8 to 1.2 inches] per year), as shown by geophysical data taken in the Indian Ocean.

The compensation for this northward movement must be within the continental crust: in 1985, north of the suture, in the region of Tibet (south Eurasion plate), a joint Geotraverse of the Royal Society and the Academia Sinica (Chinese Academy) discovered unexpectedly intensive folds and upthrusts, which would also explain the unusual thickness of crust under Tibet (up to 75 kilometers [45 miles]) and the subsequent uplift.

South of the Indus-Yarlung suture, marked movements have formed the actual Himalayas. In the north the sediments of the Tethyan Himalayas are strongly folded. South of this is the High Himalaya region, with the highest peaks. Here we find the old crystalline, the oldest core material in the whole Himalayas, the actual basis of Tethyan sediments, in thick 15- to 18-kilometer (9- to 11-mile) layers thrust 100 kilometers (60 miles) to the south over the Low Himalayas. This thrust is known as the Main Central Thrust. The lower Himalayas are characterized by their old (600 to 800 million years) sediments, which have been strongly deformed and thrust several times. Their composition resembles the sediments of the north Indian shield. The complicated mass of the lower Himalayas has also been subjected to a large thrust (Main Boundary Thrust) pushing it over the Sub-Himalayas. The narrow strip of the Sub-Himalayas, which is nonetheless over 2,000 kilometers (1,200 miles) long, forms an almost continuous range of hills, made of erosion material from the rising Himalayas and comparable with Alpine molasse. Known as the Siwaliks, their sediments reflect the history of the upthrust of the emergent Himalayas. Numerous mammalian fossil finds allow the Siwaliks to be dated with accuracy and provide evidence that the Himalaya formation occurred not too long ago.

Parallel to the history of events in the Himalayas, we can trace a similar evolution in the Transhimalayas. After the intrusion of granitic rocks that was mentioned before, a period of intense volcanic activity followed, and then after the collision came an uplift of the whole Transhimalayas. Thus evidence can be found for the existence of a high 40-million-year-old mountain range north of the suture at a time when the Himalayas as a mountain range were not visible at all. But as soon as mountain ranges are formed, the process of erosion begins and the products of this process are seen on and along the southern slopes of the Transhimalayas as a 4,000- to

The Growing Himalayas

Strong continuing rise of the mountains, including Tibet (1 cm [0.4 in] per year). Mountains are formed into their present shapes (morphogenesis), while the Indus/Ganges plain sinks.

Mountain ranges rise slowly, and erosion begins (formation of molasse). Ice Age begins.

The Tethyan Ocean narrows. Marked uplift occurs in the Transhimalayas following granite intrusion. Mount Kailas formed after the collision.

India rises slightly. To the north is the deep Tethyan Ocean, with deep-sea sediments. Indian continental plate starts to drift northward.

Erosion of the Aravallis and deposition of marine sediments into a shallow sea.

High mountain range along the northern edge of the Indian continent (Aravallis), with a deep ocean farther north.

5,000-meter (13,200- to 16,500-feet) massive conglomerate with sandstone layers intercalated.

They are like a coarse molasse but are nearly 20 million years older than the molasse of the Siwaliks. The best of these sections is in the central part of the Transhimalayas, on that most sacred of mountains, Mount Kailas. It is referred to as the Kailas molasse.

To the north of the western Himalayas follows the Karakorum, a range about half as long as the Alps. It is twice as heavily glaciated as the Himalayas and contains many light granite intrusions. Karakorum is a Turkish name, meaning "Black Gravel." The name actually comes from the pass of that name and is not really appropriate for the white mountains, since the pass itself is not a part of the Karakorum, geologically speaking. The old Turkish name "Mustagh" ("Ice Mountain") would be more suitable, but now it is only used locally for certain of the peaks.

A northern suture zone, the Shyok suture, named after an important tributary of the Indus, separates the Karakorum from the actual western Himalayas. The Karakorum, or at least the main chain, is composed of highly crystalline rocks, such as gneisses and granite. Interestingly the Karakorum shows no trace of being influenced by the characteristic crystal-

Below: *Rhubarb* (Rheum nobile) *growing at 4,500 meters (14,850 feet). The cylindrical form protects its flowers from the cold. Pollination takes place inside the cylinder. Normally a yellow color, in fall it has a russet sheen (East Himalayas).*

Above right: Meconopsis horridula, *short-stemmed blue poppy, which despite its unattractive name is the prettiest flower in the Himalayas and Tibet. At 4,600 meters (15,180 feet) in northern Transhimalayas.*

Above far right: *The delicate* Saussurea, *a type of composite, protecting itself from the cold with white woolly threads. At 4,400 meters (14,520 ft.) in the East Himalayas.*

line spur of the Indian shield. Instead it forms a flat arc, convex toward the north, parallel to the wide bow of the Pamir. The Shyok suture seems to cut off the Nanga Parbat uplift and related structures quite sharply. The old crystalline of the southern Karakorum along the Shyok suture dips steeply to the north. Here in the Hunza region the folds of white marble are famous because of the rubies that they contain. There seems to be no link between the history of the formation of the Karakorum granite with that of the suture zone (subduction melting, as in the Transhimalayas), since most of the granites in the Karakorum are much younger. The celebrated Baltoro granite, which leads up to the famous K 2, is less than 10 million years old. Similar young granite intrusions are also quite widespread in the High Himalayas, notably often in the highest peaks. On account of their light color and special mineral content (often muscovite and tourmaline) they are known as leukogranites. They broke through older structures and are often accompanied by a complicated series of dykes that contrast sharply by showing up as white veins in the walls of the highest Himalayas.

About 5 million years after the horizontal contraction phase (orogenese), the vertical movement phase (morphogenese) began and is still in progress, continuing to affect the mountain forms.

It is quite astonishing that the last upthrust not only affected the Himalayas, the Transhimalayas and the Karakorum but also the whole of the Tibetan region. With an area of 2.5 million square kilometers (1 million square miles) this region is the highest land mass on earth, and in the last million years it has risen by between 4,000 and 5,000 meters (13,200 and 16,500 feet), an average of 4 to 5 millimeters (0.16 to 0.2 inch) per year. Today the rate is close to 1 centimeter (0.4 inch); the rise is 10 times faster than in the Alps. A few years ago Chinese scientists found the remains of flora and fauna that had lived in tropical and subtropical zones at an altitude of 5,000 to 6,000 meters (16,500 to 19,800 feet) in alluvial terraces on the flank of the 8,013-meter-high (26,443-foot-high) Shisha Pangma (to the north of the Nepalese border in Tibet). Over 100 years ago the geologist Lydekker was investigating the well-bedded horizontal alluvial terraces in the upper Sutlej region (Hundes) at an altitude of 4,000 to 5,000 meters (13,200 to 16,500 feet) and found mammalian bone remains, including those of rhinoceros and hipparion (early horse), animals that had lived in tropical regions. These terraces, hundreds of meters thick, can be seen today, still completely horizontal after being lifted 4,000 meters (13,200 feet), and covering an area about half the size of Switzerland. In these alluvial regions the Sutlej and its tributaries have carved deep gorges, and here the ruins of monasteries from the time of the Kings of Guge can be seen, with the oldest and finest Buddhist frescoes in existence.

Exact dating of the upthrusts can only be achieved by re-measuring older, already determined sections, a procedure that was possible in the Alps. But in the Himalayas these older, exact data are not available. Remeasurements currently taking place on some of the well-known peaks have corrected some older mistakes, bringing to light differences of several hundred meters in some cases. In the fall of 1985 an American-Chinese expedition made a first ascent of the 7,723-meter-high (25,486-foot-high) Ulugh Muztagh, regarded then as the highest peak in northern Tibet. Simultaneously the summit height was checked using the latest measuring techniques (satellite reflection), and to everyone's surprise Ulagh Muztagh was not a "mighty" 7,723 meters (25,486 feet), but a "mere" 6,980 meters (23,034 feet), and thus lost its prestigious position of being the highest peak in northern Tibet. Questionable results of an almost sensational nature were obtained in 1986 during a remeasurement of the height of the proud K 2, the peak that dominates the Karakorum. Reflections were used from a satellite fixing the heights of three stations at the foot of the mountain, and from these the altitude of the peak was measured using radar triangulation. The Americans published their results early in 1987, and according to their figures, K 2 stood at 8,858 meters (29,231 feet), 11 meters (36 feet) more than Everest, and was thus the highest peak in the world. However, remeasurements organized in 1987 by the Italian geologist Ardito Desio on both K 2 and Everest made K 2 only 6 meters (20 feet) higher, while Everest measured 24 meters (79 feet) higher than before and stands at the new record level of 8,872 meters (29,278 feet).

Because of their spiral form, ammonites are highly prized by the Tibetans in the Himalayas and the Transhimalayas. Worn as amulets on long trips, they are often deposited as "sacrifices" after a high pass has been climbed, leading to great confusion among geologists,

who then often find them in quite the wrong surroundings. Tibetans find their ammonites in concretions in 130-million-year-old black slate on the Jurassic/Cretaceous border. The ammonites are hacked out of these concretions. A rich area is the Gandaki valley in Nepal, where the black slate layers are exposed. The gas that fuels the sacred eternal flame in the much-revered little temple of Muktinath comes from the ammonite slate of the Spiti formation. The ammonite pictured here was found by the geologist Toni Hagen in the Kali Gandaki valley.

However, even though these latest figures were obtained using the most up-to-date measuring instruments, it should be emphasized that some inaccuracy remains, and that results given to the nearest meter may not be totally correct, since drifts of snow can easily cause variations of several meters in the level of a summit.

Very little is known about the start, duration and extent of the Ice Ages in the Himalayas and Tibet. What is certain is that the next to last Ice Age was markedly more intense than all the others. Clearly in earlier times the extent of the ice was less since at the time the upthrust was only in its early phases. The period after the major Ice Age seems to have been a time that saw a marked retreat of the glaciers. In the extensive Tibetan basins there

The little-known eastern border range of Lunana, in the northern Bhutan Himalayas. Leukogranite has penetrated through the gneisses, which are covered with sediments from the Tethyan Ocean. The lower layers of sediment just cover the highest peaks. The gradual rock changes (metamorphosis) are caused by a reduction in temperature and pressure. (Sketch of the southern moraine of the great unnamed glacier that extends from Gonto La to the west.)

most probably remained considerable dead ice masses, which on melting formed many lakes, most of which had no outlet. The huge amounts of water present at the start evaporated quickly in the desert-like climate, and what had been initially freshwater become brackish and finally salty. From the salt beds that were thus formed, the Tibetans have been able to obtain the valuable salt that they use as an export product and as a bartering currency. Old strand lines where the water level once stood often mark the shores of these lakes, marking time periods rather like the rings of a tree.

In the High Himalayas many lakes were also formed at the same time by the damming effect of moraines, from the side glaciers of the last Ice Age and smaller lakes in the ice-polished rock landscape of the last glaciation. Of the larger and older dammed lakes very few remain. Quite frequently in the larger valleys of the Indus and the Shyok one can see light yellow horizontal layers high up on the valley slopes – the last remains of the sediment from the old lakes. Widespread coarse alluvial terraces in the lower valleys provide evidence of earlier floods caused by the collapse of the natural walls damming the lakes. This is happening even within historical times: In the central part of the Bhutan Himalayas the famous Phunaka Dzong lies at the confluence of two important rivers, the Moh Chu

("Mother River") and the Pho Chu ("Father River"). The Pho Chu is known to be particularly wild, but even so, about 50 years ago the monks of the Dzong were very surprised when in the middle of the dry season the Pho Chu turned into a mighty torrent of mud carrying along blocks of white granite that tore down all the bridges and destroyed part of the northern Dzong. Since this catastrophe the Dzong has been an island in the river. Thirty years later, during the geological exploration of the Bhutan Himalayas, I reached the remote source of the Pho Chu near the Tibetan border. Instead of the high mountain forest, I discovered in the uppermost valley of the Pho Chu an expanse of white granite blocks several hundred meters wide. This extended up past the tree line as far as the glaciers of the Teri Kang, over 7,000 meters (23,100 feet) high. Here there had once been a blue glacier lake, dammed in by a high moraine wall. Above it had been a wall of white granite, with an overhanging glacier. Fifty years ago this glacier suddenly moved forward, probably as a result of an unusual kind of glacier

Next double page (20/21):
Aerial picture of the southern Tibetan lake region. The frozen Zigetang Tso (top center) clearly shows earlier strand lines. Most of the lakes are the remains of much larger ones, while others are formed in depressions by fracture zones (right half of the picture). To the left can be seen fracture zones over 100 kilometers (60 miles) long. Metric camera photo from approximately 250 kilometers (150 miles) altitude (Space Shuttle), December 1983. The width of the picture corresponds to about 180 kilometers (108 miles), looking toward the north-northeast.

movement, about which little is known. Called "surging," it also occurs in the Alps and particularly in the Andes, where it is known as *huaicos* and causes widespread destruction. The ice masses of the glacier fell into the lake, causing a huge flood wave that burst through the moraine wall like a dam bursting. Flood catastrophes of this kind in the Himalayas can cause within a few hours alterations in the landscape that would normally take hundreds of years.

The great floods of Tibet that followed the Ice Ages form part of local sagas, just like the biblical story of the Flood. The sagas tell how "a Buddha of that time" took pity on the flooded land and with his sword cut a deep swath through the mountains in southeastern Tibet and thus let the water out. Today in this region is one of the deepest and wildest gorges in the world, where the Yarlung Tsangpo cuts through the chain of the 7,776-meter-high (25,661-foot-high) Namche Barwa and then flows southward as the Brahmaputra into the plains of Assam.

Many of the lakes that remain today are regarded as sacred by Buddhists. In spite of their lovely dark blue to turquoise color, they are often believed to be haunted by evil spirits, while the gods themselves reside on the highest and most beautiful peaks. Old legends tell how the foundations of

Following double page (22/23):
Aerial picture of the central Yarlung Tsangpo valley southwest of Lhasa near Shigatse. The river runs parallel to the Indo-Yarlung suture, to the south of which can be seen the dark green rocks of the oceanic crust (ophiolites). Above the Yarlung Tsangpo follows the granite landscape of the Transhimalayas. The region in the lower right-hand page belongs to the Indian continent, that in the upper left to Eurasia. Metric camera photo from approximately 250 kilometers (150 miles) altitude (Space Shuttle), December 1983. The width of the picture corresponds to about 175 kilometers (105 miles), looking towards the north-northeast.

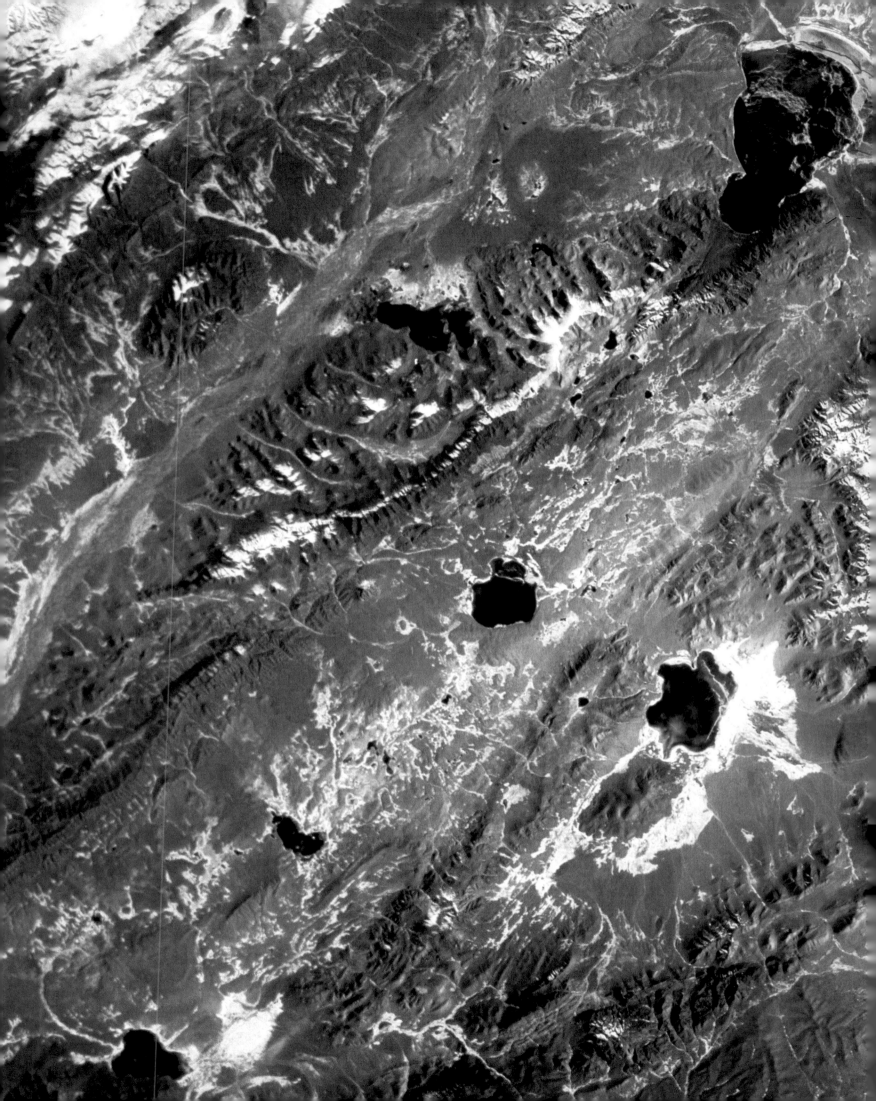

HIMALAYA
AND
KARAKORUM

(Heights in meters)

N

0   300 km

© Carta Lüthi + Ramseier Bern   180 miles

In the Buddhist search for suitable locations for temples and monasteries, it is not only the sacred lakes that play a role. Geological factors are considered, too: the famous Sakya monastery was founded near the "great white spot," which consists of volcanic rock.

In many of the monasteries of Bhutan the footprints of the famous Padmasambhava, the Lotos-born, here mostly worshiped as the Guru Rimpoche, are preserved. These were decisive in choosing the site of the monastery. It is a fact that in the cliff monastery of Taktshang and in other monasteries of eastern Bhutan, one can see round concretions in the cliffs that do indeed look like footprints.

The little monastery of Trimyer in the Barbung gorge of Dolpo in northwestern Nepal. At this site there is a great fold in the marine sediment of the former Tethyan Ocean, a nice example of the balance between religious and geologic factors.

Below: *A magnificent representation of the Buddha Maitreya on slate that is almost 400 million years old. The engraving itself is nearly 100 years old, and despite being on the outside of a small chorten in Bhutan, 4,000 meters (13,200 feet) above sea level, it is surprisingly well preserved. At the request of the Queen of Bhutan we re-located the original source of this valuable type of slate, and slate roofs are beginning to replace the unsightly, rusting corrugated iron sheets that were very common. The original shingle roof of the monastery had to be replaced because it was a fire risk.*

Facing page: *The settlement of Kagbeni, which lies on a terrace of the Kali-Gandaki river below a slope with very steeply inclined strata. Above the village can be seen the remains of earlier terraces, evidence of a periodic upthrust of this valley formed by one of the main fracture zones. One can also see the red monastery and the irrigated fields.*

important monasteries are connected with the sacred lakes, but from a chronological point of view there can be no substance to these tales. One of the most impressive and highest-situated monasteries of the Ladakh-Himalayas, Lamayuru, is said to stand on the site of a former lake: "In the olden times [historically 2,500 years ago] when Shakyamuni-Buddha inhabited this world, southern Tibet and the northern Himalayas were totally uninhabited. In the valley of Lamayuru there was at that time [geologically more than 25,000 years ago] a clear lake, home of the evil Naga spirits. An Indian Holy Man visited this lake and landed on a small island. After various sacred negotiations had been performed, he prophesied that an important monastery would be founded at this spot. He softened the evil Naga by offerings of barley, and by the strength of his will drained all the water of the lake in one direction. After he had left the lake was practically dry. Mud-lions came up out of the swamp onto a small hillock, which is still known today as Sengay-Syang [Lion Hill]."

In the oldest monastery in Ladakh, Alchi Gompa, which is famous for its splendid Buddhist frescoes, I discovered among the many Bodhisattvas a depiction of two fully manned boats, carrying prayer flags. This unlikely picture in Alchi, where the climate had been desert-like before the monastery's foundation, was perhaps a "memory" of the time 20,000 to 30,000 years ago when that area had been a region of great lakes.

Very little is known of the pre-Ice Age inhabitants. Some pieces of primitive tools from the Karewa layer in Kashmir probably indicate a pre-Ice Age settlement. Even the much easier routes used before the Ice Age and before the final upthrust are only vaguely suspected, but there were certainly other routes that preceded the ones that are used today and those documented in history.

The most important historically documented route follows the middle Indus valley and reaches the territory of the Hunza, who have a language of their own and are perhaps a leftover people from an early migration, in the northern desert valleys. The various rock engravings (petroglyphs) along this route, like visiting cards from early caravans, cover a time span of 3,000 years. Perhaps the legendary gold of western Tibet traveled along this caravan route as dealers made their way to the south. Even Herodotus provides an account of their unusual way of obtaining gold, relating the story that huge ants "smaller than a dog, but larger than a fox" fetched gold nuggets from deep holes.

Today the fierce high-altitude climate of the Himalayas and the areas that border them to the north make very specific demands on the adaptability of flora and fauna. Visitors to this region see rhubarb growing at over 4,000 meters (13,200 feet), with tightly closed leaves wrapped around in the form of a cylinder for protection against the cold. It takes on a dark russet color in the early winter. The delicate *Saussurea* shrouds itself at 4,500 meters (14,850 feet) with a thick white fuzz. The sky blue Tibetan gentian flowers only in the fall when the monsoon storms are over. The splendid, almost orchid-like *Sophora moorcroftiana*, which only emerges from the desert soil of the Transhimalayas and south Tibet for very short periods, seems not to mind the desert storms at 4,600 meters (15,180 feet). By far the most beautiful flowers of the whole Himalayas, the sky blue

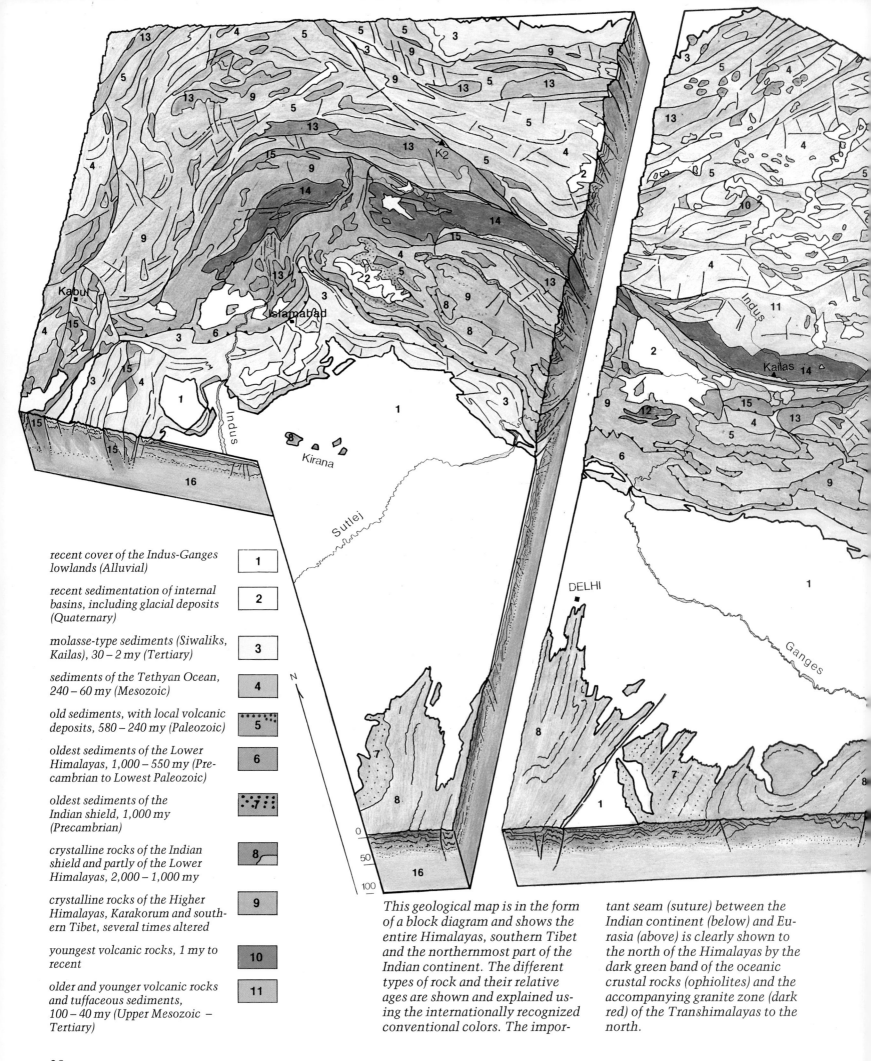

recent cover of the Indus-Ganges lowlands (Alluvial) — **1**

recent sedimentation of internal basins, including glacial deposits (Quaternary) — **2**

molasse-type sediments (Siwaliks, Kailas), 30 – 2 my (Tertiary) — **3**

sediments of the Tethyan Ocean, 240 – 60 my (Mesozoic) — **4**

old sediments, with local volcanic deposits, 580 – 240 my (Paleozoic) — **5**

oldest sediments of the Lower Himalayas, 1,000 – 550 my (Precambrian to Lowest Paleozoic) — **6**

oldest sediments of the Indian shield, 1,000 my (Precambrian) — **7**

crystalline rocks of the Indian shield and partly of the Lower Himalayas, 2,000 – 1,000 my — **8**

crystalline rocks of the Higher Himalayas, Karakorum and southern Tibet, several times altered — **9**

youngest volcanic rocks, 1 my to recent — **10**

older and younger volcanic rocks and tuffaceous sediments, 100 – 40 my (Upper Mesozoic – Tertiary) — **11**

This geological map is in the form of a block diagram and shows the entire Himalayas, southern Tibet and the northernmost part of the Indian continent. The different types of rock and their relative ages are shown and explained using the internationally recognized conventional colors. The important seam (suture) between the Indian continent (below) and Eurasia (above) is clearly shown to the north of the Himalayas by the dark green band of the oceanic crustal rocks (ophiolites) and the accompanying granite zone (dark red) of the Transhimalayas to the north.

Geological Map of the Himalayas

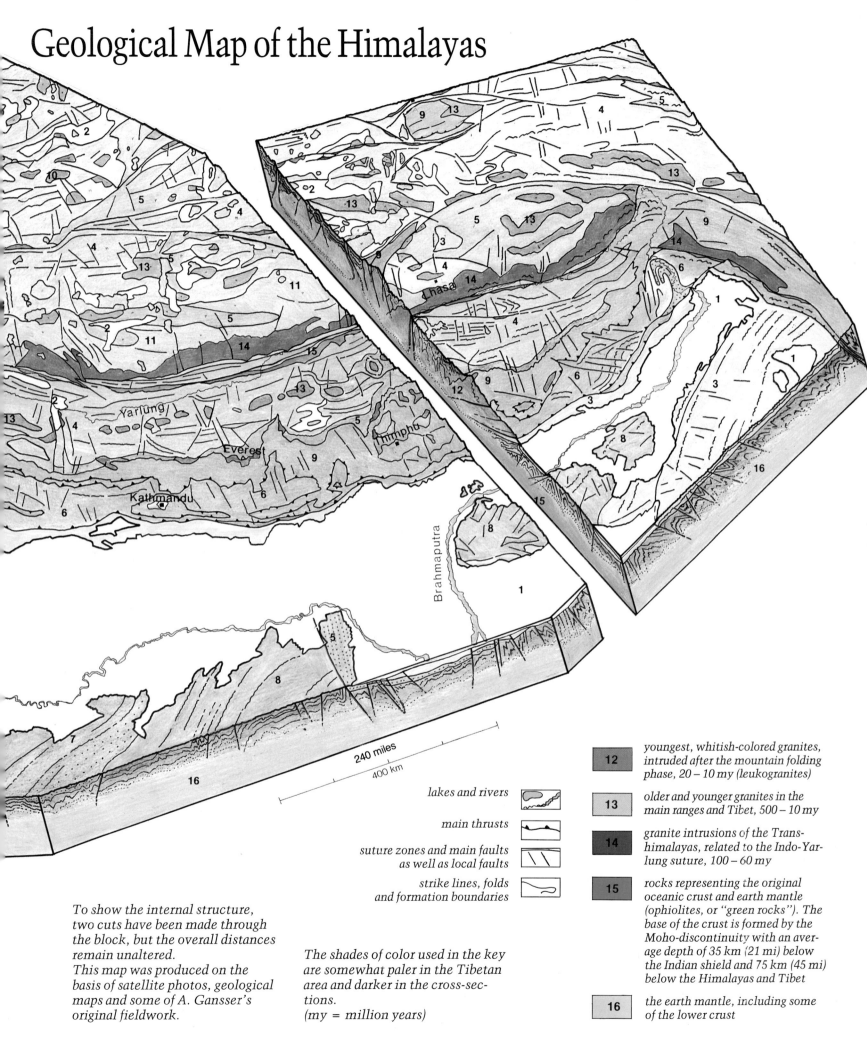

240 miles
400 km

lakes and rivers

main thrusts

suture zones and main faults
as well as local faults

strike lines, folds
and formation boundaries

To show the internal structure,
two cuts have been made through
the block, but the overall distances
remain unaltered.
This map was produced on the
basis of satellite photos, geological
maps and some of A. Gansser's
original fieldwork.

The shades of color used in the key
are somewhat paler in the Tibetan
area and darker in the cross-sec-
tions.
(my = million years)

12	youngest, whitish-colored granites, intruded after the mountain folding phase, 20 – 10 my (leukogranites)
13	older and younger granites in the main ranges and Tibet, 500 – 10 my
14	granite intrusions of the Trans-himalayas, related to the Indo-Yar-lung suture, 100 – 60 my
15	rocks representing the original oceanic crust and earth mantle (ophiolites, or "green rocks"). The base of the crust is formed by the Moho-discontinuity with an aver-age depth of 35 km (21 mi) below the Indian shield and 75 km (45 mi) below the Himalayas and Tibet
16	the earth mantle, including some of the lower crust

31

poppy (*Meconopsis horridula*), seems to fear predators more than the climate – it defends itself with spines.

It was only when the yak was domesticated that the inhabitants of the Himalayas were able to conquer the high mountains. The yak can be ridden or made to carry a heavy load. In addition, this useful animal, which makes few demands in the way of food, provides wool for making ropes, blankets, clothes and tents, as well as a rich milk that makes excellent butter, yogurt and cheese. Small pieces of this cheese are threaded like a string of pearls

Facing page: The famous Trango towers on the lower Baltoro glacier in the Karakorum, made of Baltoro granite "only" 10 million years old. A practice area for future extreme alpinists?

and carried as a sort of emergency ration. The tails of yaks have been a valuable export since early times, and the animal's droppings provide the only combustible material above the tree line; finally, the meat can be eaten. The flesh is cut into thin strips that are air-dried. The product can stand comparison with the most delicate dried meats in the world. The yak cannot survive below 3,500 meters (11,550 feet) in the tropical Himalayas; its habitat is the yak pasture region between the forests and the glaciers.

The gorges of the Himalayas, with their wild and unpredictable rivers, were impassable natural barriers in earlier times. Only with the introduc-

Above: The young granite of the Paiju group in the region of the Baltoro glacier.

tion of the suspension bridge, a Chinese invention, were continuous routes made possible. In the wild mountain jungles of the eastern Himalayas these were first made of lianas and bamboo, following a tradition thousands of years old.

In the lower Paro valley in western Bhutan there still stands an old monastery, Tamcho Gompa. Here lived the famous Thangtonggyalpo-Lama, known as the builder of iron-chain bridges, whose skills greatly improved the primitive hanging bridges. In time the art of building these iron-chain bridges spread throughout the Himalayas. The chains were forged link by link, on the spot, out of local iron supplies. Surprisingly, when a link in a chain was analyzed, the section where the link had been welded showed an arsenic content of 2.6%. Arsenic lowers the melting point of iron, a fact that had slipped into obscurity but was rediscovered in Bhutan. With the building of bridges came the construction of numerous pathways, often quite artistic, for beasts and porters along the cliff faces. It was along these routes that an efficient postal system, excellently organized by officials of

The Punakha Dzong, former winter residence of the rulers of Bhutan, now on an island following the moraine-lake flooding.

Far left: *The cause of the flood disaster of the Punakha Dzong in the source area of the wild Pho Chu, the "Father River." This is in the Lunana region, with the 7,000-meter (23,000-foot) Teri Kang in the background. Left of center one can see the granite wall with the hanging glacier, which fell into the lake below, itself the result of the valley's being dammed by moraine. The place where the moraine dam broke as well as the white granite debris are clearly visible.*

Left: *The middle Pho Chu valley, after the moraine dam broke. This region was once thickly forested with splendid tall firs, of which little trace remains. The valley is now filled with the debris of white granite blocks. Luckily the area was uninhabited.*

British India, functioned. Teams of runners carried the mail in day and night relays to even the most outlying regions.

Following the Chinese invasion of Tibet in 1950, and their unexpected advance into the plains of Assam in 1962, military roads were built in great haste in the whole of the southern Himalaya region. The location of these roads showed little knowledge of mountain road technology. Great irreparable swaths were sliced through the mountain forest, and consequently the roads have to be painstakingly repaired after every monsoon season.

Facing page: *A potentially dangerous glacier lake in northern Bhutan. The lake is dammed by moraine, and a sudden advance by the glacier or one of the frequent earthquakes could cause a catastrophic dam burst.*

Facing page: *Wild shapes caused by erosion of the whitish-yellow fine-grained sediment of the former Lamayuru lake. Age-tests on these sediments determined them to be 30,000 years old, indicating that the lake was formed in the period between the last two Ice Ages, an era that produced most of the lakes of the Himalayas and Tibet.*

The horizontal lake sediment of Lamayuru testifies to the existence of the lake, which is mentioned in local legends. One can recognize the outbreak toward the Indus valley 600 meters (1,980 feet) below.

THE GREAT RIVERS OF THE KAILAS

YARLUNG TSANGPO, INDUS, SUTLEJ, KARNALI, GANGES

From the "Center of the World," the holy Mount Kailas, flow all the largest rivers of the Himalayas and Transhimalayas. This outstanding fact, related to the upthrust of the Transhimalayas and the peculiar shape of the mountain, which allows its circumvention, is the reason that Mount Kailas is sacred to the major religions of Asia, with the exception of Islam, which is too firmly anchored to Mecca. The reason why all the rivers rise here is associated with the history of the upthrust of the Transhimalayas. The shape of the mountain makes it possible to walk all the way round it.

All the major rivers of the Himalayan and Transhimalayan region have their sources in the Kailas: the Yarlung Tsangpo (Brahmaputra) in the east, the Indus in the north, the Sutlej in the west, the Ganges in the southwest and the Karnali in the south. This unusual situation is the result of a special upthrust of the Kailas range at a time (30 million years ago) when the Himalayas were in the slow initial phase of their formation. Two of these rivers – the Indus to the west and the Yarlung Tsangpo to the east – were forced to flow in an east-west direction by the emergent Himalayas, and they could only penetrate the Himalayan range at its eastern and western extremities. Amazingly this penetration occurred at the points of highest uplift, the Nanga Parbat in the west and

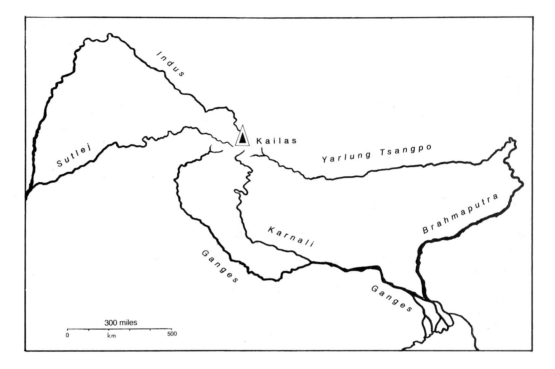

the Namche Barwa in the east. The other three rivers, however, the Sutlej, Karnali and Ganges, were not deflected by the rise of the Himalayas – they came right through the range, as some other mighty rivers that cut through the range at the highest points.

The Arun in eastern Nepal chose the very highest part of the Himalayas for its breakthrough. The gorge that it cuts between the Everest and Kanchenjunga groups is quite spectacular. In the region of its source in southern Tibet the Arun is causing erosion at such a rate that it seems as if it is attempting to join up with the mighty west-east-flow of the Yarlung Tsangpo. At the moment the sources of the Arun lie only 10 to 20 kilometers (6 to 12 miles) from the Yarlung, and the watershed is only a few hundred meters above the level of the bed of the Yarlung. In the very near geological future the waters of the Yarlung Tsangpo will be captured by the Arun and rush into the plain of the Ganges; it does not take a lot of imagination to visualize the catastrophe that this will cause.

The Kali Gandaki in central Nepal rises on the Tibetan border and cuts through the High Himalayas between the two 8,000-meter (26,400-foot) peaks of Annapurna and Dhaulagiri. Here the river follows a major north-south fault zone. This fracture passes near the little temple-village of Muktinath, where a hot spring emerges. A natural gas outlet fuels an eternal flame in one of the small temples. Both spring and flame are particularly revered by pilgrims. The fault runs into Tibet, where it affords the easiest passage in the whole Himalayas. A wide flat saddle (the exact location of the border here is hard to determine) extends from Kali Gandaki into the broad river area of the Yarlung Tsangpo. This passage through the mountains made it possible for the very early Tibetan tribes to migrate into the northern valleys of Nepal, where they founded the little kingdoms of Dolpo and Mustang. In the uppermost Kali Gandaki valley one of the fortresses of the latter kingdom can still be seen. Following the occupation of Tibet in 1950, Tibetan tribes once again passed over these heights. This time it was

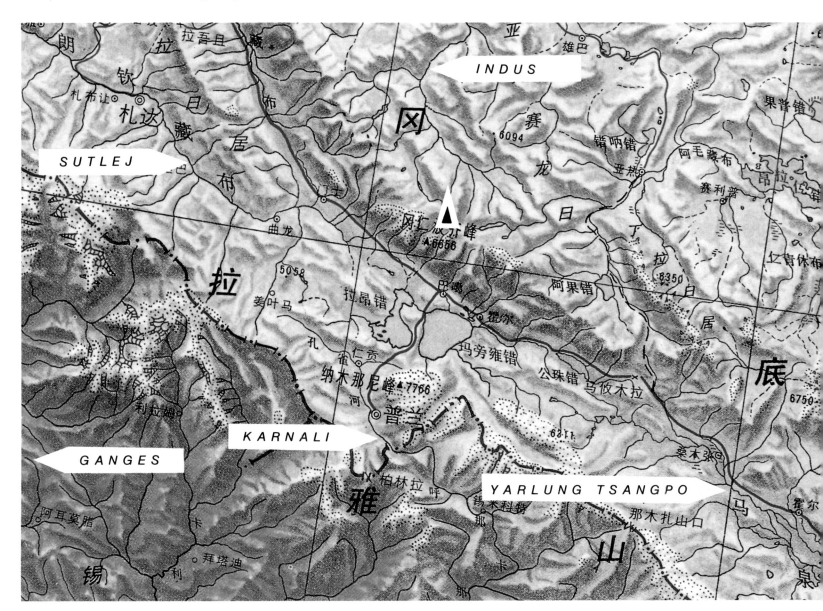

the warlike Kampas from eastern Tibet, who used Mustang as a base for attacking Chinese truck convoys as they moved along the new military roads of the Yarlung Tsangpo. The Kampas then withdrew over the Mustang pass into Nepalese territory. They were Tibet's last resistance fighters.

If we follow the great rivers that rise in the Kailas, from source to estuary, we will get to know something about them and about their regions, mountains, peoples and history.

Part of a Chinese map of southern Tibet, showing Mount Kailas and its five rivers. The width of the map represents approximately 240 kilometers (144 miles). Orientation to the north.

THE YARLUNG TSANGPO

The source of the Yarlung Tsangpo (Brahmaputra) has many arms. Southeast of the Kailas the 7,700-meter-high (25,410-foot-high) peak of Gurla Mandhata, a unique glaciated crystalline dome, dominates the headwaters. Situated between the Himalayas and the Transhimalayas, it divides the source area into its various branches.

In 1864 a British "hunting expedition" led by Edmund Smyth reached the source area of the Yarlung Tsangpo by coming from western Nepal over the extremely difficult Dakeo pass. When the members of the expedition traveled from Garbyang over the Lipulekh pass into Tibet, they were immediately attacked by armed Tibetans, who had been informed of the English plans, and so the expedition was prevented from going farther. One of their Bhotia guides, however, knew of a "secret pathway," by means of which they could travel unobserved from Nepal to the uninhabited high plateau. Even at this early time, Tibet was closed to foreigners, and this group of Englishmen were not in disguise. The Dakeo pass formed a deep cut in the eastern Gurla-Mandhata chain. Yaks were used to "plough" a track through the deeply snowed-in pass. While descending, before they reached

A view of the sacred Mount Kailas from the southwest. Beyond the Himalayas and running parallel to this range lie the Transhimalayas, a name introduced by the famous explorer Sven Hedin. The dominant position of this peak in the range is particularly noticeable from the south. Kailas is always covered with a glacial cap. Its name comes from the Sanskrit Kailasa. The Tibetans call it Kang Rinpoche ("Snow Jewel").

the highlands of the Yarlung source region, Smyth noticed some black basaltic rocks — exactly where the great suture runs between India and Asia. Even though the members of the expedition were more interested in the wild yaks that were still common in this region than in geographical research, they did in fact make the first sketch maps of this important source area. Forty years later Sven Hedin also reached the Yarlung sources. He was on his way back from Shigatse, where he had been waiting for an opportunity to get through to Lhasa. He found three source rivers, measured the volume of water in them and followed the southern arm as far as a huge glacier, which extended down from the over 7,000-meter-high (23,100-foot-high) mountain Kubi Kangri on the Nepalese border. The central and northern arms were of less interest to Hedin and so he soon went on to the region of the great lakes of Manasarowar and Raksastal. He was very proud of the

This epic Thanka from the Karmapa School comes from a series of representations of the Central Asian Gesar Saga. It depicts one of Hero Gesar's knights as he gallops across the mountains in full armor, holding sword and banner in his hands. The Gesar tradition (his home is located in East Tibet) is cultivated particularly by the Karmapas. The legends which have been woven around Gesar portray him as the conqueror of all of Central Asia and have been collected in nine or, alternatively, 18 volumes of block print, published by the Tibetan regent Reting in the 1930's.

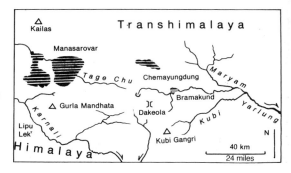

The source of the Yarlung Tsangpo. The actual source is taken to lie on the central tributary (Chemayungdung), and not on the more southerly Kubi river, which comes from the Kubi Kangri glaciers, as Sven Hedin asserted.

fact that he was the "first" European to have discovered the source area of the Yarlung (Brahmaputra). Unfortunately he did not follow the central tributary flowing from the west; this leads to a small lake that the Bothias regard as the main source of the Brahmaputra and revere as part of the Brahmin culture. From here this river, which is the actual source, can be followed farther in a more southerly direction to the Chemayungdung glacier, where the source is surrounded by little cairns and clay figurines (Tsa-tsas). Many other rivers feed the Yarlung Tsangpo on its eastward journey. It follows the geological line along the important Indus-Yarlung suture, the black and green cliffs of which – originally oceanic rocks – are sporadically seen on the southern side, while on the northern side the light granite of the Transhimalayas is an ever present feature. In sheltered areas we can see the black tents of nomads and hundreds of sheep and black yaks grazing. Steppe-like, sparse meadows predominate, often covered with quite beautiful edelweiss. Downstream the numbers of nomad tents increase and soon we reach the first houses of the Tibetans. Their firewood, consisting of desert bushes, is stored on the flat roofs, and round lumps of yak dung hang on the walls; when dry they are stored in piles. Everything is ready for the cold and stormy, but usually not very snowy, winter season.

South of the confluence with the Rake, another river that runs almost parallel to the Yarlung Tsangpo, we find Latse, the first settlement of any size. We are now 500 kilometers (300 miles) from the river's source, and the Yarlung has become an important waterway that can only be crossed at certain points using skin boats or floats of inflated sheepskin. Building bridges was not a possibility because of the Yarlung's irregular meanderings. To the south of the now quite broad Yarlung valley it will soon be pos-

The first winter snow on the Tremo La, a 4,700-meter (15,510-foot) pass leading from West Bhutan to Tibet. In the background the pastel shades of the broad Tibetan plateau in the Phari region.

sible to make out the proud fortress of Shigatse and somewhat farther in the interior the great monastery of Tashilhunpo, seat of the Panchen Lama. Yak caravans, pilgrims and small shaggy Tibetan horses add movement to the scene as they travel along the many pathways. Walls with artistically carved prayer stones (*Mani* stones) can be seen and many small stupa-chorten bear witness to the proximity of holy sites. On every house prayer flags flutter in the constant wind. Soon the broad Yarlung disappears into a narrow gorge and the caravan trails veer southward to Gyantse, the most important trading center on the north-south route, which runs over the Tremo La pass in western Bhutan to Sikkim and India. Here at Gyantse is another imposing fortress, where in 1904 its defenders offered stiff opposition to the British "punitive force" heading to Lhasa. Kumbum, the finest of all the stupa-chorten, is still regarded as the jewel of Gyantse. Along the banks of the many-branched Yamdruk Tso, a lake that was formed by the sinking of a valley and is now at an altitude of 4,400 meters (14,520 feet), the caravan trail rejoins the Yarlung, which with all its loops now fills the entire valley. High above in the granite hills are vast sand dunes, blown there from the wide valley. Eighty kilometers (48 miles) to the northeast, on the important Kyi-Chu tributary, is Lhasa. From far off the pilgrim can see two hills; on one of them is the Potala, which was founded by the fifth Dalai Lama, and the other is the Iron Mountain, the most famous medicine

center in Tibet. In the ancient center of Lhasa the houses, whose windows are decorated with flowers, stand in rows around the most holy of all the temples, the Jokhang. Thousands of pilgrims move clockwise round it along the Barkhor (an important circular road of bazaars). In the Jokhang the most revered relic in Tibet, a precious statue of Buddha, can be worshiped. When Tibet was ruled by King Songtsengampo and at the height of its power (seventh century), the king's two wives encouraged Buddhism in Tibet. One of the wives was a princess of Buddhist faith from Nepal, the

A Tibetan border patrol along the frontier between Tibet and the Himalayas, which is not very well defined in some places.

Next double page: *The morning mist disperses along the south face of the 8,080-meter (26,664-foot) main peak of the Annapurna range. This dominates the amphitheater that is the sacred source of the Modi Khola in central Nepal.*

A view of Kangtega with its fierce granite walls from the roof of the Tangboche monastery, well known for its "Yeti relics." Khumbu valley, home of the Sherpas, south of Everest.

other the daughter of the Emperor of China and also a devout Buddhist. According to tradition, the precious statue of Buddha was brought to Lhasa in the year 641 by the Chinese Princess Wengcheng as a wedding present for the Tibetan King Songtsengampo. Since the 17th century there have been as many as 20,000 lamas living in the three largest monasteries in the Lhasa region: Drehpung, Sera and Ganden.

Eighty kilometers (48 miles) north of Lhasa, on the caravan route to central Tibet, lies a glaciated mountain range with two unclimbed and practically unknown 7,000-meter (23,100 foot) peaks. This mountain chain, known as the Nyenchentanglha, which runs from the northeast toward the southwest, is often wrongly regarded as the eastern part of the Transhimalayas. We will meet its extension to the north of the great bend of the Yarlung Tsangpo. Besides having a different direction than that of the Transhimalayas, the Nyenchentanglha borders another unique feature – the world's largest high-altitude inland lake, which reflects the image of its glacier. The Nam Tso lies 4,720 meters (15,576 feet) above sea level and is twice the size of Lake Constance. In the plain on the south side of this

Facing page: One of the peaks of the long Annapurna range, at the spot where the range links up with the ridge of Machapuchare, the sacred "Fishtail" mountain. The peaks here are remarkably rugged and steep.

chain, which is crisscrossed with recent post-Ice Age faults, the largest thermal area of Tibet was discovered, with steaming hot springs. South of Lhasa, on the north side of the Yarlung, is the oldest monastery in Tibet, Samye, which was founded by Padmasambhava in 770. Somewhat farther downriver we find the opening of the actual Yarlung valley, which enters from the south out of the mountains of Bhutan. According to one of the many ancient legends, it is the origin of the Tibetans and of the Yarlung

"Edmund Hillary and Sherpa Tensing spent the night before May 29 in camp 9. Setting off at 6:30, carrying their 13.5 kilogram [29.7 pound] oxygen apparatus, they reached the south peak at 9:00. A short descent and then up toward the main peak. Splendid weather. After an hour a cliff-ledge, extremely demanding. Then the steep, narrow ice-ridge with dangerous cornices, left and right the abyss. The summit. May 29, 1953, 11:30 a. m."
Toni Hiebeler in Himalaya and Karakorum, 1980.

Above: The Everest region seen from the air. Section of a metric camera photo, taken from an altitude of 250 kilometers (150 miles), 1983. The summit itself lies roughly in the center of the picture, covered by the familiar wisps of cloud. Looking towards the northwest.

Right: The famous north face of Everest (Chomolungma). Here the first British expeditions of 1923 – 1924 came to a halt, but they had reached an altitude of 8,500 meters (28,050 feet). In 1975 a big Chinese expedition succeeded, with one woman and seven men from Tibet, and one Chinese. The attempts and the ascent were made along the east ridge, left in the picture.

dynasty, from which the valley derived its name. Here stands one of the oldest buildings in Tibet, the Yumbu Lakhang, a sort of fortified monastery, which in one way is a forerunner of the Dzongs, which are quite common throughout the Himalayas and particularly in Bhutan. These buildings house both worldly domination and monastic piety under the same roof.

Since 1950, and in particular since 1959, great changes have taken place along the mighty Yarlung Tsangpo and its tributaries. Many of the nomads' tents have disappeared and a military road has been constructed to the south of the Kailas into western Tibet. To build it, materials from prayer walls and chorten were sometimes used. The great monastery of Ganden has been completely destroyed and those of Sera and Drehpung badly damaged. The medicinal center on the Iron Mountain in Lhasa has disappeared. It was only because of the intervention of Chou En-lai, China's former premier, that the Potala itself was saved from the destructive zeal of the Cultural Revolution. From the airport on the southern bank of the Yarlung Tsangpo the new road leads across the first modern bridge in Tibet and into Lhasa. The city itself, like other places along the river, has grown enormously. The Barkhor in front of the Jokhang has been made into a huge open space. From here a new road system, started in 1959, leads past the Potala and to the west, where close to the summer palace of the Dalai Lama a tourist hotel was built in 1985 to accommodate the foreign visitors who have been coming to Tibet since 1980 in ever increasing numbers.

Let us now continue to follow the Yarlung Tsangpo farther to the east. Here apart from some new settlements, like the one around the old monastery town of Tsethang at the mouth of the Yarlung valley, little has changed. Broad flood plains with conspicuous terraces and sand dunes alternate with short gorges. In this section the river is "only" 3,000 meters (9,900 feet) above sea level, and so the natural (and cultivated) vegetation has thickened, with birch and oak forests now in evidence. The slopes leading up to the Himalayas are more densely wooded in their upper reaches.

Above the mountain jungle we can discern the glacial mountains of eastern Bhutan. They are dominated by the 7,600-meter-high (25,080-foot-high) Kunla Kangri, which lies on Tibetan territory, and farther east by the 7,100-meter-high (23,430-foot-high) Kangto group, all little known and as yet unclimbed. The passes in between the peaks of this eastern part of the Himalayas have become lower, and it would be easier to cross here were it not for the dense mountain jungle that reaches almost up to the watershed. In 1959 the Dalai Lama chose one of the routes through this area to make his escape from Lhasa, and the Chinese crossed this mountainous jungle in their unexpected advance in 1962.

By the Treaty of Simla in 1914, the watershed of the eastern Himalayas was accepted as the border between British India and Tibet, known as the McMahon line. However, it has never been accepted by China, and since 1950 there have been repeated border incidents. There were conflicts not only here but also in the border region of Ladakh, where the Chinese annexed the vast uninhabited highland area of Aksai Chin, which the Indians claimed was theirs. The Chinese moved in and built a military road before India was aware of what was happening. The buildup of Chinese troops along the McMahon line began early in 1962 after a long period of prepara-

Yaks are a sturdy species of cattle, eminently well adapted to life in the highlands and mountains. An average animal weighs about 200 kilos (440 pounds). A yak cow produces only about one liter of milk per day, but the milk has an extremely high fat content.

Facing page: *The commonest trees in the high, damp forest of the East Himalayas are firs and birch, with a thick undergrowth of rhododendron and mountain bamboo.*

51

Right: *Young and old enjoy a Lingga feast, the "Time of the Gardens," in the festively decorated tents.*

Below: *A performance of a Tibetan play at the Zhotan festival. In earlier times such performances were only allowed in the presence of the Dalai Lama in the summer palace in Lhasa, but today they are open to all.*

Right: *The staple food of the Tibetans consists of tsampa, roasted flour made from highland barley. It is made into small balls and eaten with butter tea.*

Facing page: *The Bazaar on the Barkhor, the road around the Jokhang temple in the center of Lhasa. Above the two Tibetan women hang huge bundles of prayer flags.*

The Lingkor of the Sera monastery to the northeast of Lhasa leads through this imposing spot, strewn with round granite boulders that invite one to meditate. The lamas recognized this long ago and painted religious themes on the blocks. A less appealing use is made of some similar granite blocks to the east of Sera. Here dead bodies are laid out and left to the vultures for "heavenly transport." The granite near Lhasa is 40 million years old.

tion. On the Indian side the buildup was at first taken to be an escalation of the border conflict. Only when it was too late did India recognize what the threat really was. To defend their territory, the Indians used troops unaccustomed to mountain warfare, and when the Chinese launched their attack on October 20, 1962, beginning with massive artillery fire from the wooded heights, the Indians down below in the narrow valleys were badly beaten. After 30 days the Chinese reached the lower hills and the plain of Assam and then, unexpectedly, they withdrew.

The area south of the McMahon line is known as the N.E.F.A. (North Eastern Frontier Agency) or more recently as Arunachal Pradesh, and today,

together with Nagaland, it is regarded as one of the states of India. However, the Chinese still lay claim to this region of the eastern Himalayas, which remains closed to foreigners, and it will not easily find peace.

At its eastern end the range of the Himalayas rises once again, into the extremely wild and scarcely known 7,800-meter-high (25,740-foot-high) Namche Barwa group, the highest part of all the eastern Himalayas. The Yarlung Tsangpo, now up to a kilometer (0.6 mile) wide, approaches these mountains slowly, then suddenly narrows to only 90 meters (297 feet) and crashes down between huge cliffs into a deep gorge. In the thirties, British botanists and ornithologists were the only Europeans to have observed this

North of Lhasa, at the foot of the unique Nyenchentanglha chain, the biggest thermal region of Tibet was discovered. A steaming lake had been spoken of since time immemorial. Recent borings several hundred meters deep have released superheated water that gushes out like a geyser. The cause of this phenomenon is a recent fault zone along the Nyenchentanglha chain, the western part of which is shown here.

spectacle. Now Chinese scientists are active in the as yet unclimbed Tibetan Namche Barwa group. The passage of the Yarlung Tsangpo through the Namche Barwa chain is probably the most spectacular and, until now, least-explored gorges in the world; to the south lies Namche Barwa itself (7,800 meters [25,740 feet]) and to the north the Gyala Peri (7,100 meters [23,430 feet]). On the north side of Namche Barwa steep glaciers up to 10 kilometers (6 miles) long extend down into the gorge. Huge ice avalanches are by no means rare in this region. Here too, one of the great Himalayan rivers has chosen one of the highest sections of the chain to break through the mountains, a fact that is not easy to explain, particularly in this case, unless one believes in the legend of the great lama who cut a gap with his sword to release the flood waters of Tibet. Initially the great gorge runs to the northeast, then turns sharply to the southeast. At this point the Yekhung Chu flows into the Yarlung gorge. It drains the little known Nyenchentanglha group, which lies to the northwest, a heavily glaciated region over 7,000 meters (23,100 feet) high, actually a continuation of the chain of the same name to the north of Lhasa. The river runs from the northwest to the southeast, following the major fault zone that sharply cuts off the Himalayan chain stretching away to the northeast. The hot springs along this zone testify to the fact that the shaping and growth of the

Facing page: View from the fortress of Gyantse looking down on the old town and away toward the north. The monastery settlement, surrounded by a great wall, is now partly in ruins. The main monastery and the Kumbum are also visible.

Below right: Statues of the great Tibetan "priest-kings" of the seventh and eighth centuries in the "Maitreya" chapel of the monastery. The wooden statues date from the 15th century and represent Songtsengampo (609 – 649), Thisongdetsen (755 – 797) and Ralpachan (817 – 836).

Above: *The jewel of Gyantse, the Kumbum, built about 1414 – 1424 but still in good condition today. Pilgrims walk around this "Stupa of the 100,000 Pictures" in a clockwise direction. This monumental chorten is regarded by the Italian Tibetologist Giuseppe Tucci as the most important example of Tibetan art.*

mountains is still going on. The Yarlung itself continues southeastward in its gorge, running through extremely dense rain forest. At Medog, now only 1500 meters (4,950 feet) above sea level, it turns to the southwest. Past Tuting – and we are now already in the N.E.F.A. territory – it is again a broad river and reaches the plain of Assam. Along this last stretch the Yarlung is known as the Dihang. Coming out of the mountains, it changes its name again and flows comfortably along as the Brahmaputra (the river of the god Brahma), now several kilometers wide and divided into many branches, heading westward through the plain of Assam. It is forced to narrow again somewhat by the Shillong massif in the south, then flows on

It was formerly called Rasa, "Land of the Goats," only becoming known as Lhasa, "Land of the Gods," in the mid-7th century. Songtsengampo, the first of the great kings of Tibet, made it his capital on the Kyi-Chu, the "River of Fortune." The king's headquarters were usually in a military encampment, but he constructed residences for his two foreign wives, the Nepalese Princess Brikuti, who lived in the castle on the red hill, and the Chinese Princess Wengcheng. Each came to Tibet with a large retinue of learned men, artists and handworkers. These were "dynastic marriages," insisted upon by the then mightiest ruler in central Asia as a means of ensuring peace and well-being for his kingdom. These wives helped the king to introduce Buddhism and they also promoted the trade routes, thanks to which the importance of Lhasa, with its central position, began to increase.

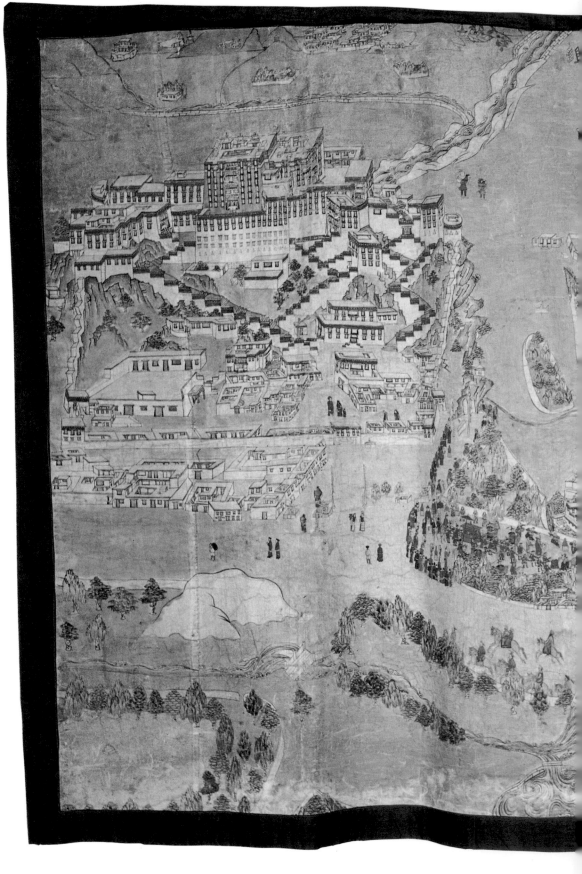

through Bengal and turns gradually toward the south (Bangladesh). Following the western edge of the Shillong massif, which is part of the Indian shield, it finally unites with the Ganges before opening into the Bay of Bengal. In the Bay of Bengal these two rivers together form the largest known submarine delta. The delta consists of material that has been eroded from the still growing Himalayas.

Like parts of a huge arch, the Yarlung in the north, the Dihang in the east and the Brahmaputra in the south combine to flow as the great river round the East Himalayas, arguably the most interesting, but at present the least known, section of the whole 3,000-kilometer-long (1,800-mile-long) mountain range. In the dense jungle there are still primitive tribes, which for many years added an extra degree of difficulty to the task of exploring a

Thanka with a plan of Lhasa – such guide maps for pilgrims hung on monastery walls. On the right the old town, with Tsuglakhang, Barkhor and Ramoche (left), and on the left the road leading over the "turquoise bridge" to the Potala.

Right: *Ornament on the roof of the city temple (Jokhang) in Lhasa. One of the oldest Buddhist symbols is the "wheel of knowledge," which Buddha himself first set in motion during his first sermon in the Gazelle Park of Sarnath. Since then, it and the listening gazelles have been a symbol of the living message of Buddhism.*

Above: *A lama cleaning the statue of the protecting god Thowo-Menra Tsegpa in the monastery of Drehpung. According to a letter written by the fifth Dalai Lama (1617 – 1682), this god put an invading Chinese army to flight.*

region where the climatic conditions and intense monsoon rainfall region made exploration hard enough anyway. The foothills of Assam rank among the wettest places on earth in terms of rainfall. Along the Dihang is the homeland of the Abor tribe, warlike jungle dwellers whose weapons include spears, long swords and poison arrows. From the very first contacts, the athletic Abors were hostile to "foreigners" in their region. Southeast of the Abors' territory in the Assam Burma border area, live the Mishmi. To the north, and particularly to the west of the actual Yarlung Tsangpo bend, out as far as the Bhutan border, the real mountain tribe of the Monpas makes its home. Only to the east and to the southwest of the great bend do we find small enclaves of the Lopas and Denpas, where the men often wear black turbans and smoke long pipes, a custom shared by their women. In higher regions these people usually live in wooden huts, with shingle roofs often weighted down with stones; in lower regions the huts are made of bamboo. The Monpas build stone houses, often with horizontal beams in the walls, and the result looks rather like the construction of primitive English cottages. In contrast to the Abors, most of these tribes are friendly toward newcomers, unless they feel they are being forced out of their homeland, which is all too often the case. These are tribes of Indian-Tibetan-Burmese origin, and their beliefs still retain ideas of animism and shamanism. The influence of Buddhism is only slightly in evidence in the Monpa tribe.

At the beginning of the 19th century, one of the major puzzles that the British Indian Survey had to solve was the so-called missing link — the connection between the Yarlung Tsangpo and the Brahmaputra. The Yarlung Tsangpo south of Lhasa was a known factor, so was the lower region of the Dihang and its entry into the Brahmaputra. But were these the same waters? Didn't the Yarlung flow into the Salween? Exploration began with the Dihang, but several efforts failed because of Abor hostility, their devastating attacks on the newly planted tea gardens in the Assam foothills causing quite a stir. Usually the Abors allowed the Indian troops to penetrate into the jungle, and then they would mount fierce attacks from behind and cut them down. The Indian survey then tried to solve the puzzle by approaching from the Tibetan side, but Tibet was forbidden territory; so the survey sent in groups of Pundits, natives mainly from Sikkim who were trained by the survey to be experts in the field. The most famous of the Pundits, Kinthub, managed to reach the spot where the Yarlung vanished into the deep gorge of the Namche Barwa, but only after ovecoming great difficulties on the way. It was impossible to penetrate the gorge, and so it was decided, according to Kinthub's report, to solve the problem in the following relatively simple way: Marked logs would be thrown into the Yarlung at the start of the gorge, and a special group would then try to locate these logs in the lower section of the Dihang, which is where they would appear if these waters were really the same. Kinthub was charged with carrying out this project, but unfortunately he was taken prisoner. Down at the lower end of the Dihang the other members of the expedition vainly awaited the arrival of his logs. Kinthub managed to escape a year later. He decided to try again and had 50 logs marked with iron, which he concealed in a large cave. He then went indirectly to Lhasa, where he found a Sik-

Next double page: Reflection of the north face of the Potala in a little lake in the morning sunlight. The actual temple lake lies to the right of the little wood. The ancient willow trees show an unusual growth pattern, with a definite spiral tendency in a clockwise direction – the way Buddhist pilgrims go around temples.

kimese to whom he dictated a letter to the survey, giving the date on which the logs would be thrown into the Yarlung. The Sikkimese set off for Darjeeling, and Kinthub again reached his cave at the start of the Yarlung Tsangpo gorge, this time with little trouble. On the set date he began to throw his logs into the river, 10 each day. This was in the middle of November 1883. After he finished, Kinthub tried to get through the valleys south of Namche Barwa down to the Dihang. He almost made it, but at the last moment he was attacked by the Abors and had to flee again. Four years later he managed to reach Darjeeling. His letter had never reached the

The Jokhang ("House of the Master," the Buddha) in Lhasa is the holiest spot in Tibet. Built in the seventh century and greatly enlarged in the 17th, this building is the heart of the city. Countless devout pilgrims, often traveling great distances, come here daily to worship a most sacred statue of Buddha, the Jobo Shakyamuni. The outer court is also the scene of daily religious rituals.

61

Facing page: *Yak-leather boats on the Kyi-Chu, a river that comes via Lhasa and enters the Yarlung Tsangpo. These boats can be carried by one man and are used on the rivers in Tibet for transporting both people and goods. In former times the upper classes used to take boat excursions from Lhasa down to the Yarlung Tsangpo junction.*

Next double page: *The Yumbu Lakhang, the "Fortress of Life" or "Temple on the Tamarisk Hill" with its elegant tower, is taken as a symbol of Tibet. It stands high above the Yarlung valley, alongside the temple of the patron saint of Tibet, Tara Dolma. This is to the south of the district capital of Tsethang, near where the pyramid-like graves of the mummified early* kings were erected. Its construction is credited to Nyathitsenpo, the founder of the Yarlung dynasty, and it is not only the oldest fortress-like building in Tibet but also the oldest still-used fortress in the world, being over 2,000 years old. Completely destroyed during the Cultural Revolution (1966 – 1976), it was faithfully rebuilt according to the old plan and finished in 1985.

Over great stretches the Yarlung Tsangpo is practically level, and its many meanderings have formed huge sandbanks where the silt carried along has been deposited. These desert-like sand dunes are the result, particularly in the region south of Lhasa. Picture taken near the Samye monastery.

There are probably few mountains on earth that guard their secrets as well as the Namche Barwa and Gyala Peri groups, through which the Yarlung Tsangpo makes its way in the world's largest gorge. Today the area is being explored by the Chinese, but logistic difficulties and the climate make it a hard task. The 3,000-kilometer (1,800-mile) chain of the Himalayas ends here – how and why is still an open real question.

The largely unknown and heavily glaciated massif of Gyala Peri, north of the 7,800-meter (25,740-foot) Namche Barwa. The Yarlung Tsangpo forces its way through this wild massif in the world's largest gorge – quite impenetrable. Aerial photo looking toward the south.

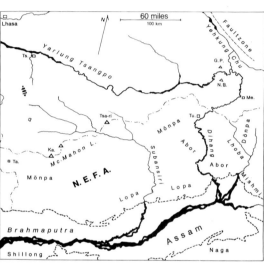

The Yarlung Tsangpo/Brahma-
putra loop: G. P. = Gyala Peri, Ka
= Kangto, Me = Medog, N. B.
= Namche Barwa, Ta = Tawang,
Ts = Tsethang, Tu = Tuting.

survey and so his 50 logs had floated down the Brahmaputra unnoticed, and on out to the sea.

In 1899, Lord Curzon, the Viceroy of India, tried a new approach. Obsessed with the thought that the Russians might be attempting to gain political influence in Tibet, he sent Younghusband to Lhasa with a military mission in 1904. In the meantime there had been an increase in the extent of Abor atrocities, and in October 1911 a new punitive force under General Bower was sent to the Abor region of the Dihang. This troop contained 800

The Lopa men of Leyn are hunters. The man here, hacking firewood with his bush knife, seems as reluctant to be separated from his bow as does the woman from the young bear.

Gurkhas, specially trained for jungle warfare, and 3,500 almost naked Naga warriors, armed with spears and keen to do battle against the Abors. Their enthusiasm was dampened, however, when General Bower decided not to let them bring home the heads of the Abors as trophies. Faced with an invading force of this size, the various Abor tribes joined forces for the first time to defend their territory. They cut through the liana ropes of the bridges, destroyed pathways, piled up tree trunks at narrow points between cliff and river, and dug out traps into which they put poisoned bamboo spikes. At strategic points they stored tree trunks and rocks high above paths, which they hurled down as the enemy troops came through. General

Bower's plan was to advance very cautiously so as not to fall into an ambush. The Gurkhas reconnoitered the terrain, removed obstacles and cleared away the nearby jungle. This slow progress (in a month they managed to clear no more than 40 kilometers [24 miles]) gradually wore down the Abor resistance, but it also wore down the Indian troops. Fourteen consecutive days of rain, despite this being the supposed dry season, and a drastic increase in the number of cases of malaria undermined their morale. Nevertheless, they managed to overcome the last pockets of resistance, not

Tribes that still live as they did long ago, hunting in the highland jungles with bows and arrows, can be found today in the southeast, which the Chinese call Nan Shan, "South Mountain," and which is shown on Indian maps as Arunachal Pradesh, "Land of the Rising Sun."
In the Middle Ages in Tibet much was spoken of the wild tribes that lived in this region, which were probably related to the headhunting Nagas of Assam. From the 12th or 13th century onward, this area gradually opened up and pilgrim routes and bridges were built. Among these routes was the one to the sacred mountain Tsa-ri, about which there are many tales and legends.

least because of the superiority of the Maxim machine-gun over the bows and spears of the natives. The surviving Abor chiefs began to capitulate, and at Christmas 1911 the punitive expedition was ended. Exploration of the Dihang could now begin again, but years went by before it was established (without the log experiment) that the Yarlung Tsangpo and the Brahmaputra were the same river. The "missing link," however, could still not quite be put into place. There remained 70 kilometers (42 miles) of the Yarlung gorge to explore, and to some extent it is still that way even today. Farther to the west there also remain some undiscovered secrets in the eastern Himalayas, where the Monpa tribes live. Here, on the upper reaches of the

In the remote and thickly wooded mountains of southeast Tibet the Monpas still hunt today with bows and arrows.

Subandsiri river lies the almost 6,000-meter-high (19,800-foot-high) Tsa-ri, the most sacred mountain in southeastern Tibet.

The tiny state of Sikkim, which is under Indian rule, acts as a buffer between the eastern and central Himalayas. B. C. Olschak wrote of it: "This state between the glaciers and the jungle is a hidden land among the high mountain gorges. In olden texts it was actually called 'Hidden Land' (Basyul) or 'Land of the Gorges' (Rong-yul). It lies embedded in the protective wall of the Himalayas, between the glaciers of the north and the jungles of the south. It is the 'Hidden Rice Valley' of the old texts, a fertile, hilly land, surrounded by huge peaks from 6,000 to 8,000 meters (19,800 to 26,400

Facing page: A Monpa mountain village. There are about 40,000 Monpas – the largest ethnic minority in the eastern Himalayas.

A string of mules and pack horses on the way to market, carrying butter churns for the preparation of butter tea. In the outlying areas of the eastern Himalayas roads and modern means of transport are still hardly ever seen.

feet) high. In the words of its last king, Paldan Thondup, Sikkim's pride does not lie in its strength of arms, nor in its bravery on the battlefield. The heart of the people has always been given over to religion, peace and benevolent acts, and its finest sons have always devoted themselves to the study and the practice of their belief."

The western end of the eastern Himalayas, between the Yarlung Tsangpo in the north and the Brahmaputra in the south, where the journey southwards to the sea has begun, is one of the most beautiful areas of the whole Himalayan region, the incomparable kingdom of Bhutan.

B. C. Olschak wrote in *Bhutan: Land of Hidden Treasures:* "... it is a

'Land of Fortresses' with a 'Fortress Language' (thus called because the famous Bhutanese fortresses, once the centre of the military, civil and administrative power, are still the seat of the government and the main temple of the district and the longest and finest chain of glacier mountains, full of still hidden treasure. Towards the middle of the northern border rises the Kangkar Punsum, 7,550 meters [24,915 feet] high. Its name, full of promise, means 'White Glacier of the Three Spiritual Brothers,' recalling the once peaceful co-existence of three races, the Tibetans, the Bhutanese and the Monpas of the south-eastern Himalayas – now once again slowly opening their borders. Far to the east of the giant glaciers rises the Zhug-thikang, the 'Throne of the Gods' of Kurto. At its foot lies Sengge Dzong, the 'Lion Fortress'. For travelers coming from the north, Bhutan was the

Facing page: A thickly wooded mountain valley in the eastern Himalayas, following heavy monsoon rain. Here the monsoon is particularly intense and lasts from May to October.

Three generations of a Donpa family. In the tropical parts of the Yarlung Tsangpo the men wear black turbans and are great pipe smokers – as are the women.

'Paradise of the South'. In old texts it was also referred to as the 'Lotus Garden of the Gods – full of sandalwood forests and fragrant herbs'. Medicinal herbs have been one of the exports of this area since time immemorial. For the Indians in the south this was the 'Land of the Bhutias,' from which the name 'Bhutan' derives. The Bhutias, as all the Tibetan tribes in the north-east of India were called, came slowly down into the south-eastern Himalayan region starting about 1,500 years ago. Exact descriptions of the four southern Mon districts existed a long time ago. In the north is

Next double page: *Near the great loop of the Yarlung Tsangpo = Brahmaputra. A view of the village and monastery of Demo Chemnak across to the Kongpo Bonri, the most sacred mountain of the Bon religion. Hidden by clouds to the right is Namche Barwa, 7,756 meters (25,595 feet) and as yet unclimbed.*

The watershed of the shimmering Himalaya glaciers forms the northern border of Bhutan. It is also a climatic border – separating the "Southern Garden of Paradise," where rice grows in altitudes up to 2,800 meters (9,240 feet) and multicolored giant rhododendrons flourish up to 4,000 meters (13,200 feet), from the dry lifeless cliffs and ice of the north.

The easternmost and least known of the mountains on the Bhutan border, Garula Kang. It rises to 6,500 meters (21,450 feet), with the forest reaching up to 4,100 meters (13,530 feet), where the tongues of the glaciers meet the luxuriously thick rhododendron undergrowth.

Punskha, the 'Flowering Valley of the Abundant Southern Fruit,' where mandarins, sweet bananas, huge citrus fruits and sugar cane flourish. To the south lies Pasamkha – now called Buxa – the 'District of All Wishes,' at the foot of the Himalayas, where goods from the north are traded for the products of the south. In the west is Dalikha, the 'Walnut Tree Region,' now called Kalimpong, an area which once belonged to Bhutan. To the east is Dungsamkha, 'the Land of Longing and the Silver Pines.'"

Nowhere else has the beauty of the old traditions been so authentically and harmoniously maintained as in Bhutan. True, the newly built highland road has opened the way for tourism, but the country has not allowed itself to be swamped by this development. Thanks to the natural diplomatic talents of King Jigme Dorje Wangchuck, who died in 1972, Bhutan became a constitutional monarchy. This tiny state, sandwiched between two huge ones, India and China, makes use of the technology it needs but also preserves what was good in the past. In this region, which is protected to the north by the watershed of the Himalayas, the mountain gods live on, and Buddhism flourishes as the state religion in the Drukpa-Kagyu school. The highest mountain in Bhutan, the "Glacier of the Three Spiritual Brothers" (Kangar Punsum), symbolizes the wish for peaceful coexistence shared by the Bhutanese, the Tibetans, and the native Monpas and other tribes who sought refuge and found peace in this area.

A festive procession of members of a Bhutanese monastery, on their way from the main temple to the royal palace. They are carrying the famous round Buddhist flags, which spread the truth of their teachings equally in all directions.

THE INDUS

Of all the Kailas rivers, the Indus is the one that flows farthest to the north into the Tibetan highlands. Its headwaters used to be quite short rivers, ending in a basin with no outlet, until a further upthrust of the Tibetan highlands occurred. The river then found its way through to the west. There, following the geological path formed by the suture, it became the life-giving water supply for Ladakh and Baltistan, the northern part of Pakistan.

We've returned to the sacred Kailas, looking northward toward the countless russet and yellow chains of the Tibetan highlands. Exactly on the north side of the Kailas chain is the source area of the second largest Himalayan river, the Indus. Like the Yarlung Tsangpo, the Indus has its beginnings in a number of arms, but the scale is somewhat smaller. Approaching from the Kailas, Sven Hedin discovered the source in 1907. Since then it seems that there have been no other Europeans in this area. Again like the Yarlung, the Indus is fed by three tributaries. Based on the amount of water carried, the actual source river would be the Lungdep

Nomad tents in the source area of the Indus. The west and north of Tibet is nomad country – over great stretches here there are no permanent settlements and no monasteries. The life-style of these people has hardly changed for hundreds of years.

Chu, which rises in the south near the Kailas. However, Sven Hedin's Tibetan guide led him to the northeastern tributary, the much less important Bokhar Chu, in the lower reaches of which several springs issue from a white porous chalk. On top of this chalk layer stand several "stone men" (cairns), and numerous finely carved *Mani* stones and little clay figurines (*Tsa-tsas*) just lie there. The place is referred to as Senge Khambah, source of the "Lion's Mouth," a name by which the upper Indus is also known. From this, its official "source," the Indus flows through a wide, rather monotonous highland with barren desert-like hills. The region is practically uninhabited, although here and there we encounter nomads with their black tents. Farther downstream the Indus gradually makes a turn toward the west, and a new military road follows its course. The new military camps with their mud and sheet metal barracks are certainly no decorative addition to the landscape.

Near the old monastery site of Tashigang the Indus reaches a wide valley that runs toward the northwest, with the once important but now disused trading center of Gartok to the southeast. This valley follows the famous

Tinkar lies in a remote side valley in northwestern Nepal, near the 5,100-meter (16,830-foot) pass that leads into Tibet. But even this village, with only 200 inhabitants,

Indus-Yarlung suture zone, with the granite of the Transhimalayas visible to the north. The same valley leads farther off to the northwest, passes the fjord-like Pangong Tso to the south and then becomes part of the Shyok valley; the Shyok comes down from the Karakorum pass, flows south at first along the Karakorum fault and then swings sharply northwest by the little town of Shyok. Here it follows the second suture, which farther to the northwest is known as the Shyok suture and forms the border with the Karakorum. The geological properties of this area make its topography par-

has its own temple, with prayer flags fluttering on top. A surprising find here is this mural, which is a map of the region around the sacred Mount Kailas. In addition to the conically shaped Kailas one can see the round sacred Lake Manasarowar and the nearby monasteries, once under Bhutanese control but now largely destroyed.

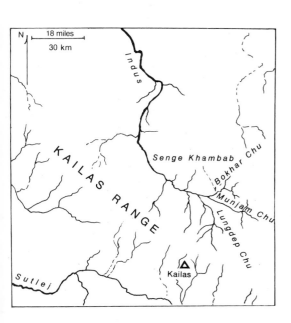

The source of the Indus near the
sacred Mount Kailas.

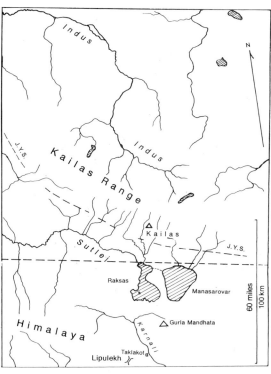

The lower half of this Landsat photo, taken on March 16, 1977, shows the snow-covered Kailas group (Transhimalayas), with Mount Kailas itself at the center of the southern edge. This stands out very clearly because of the Indus-Yarlung suture (I.Y.S.). South of Mount Kailas we can just make out the northern tip of Lake Raksas, from which the Sutlej emerges to the west. North of Mount Kailas, on the northern slopes of the Kailas chain, we find the three sources of the Indus. Farther north, in the upper half of the picture, there is an area of broad plains, basins with no outlet, and wildly strewn mountains that form a remarkable composition, dominated by volcanic rock. Most of the plains were once great lakes that filled up and dried out over the years. (Taken from a height of 900 kilometers [540 miles.])

ticularly striking. Meanwhile, the Indus, having reached the Gartok valley region near Tashigang, now flows among wild black hills, which document the oceanic rocks of the suture. It follows this zone for 100 kilometers (60 miles) and then breaks through the granite of the Ladakh chain.

We have now left Tibet and are on Indian soil as we follow the broad val-

In his lap this Buddha is holding a symbol of the most sacred mountain, Meru, in the form of a rock crystal. He is one of the "35 Buddhas for the Forgiveness of Sins" and is called Shailendraraja Jina, the Victorious, King of the Mightiest Mountain, of the Center of the World, long known from old Hindu texts as the residence of the gods. On mythological maps this mountain is drawn in the region of Pamir and later was taken to be Mount Kailas. This Buddha and the rest of the group of 35 form part of the "Thousand Buddhas" often depicted on the walls of the main temples. An original text describing them is said to have come from China to Tibet as early as the seventh century, a "guide to the age of happiness," at which time the 1,000 Buddhas appear and come to the aid of sufferers.

ley, now characterized by the Indus-Yarlung suture, which makes a cut over 300 kilometers (180 miles) long through the ancient kingdom of Ladakh in a northwesterly direction. Like the Yarlung Tsangpo, the course of the Indus alternates between wide plains and short gorges, accompanied by signs of an old culture – numerous monasteries on the hills or on the cliffs,

Below: *The deserted granite landscape of the Transhimalayas (Ladakh chain), north of the monastery of Thikse. Clearly visible are the young (light) granite rocks that have intruded through the older (dark) ones.*

This Landsat photo, taken on April 13, 1977 from a height of 900 kilometers (540 miles), covers the area to the south of the fjord-like Pangong Tso (Tso = lake), which is 150 kilometers (90 miles) long and lies at 4,250 meters (14,025 feet). It forms the border between the eastern Karakorum, Ladakh and the western Tibetan highlands. The Indus flows through the middle of the picture, from southeast to northwest, from Tibet into eastern Ladakh. On the river, almost in the center of the picture, lies the once important little trading town of Tashigong (Ta). The great Indus-Yarlung suture (I.Y.S.) runs diagonally through the whole area, as the border between the Indian continent in the southwest and Eurasia (Tibet) to the northeast. At Tashigong the Indus-Yarlung suture splits into the zone that leads to Ladakh and the Shyok suture (Sh.s), which runs off farther to the northwest. In the lower left part of the picture the Morari Tso, at 4,500 meters (14,850 feet), stands out. North of the Indus, in the Ladakh region, the snow-covered granite chain continues, passing north of the capital, Leh. East of Tashigong as well as to the south of the Indus in Ladakh the unusually dark cliffs mark where the oceanic crust rocks (ophiolites) have been forced up.

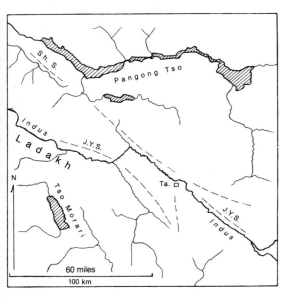

With a length of 150 kilometers (90 miles) the Pangong Tso is the longest of the fjord-like lakes in the border area between the Transhimalayas and the Karakorum. The contrast between its deep blue waters and the bare but colorful mountains nearby, inspired Sven Hedin to paint one of his best watercolors. The sunken valley of Pangong Tso is reminiscent of the complicated Yamdrok Tso south of Lhasa.

Even over 5,300 meters (17,490 feet) high in the Himalayas one can still find flowers in bloom (here Sedum rhodiola). Picture taken on the Stakspi La between Ladakh and Zanskar, just below the snow line.

No less than 2,500 years ago, Arhat Bakula made a pilgrimage into the northernmost regions of the Himalayas and the Karakorum. He is holding a jewel-spitting mongoose, a symbol of his wish to relieve the poverty of the mountain folk. In Ladakh, where he was the first to preach the message, he still lives on after numerous successive reincarnations and is worshipped as the Bakula Lama.

Right: *Bird's-eye view of the Indus near the monastery of Alchi. Every traveler in Ladakh follows the course of the Indus for long stretches. The muddy brown river soon makes a wide arc through Baltistan into northern Pakistan. This flood plain is very fertile. In the 11th century one of the jewels of Buddhist monastic skill was built here, with the most splendid wall paintings.*

Facing page and below: *Leh, the capital of Ladakh, has almost 10,000 inhabitants and lies at the same altitude as Lhasa (3,650 meters [12,045 feet] above sea level). Reminiscent of the Potala in Lhasa, the former royal palace that was built in the early 17th century was already in ruins by the 19th century. In earlier times Leh was an important transit point for*

irrigated fields, and most impressively the capital Leh, with the king's palace dominating everything else. It was built at the start of the 17th century by King Sengge Namgyel, the greatest of all Ladakhi rulers. Below the palace, in the town itself, there was always a lively trade in the market streets, which are lined with poplars, and a mixture of Asiatic peoples of all races. However, Leh's pre-eminence as a trading center came to an end with the Chinese invasion of Tibet. Now there are military encampments and an airport between Leh itself and the several arms of the Indus.

pilgrims and caravans on the way to Yarkand and Lhasa. Today it is the last stop for foreigners on the scenic road from Kashmir. There is now a military road over the 5,500-meter (18,150-foot) Kardung La into the Shyok valley, one of the highest road passes in the world. Above: View from Leh toward the Kangri group.

The wide valley is framed by the bare granite mountains to the north and the very orderly chain of the Zanskar in the south. A well-bedded molasse forms the immediate southern edge. Then come the dark rocks of the suture, and farther away still the extremely rugged limestone mountains, split by incredible gorges – important routes down into the southern valleys. The southern end is formed by the glaciated Zanskar chain, over which towers the 7,135-meter-high (23,546-foot-high) Nun-Kun group. The

Faces along Karakorum Road

Particularly striking among the crowd are the long-headed, large-nosed men who wear great beards with the tips dyed red and turbans artistically wound around their heads. They are reminiscent of the Dards and other Indo-European tribes. The "top hats," with their earflaps folded up,

glacier passes stand at over 5,000 meters (16,500 feet) and are particularly impressive. They form an important climatic division – we are now leaving the dry highland climate of Ladakh and entering the southern high altitude forest region with its birch and firs, before gradually reaching the real mountain jungle, which is usually quite light but greatly influenced by the seasons. In the isolated villages most of the houses are wooden, usually covered with shingles. Astonishing wood carvings adorn many of the temples, which are dedicated to local saints.

Ladakh, too, has unfortunately suffered "militarization." Along the new military road we encounter hundreds of trucks, bringing supplies to the many army camps. A strikingly high proportion of the soldiers are dark southern Indians, who, despite being well equipped, always feel cold. At the beginning of winter in 1975 – Ladakh had only been opened to out-

are also remarkable, worn here by two Ladakhi women with prayer beads. To the right is a Kan woman with a pretty felt hat; next to her the portrait of a smith from Chilling. One often comes upon lamas dressed in Tibetan monks' habits with their horns.

siders in 1974 – the three of us were the first foreign geologists to do field-work in the area. On November 7 winter began. The Zoji La, the only pass through to Kashmir, was already snowed in, and we got hopelessly stuck with our jeep on the north side. So that we would not have to spend the whole winter in Ladakh, we attempted to cross the Zoji La on foot, carrying heavy packs. At 3,530 meters (11,649 feet) this is the lowest pass in the entire Himalayas. In the evening, when we reached the pass, the snow was already over one meter (3.3 feet) deep, and even more laid on the south side. And avalanches of new snow were sliding down the steep southern slopes. We fought our way along the military road and in the middle of the night in

Left: *The snake-shaped bonnets worn by the women in northern Ladakh, which represent their fortunes, catch one's eye. The peraks have widely protruding earmuffs of black lambskin and curve forward over the wearer's forehead; they often extend far down in back. Artistically applied turquoise stones decorate the cap. Jewel necklaces and amulets revealing a woman's wealth are worn with the bonnet.*

Above: *A wedding dancer wears the richly decorated five-leaf crown.*

a snowstorm we came upon a truck convoy that was completely blocked in and in deep snow near an extremely steep avalanche slope. As we made our way past the trucks in the deep snow, a small flashlight came on and a southern Indian soldier asked in a friendly voice, "Do you want a cup of tea? That's all we have." It was only days later that the blocked convoy could be rescued, using special snow ploughs brought up from Ladakh.

At Khalsi, a small trading center north of Lamayuru, the Indus leaves the wide valley of Ladakh and disappears into a bare, impassable granite gorge, heading off to the northwest. From Lamayuru the military road leads over

Next double page: *There is no place like Ladakh for observing the variety of tribes and heritages, especially at the bazaar in the capital city, Leh, where a cheerful crowd mills about, or at the religious festivals, where the headgear alone indicates background and customs.*

93

The black-hat dancer performs in the mystery plays that are held on monastery holy days in the temple courtyards, here in Ladakh, as well as in Sikkim and Bhutan. This is a grand play enacted in beautiful costumes that wordlessly commemorates an important real-life drama of bygone days by means of

movement and dance. It deals with the victory of good over evil, as illustrated for example by the assassination of the treacherous Tibetan King Langdarma, who wanted to eradicate Buddhism and convert the temples into bars. A solitary yogi decided to take action against him. Disguised as a Shamanist black-hat dancer, he entered the court and fascinated Langdarma so completely that he was able to stab the king to death, thus putting an end to the Yarlung dynasty in Lhasa during the midninth century.

Left and below: *Among Ladakh's fortresses and fortified monasteries, Thikse is exceptional. A typical example of monastery design with its tapering walls, it climbs high up the hill. It is located on the road to Hemis about 17 kilometers [10 miles] from Leh and was supposedly founded in the 15th*

century. The Buddha of the Future, Maitreya, is held in high esteem here, where frescoes of the 84 Mahassidhas, the "Great Miracle Workers," shine from the walls of the courtyard. The monks' living quarters cling to the hillside below the main building. Here, as in all monasteries, the lamas beat the large standing drums to summon the faithful to religious ceremonies.

Facing page: *A little-known relief of Buddha Maitreya carved into rock on the Suru river in Zanskar. This carving was rediscovered by the geologist Kaspar Honegger 10 years ago.*

the 4,100-meter-high (13,530-foot-high) Fatu La, then over the 3,720-meter-high (12,276-foot-high) Namika La, after which it follows the Wakha Chu until it reaches the important center of Kargil, where a strong Islamic influence is evident. Probably no other area in all of Asia has such a sharp dividing line between Buddhist and Islamic cultures. In Kargil and the other small villages of the Suru valley the colored domes of the mosques and their delicate minarets glisten in the sun. The houses themselves, mostly mud and wood constructions, are rather drab by comparison, but the streets are enlivened by the colorful clothing and the obligatory head-

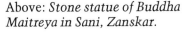

Above: *Stone statue of Buddha Maitreya in Sani, Zanskar.*

Above right: *Bronze idol from Kashmir dating from around the 12th century. In the Ladakh of about 1000 years ago, the Light did not yet shine out of the East. At that time, Kashmir was a center of Buddhist scholarship and many impulses came to Ladakh from the West, as did this outstanding statue of a bodhisattva that today is housed in Hemis monastery.*

wear of the women. The broad Kargil basin and its impressive river terraces (now mainly used as military training grounds and depots) are separated from the Mulbeck valley, which lies to the east by the 12-kilometer-long (7-mile-long) Wakha gorge. Suddenly, at the eastern end of the gorge we find ourselves transported into a Buddhist landscape. Surrounded by intensely cultivated fields, we see the tidy white-painted Tibetan houses; on the flat roofs lies firewood for the coming cold, but not usually very snowy, winter. Chortens and little temples line the trails, and monasteries perched on steep hills dominate the scene. The strange looking limestone cliffs seem to have been put here expressly to have monasteries built on top of them and to be used for artistic carvings. This is particularly so in the mon-

astery town of Mulbekh. The unusual landscape is characterized by the exotic limestone masses thrust up from the deep ground along the suture zone. The Buddhists, with their love of nature and their vivid imaginations, must have felt inspired to perform artistic feats by these rocks from the oceanic crust and, in fact, by this whole landscape.

The Indus also has now reached Islamic territory, but in the steep and desert-like granite gorges there is little sign of the change. This area was never inhabited and no caravan trails went this way. Today this is a "no entry" area, a military no-man's land. The Indus gorge does not reopen until we reach Skardu, formerly an important transit point on the way from Kashmir via the Burzil pass and the high Deosai plateau into the Karakorum. Skardu lies in a wide desert valley with high river terraces and sand dunes. Opening into the Indus from the northwest is the broad Shigar river, which drains the eastern Karakorum. It rises from the Baltoro glacier, which we noticed before because of its young granite with the imposing

Facing page: *Bridge over the Barai Nala in Zanskar.*

Above: *The Head Lama of Karsha monastery.*

Above right: *Karsha monastery in Zanskar. The first missionaries from the Gelugpa school ("The Virtuous"), founded in Tibet in 1419, reached the western Himalayas after only 10 years. Karsha is one of the monasteries they established. Those in Zanskar are usually simpler than the ones located in neighboring Ladakh, but they also are less spoiled.*

Trango towers. In Skardu it becomes apparent that since leaving Ladakh and passing through the granite gorge, the Indus has doubled in size.

Thirty kilometers (18 miles) southeast of Skardu, the Shyok joins the Indus. At this confluence, it is worth noting, both rivers are exactly the same size, though the Indus has come twice as far. The explanation for this phenomenon lies in the tributaries of the Shyok, which nearly all come from large, active glacier areas. At times in the past, when some supply rivers of the Shyok have been dammed by rapid glacial advances, there have frequently been serious flood disasters. In 1840 an ice barrier is said to have blocked the upper course of the Shyok and formed a lake 16 kilometers (9.6 miles) long and 150 meters (495 feet) deep. Six months later a 10-meter-

Buddha Maitreya in Mulbekh, Ladakh, carved into a huge limestone block. The limestone, which often forms steep hills, has been pushed up from unknown depths along the Indus-Yarlung (Brahmaputra)-Suture rivers. Small monasteries are often perched atop the hills or frescoes adorn their sides. The Mulbekh area is a classic example of this landscape. This monument

from the eighth-ninth centuries bears the following inscription from the Ministry of Jammu and Kashmir: "This statue of Maitreya was carved probably in first century B.C. during Kushan period. According to Buddhist belief the fifth Buddha will be Maitreya in the series of one thousand Buddhas who are to visit this world. Certain inscriptions perhaps in the Kharoshti script on the back of the rock are reported to have been buried. This is a land mark in the history of Ladakh and we must strive hard to preserve it."

high (33-foot-high) wave swept through the valleys, destroying everything in its path. Where the Shigar meets the Indus there was once a large lake, sediments from which are clearly seen in the prominent terraces of Skardu.

Leaving the Skardu basin, the Indus again flows through a deep gorge. There is now a bravely located military road that bypasses the once impassable gorge along the north face. The last section of the gorge is composed of the old crystalline wedge of the Indian shield, on the west side of

which the Indus makes a sudden sharp turn north, as if to flow around the rugged 7,300-meter-high [24,090-foot-high] Haramosh range to the north, and then goes south again to join up with the Hunza river. The wide valley of the lower Hunza river leads to the important Baltistan town of Gilgit, a former transit town on the north-south route along the middle Indus. This route followed the Hunza river to the north through the chain of the Kara-korum close to the unpredictable Pasu glacier that regularly fills the whole valley and causes dangerous damming of the rivers. Today the Pasu glacier

Below: *Ladakh. The valley of Shey with the many, mostly ruined, chorten. These chorten are the Tibetan – and also Ladakhi – form of the Indian or Nepalese stupa. This is really a burial place where the ashes of the dead, usually the devout, are kept. The chorten represent the universe.*

Right: *Coming from Srinagar one passes over the 4,100-meter (13,530-foot) Fatu La and reaches Lamayuru, one of the most famous monasteries in Ladakh, which was constructed in its present form in the 16th century. As if they had grown out of the rock face, its buildings nestle against the cliff in this rugged landscape. It belongs to the reformed yellow "school," which worships a superb statue of Avalokiteshvara, the Bodhisattva of Mercy here, in his eleven-headed and thousand-armed form. There is also a large library that houses the holy scriptures of the Tanjur and the Kanjur.*

In addition to the many Bodhisattvas, the anteroom of the Alchi monastery – the oldest still maintained in Ladakh – also contains a representation of two manned boats with flags flying (detail here). The appearance of boats in a monastery in a region that has been desert-like since the monastery's founding could be a way of preserving the notion that there were lakes in this region, whose existence in prehistoric times has been proven and which are mentioned in the legend of the Lamayuru monastery.

104

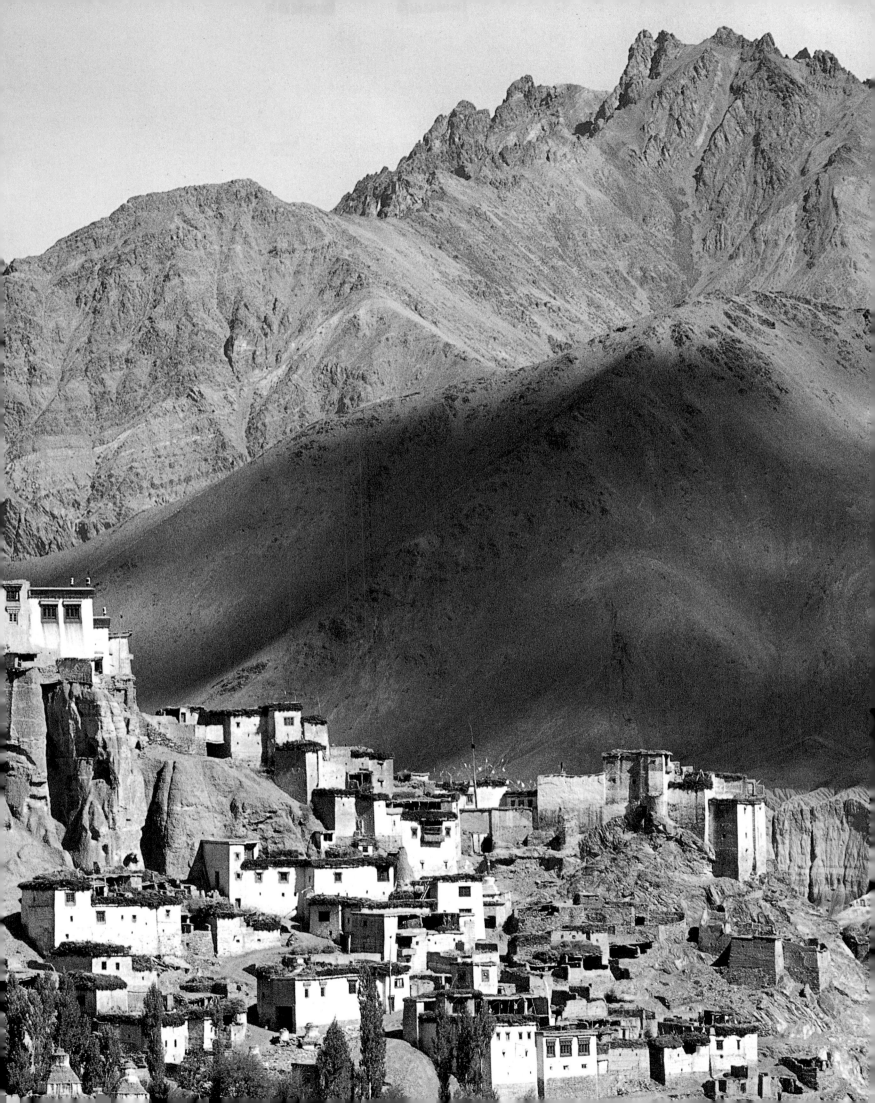

is still a fearsome problem for the new Karakorum road that the Chinese have built. At the foot of the wild Karakorum we can admire the old castle of the Emir of Hunza. It is a reminder of the days when the industrious Hunza were spread over a very wide area. Little is known of the origins of the Hunza. With their own language they could be a leftover people from past migrations. A large cliff on the northern route out of Hunza is covered with carvings of stylized mountain goats – perhaps a memorial to the Hunza's origins? Even today the intensely cultivated fields make quite an impression, the water for them being brought from the wild gorges along a

Above: *The old castle of the Hunza Kings, on the south side of the Karakorum. Hunza lies on the important Indus caravan route, and the Hunza people, with their own language, Burushaski, could be a remnant of migrations that followed this route. In the white marble layers in this area rubies are still found today.*

complicated channel system often along vertical cliff faces. Despite, or perhaps because of, the extremely harsh conditions under which they live, and perhaps because of the simple but nutritious products that they grow, the Hunza are among the healthiest peoples of the Himalayas.

Farther to the south we can already make out the glaciated massif of the 8,125-meter-high (26,813-foot-high) Nanga Parbat, which shuts off the broad valley of the Indus to the southwest and then forces it off to the west. The river now flows along the northwest flank of Nanga Parbat through the

Landsat photo taken on September 9, 1976. It shows the highly glaciated region of the eastern Karakorum and covers an area of 32,400 square kilometers (12,960 square miles). The snow line lies at about 5,000 meters (16,500 feet) and the lower part of the great glaciers is usually snow free. To the lower left the Baltoro glacier can be seen, with the Trango towers to the northwest and K 2 at the northern end. On the northern side the Karakorum is bounded by the Yarkand river system, which flows in the direction of the Pamir. The Karakorum pass (K. P.) leads off in the direction of the Yarkand source area.

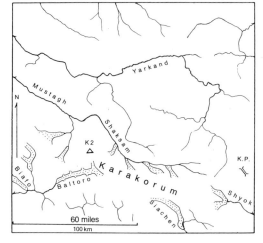

Facing page: Polish mountaineers on the north side of the northeast ridge of K 2. In 1976 they were attempting a new route, but when they were only 200 meters (660 feet) below the summit, the weather turned against them and forced them to descend.

Next double page: The south face of the eastern Karakorum showing the area where the Hushe joins up with the Shyok. The great flood plains are crisscrossed with hundreds of small streams. A contrast between the mountains and the plains.

wide gorge of Chilas. In this section we find the finest rock carvings, providing a record of over 3,000 years of caravan traffic along this north-south route. Here the climate is still dry, and the huge and solid granite cliffs along the banks of the Indus are covered with a shiny sort of desert varnish or lacquer. Predominantly manganese and iron oxides form a weathered crust on the surface of the rocks because of evaporation. This dark layer is particularly suitable for carving or chiseling figures or symbols, and once inscribed, these light marks remain for centuries. Here the Indus has another surprise in store for us: it is now only 1,000 meters (3,300 feet) above sea level and the peak of Nanga Parbat is only 21 kilomet-

Facing page: The Shyok flows along the East Karakorum, alternating between narrow gorges and broad flood plains, which form a complicated web of streams during the dry season but are completely flooded in spring and summer.

ers (12.6 miles) away. Along this stretch we notice the incredible over 7,000-meter (23,100-foot) difference in altitude. And steaming springs add to the surprise.

To the west of Chilas the Indus changes direction once again and begins a gradual turn toward the south, before finally flowing off in this direction. This change in direction is accompanied by a change in climate, too. After

A new suspension bridge over the Hunza river, strong enough to hold small trucks.

As the highest section of the West Himalayas, the 8,125-meter (26,813-foot) Nanga Parbat range runs almost perpendicular to the Himalayas and Karakorum, rather than parallel to them. This range borders the lesser known 7,300-meter (24,090-foot) Haramosh to the north, with a sharp boundary along the Shyok suture against the Karakorum, just before the Indus breaks through between the two peaks in a deep gorge. Here one can see huge folds and altered (metamorphic) rocks of the Indian shield, forming the northern spur, which is responsible for the peculiar position of Nanga Parbat. Drastic changes in the weather are quite common here and often lead to natural catastrophes.

At 8,125 meters (26,813 feet) Nanga Parbat is the highest peak of the Kashmir Himalayas (Pakistan) and the world's ninth highest mountain. In 1985 there were no less than 12 expeditions up this mountain, three of which reached the summit. In 1953 Hermann Buhl was the first to reach the summit, traveling alone via the northwest face.

the dryness of the western-oriented valley, the climate now begins to get somewhat wetter, once the south winds start to exert an influence in the now southward-oriented valleys. Following the low bushy vegetation, we here begin to encounter birch and firs, and still farther south we meet oak forests. Even in this region of the West Himalayas the climate remains relatively dry, with short intervals of a comparatively weak summer monsoon.

The religious landscape of Ladakh is characterized by old rock reliefs and drawings, which testify to the fact that Buddhism had a very early start in this region, in fact, flourishing during the first century B.C. and the first century A.D. Perhaps it had been introduced even earlier by missionaries, as the old legends would have us believe. It is certain that during the time of the Emperor Ashoka in the third century B.C. not only were monks active in Ladakh but also pupils of Buddha, the first Arhats.

Right: *This collapsible "traveling Thanka" is made of bronze and depicts the Buddha of the future, Maitreya. Between the rampant lions in the lower section one can see a lama with a prayer mill, a typical motif in old Ladakh.*

South of Patan, where earthquakes are quite frequent (the Indus crosses the southern suture zone here), there are more gorges. On the steep slopes one can see traces of older pathways, often with stone steps cut into the cliffs. Most of these paths run along the left flank of the valley, linking the little mountain villages to each other; today these villages are cut off from the main traffic, since the new Karakorum road runs along the right bank. The architecture of these little villages is noteworthy on account of the fortress-like temple towers, with their richly carved wooden upper stories.

There are similar buildings in southern Zanskar and near the southern tributaries of the Sutlej at altitudes between 2,000 and 3,000 meters (6,600 and 9,900 feet).

Before the Indus finally widens out, the Karakorum road veers off below Besham over an imposing suspension bridge built by the Chinese, an example of a technique that was developed in the Himalayas thousands of

Cliff engravings along the Indus near Chilas in northern Pakistan. Along the old caravan routes, a branch off the Silk Road, traders and pilgrims have left us interesting pictures and inscriptions at certain points in the Indus valley. It

years ago but which was originally a Chinese invention. The next Indus gorge is still largely unknown territory; there are no access roads and the tribes that live there are by no means friendly. Where the river finally leaves the highlands, it reaches a wide valley with some low hills, and here it is blocked by one of the largest dams in the whole of Asia, the Darbela, behind which the water backs up into a vast lake. To dam a river of this size is a difficult technical enterprise, particularly when a geological fault zone runs right across the dam. For this reason the dam has never been com-

was only when foreign researchers had access to this region, following the completion of the Karakorum highway, that these pictures were recognized as mostly dating back to the sixth and seventh centuries. Here one can clearly see a depiction of Buddha and the stupa shrine.

pletely watertight, and down low on the dam wall water seeps out as if from springs. Like the Ganges and the Brahmaputra, the Indus carries along vast quantities of mud and sand that will quite rapidly reduce the volume of the basin behind the dam, especially during the monsoons. It was not even possible to house the turbines in solid cliffs since the faults run along these, too. Thus the Darbela is proving to be something of a "white elephant" and it has never yet operated at its full capacity.

After the great western tributaries, like the Kunar and the Kabul, have emptied into it, the Indus finally leaves the mountains, to the west of the famous salt range, a chain of hills made of salt 600 million years old and

In the remote mountain valleys of the south, between the Sutlej and the Indus, in the open forests of pine and oak, these wooden tower-like buildings make quite an impression. Often they are decorated with elaborate wood carvings. They are in fact a kind of temple, dedicated to local deities. The lower part is made of logs, sealed with whitish mud, which gives a black-and-white-striped effect.

Right: *In the villages on the south side of the Zanskar range, one can observe the transition from the flat Tibetan-style houses to the Kashmir-style shingle-roofed wooden houses. In the Tibetan houses the different levels are still connected by Tibetan-type ladders, made out of tree trunks.*

forming the southernmost bastion of the West Himalayas. After flowing through the wide plains of Punjab and Sind, the Indus reaches the Arabian Sea to the east of Karachi, passing on its journey the ruins of Mohenjo Daro, the oldest cultural site in India. The Indus, too, has created a huge submarine delta, nearly equal in extent to those of the Ganges and Brahmaputra. The mighty Murrey Ridge, the submerged backbone of the Arabian Sea, disappears in the recent delta deposits, which here also have been partly carried all the way down from the rising Himalayas.

*In many of the mountain villages
on the forested southern slopes of the Himalayas,
artistic wood carvings decorate window frames and balconies,
but the little wooden temples
of the southern Zanskar chain
have quite a unique style in their motifs.
The forms represented here are noticeably different
from the Hindu and Buddhist motifs.
They are thought to reflect
a little-known form of animism.*

Next double page: The Indus below Skardu. In the evening light the slowly flowing river looks more like a lake. In prehistoric times there was a lake here in the Skardu basin where the Shigar joins the Indus.

The Indus and the Brahmaputra manage to overcome the barrier of the Himalayas only by means of great detours, but the other three Kailas rivers deal with the obstacle in a much more direct way.

In the same remote villages on the south side of the glaciated Zanskar chain, these interesting wood carvings can be seen, but as yet they have not been studied in any detail. Certain motifs are reminiscent of those of Maya sculptures in Central America.

119

THE SUTLEJ

Officially the source of the Sutlej is in the Raksas valley, but only when the water level is high can the river be seen emerging from the Lake of Demons. The water seeps along, partly underground, through gravel. The first major tributary rises in the south at the Darma La pass through the Himalayas, and since the tributary brings in a greater volume of water than the Sutlej, it is sometimes designated as the river's real source. The next river to enter is the Shib Chu, which also comes from the south and is of particular interest. Here begins the great alluvial basin of the Sutlej, the region of Hundes, with its spectacular horizontal terraces sliced through by steep gorges, in which famous mammal bones were found

Mythological representation of the cosmic mountain Meru, the "Center of the World"; a fresco in Likir monastery (Ladakh). The familiar world view of Indian cosmology was adopted by the Tibetans and transferred to Mt. Kailas.

In the 17th century, when India was under the rule of the Moguls and the name of Buddha had practically been forgotten in the homeland of Buddhism, Christian missionaries came to Tsaparang. In 1624 Antonio de Andrade (1580 – 1634) was the first European to cross the Mana pass and enter west Tibet, where he was astonished to find a Buddhist kingdom in the Himalayas. His description of "a long and dangerous journey" appeared in 1627, printed in Augsburg. This was the first report on the Buddhist way of life, so similar to the Christian that at first it was met with astonishment and incredulity.

over 100 years ago. Also along the Shib Chu lie the eastern outposts of the cave monasteries, which date from the time of the kingdom of Guge.

Fifty years ago I discoverd one of these monasteries, long abandoned and forgotten, in the vertical cliff wall right at the spot where the Shib Chu disappears into a cavern – only reappearing much farther to the north. We decided then to descend into the Shib Chu gorge. From our campsite on the river we had an unforgettable view. All around the valley were several-hundred-meter-high walls with vertical steps in them. In the walls themselves there were hundreds of caves, some of them manmade. Was anyone still there? For days we traveled through the area and found it to be uninhabited; we even discovered a whole "town" up on the cliffs, but it was a ghost town, abandoned, and probably long forgotten. For our camp we chose a large cave lower down, the entire roof of which was covered with a thick crust of soot. There were little niches in the wall of the cave, and in one of these niches we found a Buddha statuette, very artistically carved out of serpentine. We climbed from the lower part of the "town" to the higher levels; the climb was not always easy going. In places the cliffs have fallen, and ladders must have been used at one time, but there was no trace

of them now. Galleries in the cliff face connect the various caves, and as we went along we suddenly found ourselves in a part that had not been blackened by soot. There we discovered a fallen altar and a great pile of papers that proved to be pages out of typical Tibetan books. We also found scrolls of cloth with perfectly preserved paintings on them, depicting interesting god-like figures. The whole floor was littered with little molded clay figurines (Tsa-tsas). We were in what must have been a temple. A low corridor led to another cave, whose entrance had been half walled up. We stood

Zanda, the Tholing of ancient times, in the kingdom of Guge, western Tibet. Today the temple area lies largely in ruins, but in the 11th century it was the most important religious center in western Tibet. Here the famous learned monks Rinchenzangpo and Atisha translated important texts from Sanskrit into Tibetan.

The steep sides of a canyon near Tholing. The rivers have cut such gorges up to 700 meters (2,310 feet) deep, and the shapes and colors are spectacular. The routes to Tholing and Tsaparang in the former kingdom of Guge follow these valleys sliced deep through the horizontal layers of sediment. Over 100 years ago the remains of bones of tropical mammals were found here, further proof of the latest 4,000-meter (13,200-foot) upthrust of the Himalayas.

One of the most impressive of the Landsat photos, this one was taken on November 19, 1976 from a height of 900 kilometers (540 miles). It shows the upper Sutlej region. In the center of the western half the highly eroded gravel terraces are quite visible: this is where the bones of the tropical mammals were found. In the middle lies the ruined town of Tsaparang (Ts), capital of the former kingdom of Guge. The Sutlej and its tributaries usually form these steep-sided gorges. On the lower right edge of the picture, the Shib Chu flows into the Sutlej, and the cave dwellings (X) discovered in 1936 are also here. To the northeast of the broad basin runs an imposing mountain chain, which separates the basin from the sunken area running from southeast to northwest along the very noticeable Indus-Yarlung suture (I.Y.S.). This is the site of the once important trading center of Gartok (Ga). To the northeast the Kailas chain of the Transhimalayas. The southwest corner of the photo shows the Himalayas with the source rivers of the Ganges and the important Mana pass.

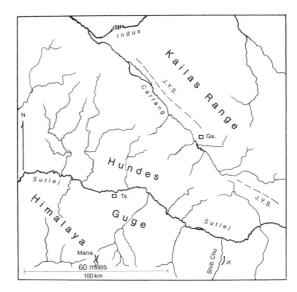

there in amazement – the mud-covered walls were decorated with brilliantly colored frescoes. There were other rooms too, probably the lamas' sleeping cells. High up in the wall there was another separate cave, painted in bright red, but our attempts to climb up to it were futile; a large section of the cliff must have fallen away.

After many hours of exploration we returned to our own "residence." Toward the Himalayas it looked very dark, with black storm clouds hanging in the south. We could hear distant thunder. Then it suddenly grew very dark, and an eerie night began. I could not sleep properly – all the things

The fortress hill of Tsaparang, once the capital of the kingdom of Guge. The bottom of the Sutlej valley is only 3,700 meters (12,210 feet) above sea level here, and so barley can be grown, a prerequisite for any permanent settlement in Tibet.

we'd found kept going around in my mind. I could see the little serpentine Buddha sitting in his niche, weakly illuminated by some external light. He smiles, begins to grow and reaches an enormous size. In all the caves I now see little serpentine Buddhas. They all begin to grow, then climb out of their caves and come down to the entrance of ours. The crash of a falling rock wakes me up, and a huge black bird flies out of our cave on silent wings. Our little green serpentine Buddha is still there in his niche.

For a distance of 200 kilometers (120 miles) the Sutlej and its tributaries now flow through a region with a completely chaotic arrangement of cliff fortresses. This is the old kingdom of Guge, and there are many signs of that culture still to be seen. The renowned Lama Anagarika Govinda, him-

Facing page: Looking out over the canyon landscape near Tholing and Tsaparang. Around the year 1000, to the west of Kailas on the Sutlej river, one of the most important cultural centers of Tibet sprang into life. From here there were natural links to other centers of Tibetan Buddhist culture, such as Spiti and Ladakh. These links were maintained until the Indo-Chinese border conflict in 1962.

Below: *Tsaparang was conquered by Ladakh in 1630, signifying the end of the kingdom of Guge, which had existed for over 600 years. Since then the palaces have fallen into ruins and the monasteries have been left empty. It was only much later that this area of great natural beauty was rediscovered by Western explorers (1933) and scholarly pilgrims (1948).*

Facing page, top: *This tiny serpentine Buddha is only 7 centimeters (2.8 inches) high. Extremely rare, it is the only one of its kind to be found in the sunken temple city. Light green serpentine rock is quite common in this area.*

self of German origin, was the last researcher to visit these sites, just before the Chinese came into Tibet, and his wife, Li Gotami, made copies of many of the works of art. The lively descriptions he gives in his book *The Route of the White Clouds* provide a fascinating picture of this unique landscape: "For us it was almost paradise, a magical world of extraordinary cliff shapes, that had crystallized to form huge towers, rising hundreds of meters into the deep blue sky, like a magic shielding wall round a green oasis that was watered by springs and quick-flowing mountain streams.

The ridge on top of the cliffs was studded with temples, chorten, monastic buildings, and the ruins of old castles and fortresses, and from up there one had a splendid view of the valley, with its phalanx of tower-like cliffs, standing in rows one behind the other like organ pipes, all pierced by the hundreds of cave dwellings with their window openings. The greatest surprise, however, was the main temple, which was not only undamaged but was crowned by a golden roof that shone among the cliffs and the ruins like a lost jewel – a symbol to evoke memories of a past splendor and a faith that flourished here when the valley was the home of thousands of people, ruled by a wise and devout king. The remains of the old frescoes led us to the conclusion that this temple had been built toward the end of the tenth century A.D. – over a thousand years ago!"

The towns of Tholing and Tsaparang, now in ruins, lie in the alluvial region of the Sutlej. In 1076 Tholing became famous for the great religious council held under King Tselde, which all the religious dignitaries of Tibet attended; it was a triumph for Buddhism in Tibet. In 1625 the Portuguese missionary Antonio de Andrade came to the royal town of Tsaparang, where the credulous and tolerant king allowed the priest to set up a mission station. Lama Govinda writes about the tragic outcome of this enterprise, beginning with a quotation from a letter from the king to the Jesuit priest: "We, the ruler of mighty kingdoms, greet the arrival of Father Antonio in our country with great pleasure. So that he can teach us the holy scripture, we hereby appoint him Head Lama with the full authority to instruct our people in the holy scripture. We will not allow anyone to hinder him in this undertaking, and we will give orders that land be allotted to him, and every assistance that he needs in order to build a house of prayer."

But the king, in his trusting goodness, never suspected that the newcomer was not there for a genuine exchange of noble ideas and to strive toward a common goal but instead had the intention of refuting what others had taught before him and replacing these teachings with what in his eyes was the one and only truth.

The goodwill that the king had shown toward the outsider evoked mistrust among the Buddhist priests. This suspicion was aroused by the intolerant behavior of the newcomer, who would neither recognize nor tolerate any ideas but his own. As the king showed more and more favor toward the foreigner, so the dissatisfaction of the Buddhist population grew, and the king's political opponents saw here the possibility of overthrowing him. This indeed happened, and the Guge dynasty and the might of Tsaparang came to an end. Around 1650 the kingdom of Guge disappeared from the map of Tibet and came under the rule of Lhasa.

Andrade left Tsaparang in 1630 and returned to Goa, where he continued his mission. He was poisoned there a few years later. At this time Tsaparang was conquered by the army of the King of Ladakh and completely destroyed. A companion of Andrade, called Marques, who was in India at this time, hoped to be able to revive the idea of a mission on the Sutlej. In the company of other Jesuits he was attacked on the Mana pass by Tibetan guards and taken prisoner. His companions managed to escape, but Marques himself was never heard of again.

The uncertain fate of converted Christians in Guge provided an incentive for further Christian missionary undertakings. A 28-year-old Jesuit, Father

Ippolito Desideri, managed to get the support of the Pope for another missionary expedition to western Tibet. Early in 1714, Desideri traveled via Goa and reached the court of the Mogul emperor, whose power was at that time on the decline. The real power in India then had been taken over by the great English and French trading companies. Desideri, however, found unexpected support from a Portuguese noblewoman, Dona Juliana. Thanks to her influence on the last Mogul emperor, permission was granted for Desideri's journey, the lady herself providing the necessary financial support out of her own pocket. A second missionary, Emanoel Freyre, who had been very much in the shadow of the enthusiastic Desideri from the beginning,

View from the fortress hill of Tsaparang over the canyon valley of the Sutlej. When the first foreigners were readmitted to this territory in 1985, they were rewarded with such magnificent panoramas, stretching away in the distance to the snow-covered Himalayas on the Indian border.

was appointed leader of the expedition. The group reached Srinagar in the fall of 1714 but found the only passage into Ladakh, the Zoji La, already closed. The members of the expedition had to spend the winter in Srinagar. Desideri was charmed by the Mogul gardens and the lakes, but Freyre saw only stinking ponds and heaps of rubbish – typical of the totally different outlooks of the two priests, which was in evidence throughout the entire trip. The journey across the Zoji La in the early summer of the following year was fraught with "indescribable difficulties." Passing via Leh, the two completely exhausted Jesuits reached the border town of Tashigang, which

The ruins of Tsaparang. All signs that this was once the seat of the rulers of Guge have long since disappeared, but luckily the little temple still stands, the "Palace Chapel" of former times.

lay between Ladakh and Tibet and was the site of an old monastery. The rigors of the journey had almost completely eclipsed its real purpose, which had been to reach Tsaparang. With the hardships of crossing the Zoji La fresh in mind, they decided not to return to Kashmir, as they had originally planned, but to continue via Tibet into India. However, because of the many bandits this route could only be traveled by large, well-armed caravans, and so the two waited in Tashigang for a caravan to arrive. The prayers of the fathers were answered, for along came a pretty and intelligent

Tartar princess, who was on her way to Lhasa with a vast entourage. Desideri's charm won the princess over, and the "two lamas from a distant land" were allowed to travel with her.

While the princess's caravan was camped by Lake Manasarowar at the end of November 1715, Desideri learned that in a cave up on a high glacier mountain had lived Padmasambhava, the founder of the Tibetan religion, and that pilgrims walked all around this mountain, which they called Ngari Niongar. It was in fact Mount Kailas! Desideri thought that here he would be able to see the sources of the holy rivers Ganges and Indus, and after crossing the Maryum La he discovered the source of the "Tsangpo" river, which the caravan now followed in an easterly direction. The Tsangpo confirmed Desideri's theory that all the great rivers had their source in the Kailas.

In March 1716, ten months after leaving Kashmir, the caravan reached Lhasa, where Desideri was to spend the next five years, enjoying the hospitality of the sixth Dalai Lama, who held him in high esteem. The beautiful Tartar princess left Lhasa after a short while to become a nun in a distant convent.

When Desideri died in Rome in April 1733, the vital manuscript containing details of all his research in Tibet disappeared completely. It was not found until 1875, in Pistoia, Desideri's hometown, in very mysterious circumstances. This comprehensive document aroused great interest, but unfortunately another 30 years passed before it was published. In it can be found an assertion that the Yarlung Tsangpo links up with the Brahmaputra, a statement over which geographers and cartographers argued for 150 years.

The old kingdom of Guge ends at the spot where the Sutlej, running through gorges of ever increasing depth, breaks through the Himalayas, east of the 6,980-meter-high (23,034-foot-high) Leo Pargial. The way around these impassable gorges is over the Shipki pass, which leads into the high valley of Poo. There are still Tibetan tribes living here, who used to have frequent contact with the Tibetans who lived on the north side of the Shipki pass, but little to do with the Indian people who lived less than a day's journey to the south. Along the Sutlej, now surrounded by woods, and its tributaries, we encounter first the Bhotias and then farther south the Indian tribes. The plentiful supply of oak and pine has enabled these people to build a variety of wooden constructions, ranging from simple log huts to elegantly carved wooden houses with shingle roofs and, where slate is available, stone slabs. The temples are most interesting, tower-like buildings, dedicated to the local gods, and they have carved wooden pergolas and, lower down, wooden beams set into the white-painted mud walls.

The Sutlej takes its leave of the Himalayas through a final steep gorge, overlooked by Simla, the summer residence of the former British Indian government. In a wide basin, the now many-channeled Sutlej deposits all the material it has eroded, before flowing on through the heavily irrigated plain of the Punjab. In Pakistanian Punjab the Sutlej joins up with the Indus.

Next double page: The Sutlej valley near Tholing (now Zanda). One of the rare bridges still spans the Sutlej at this point, the river here running in many channels between the sandbanks. Recent redefinition of borders has meant that this area is off the main routes and it remains very sparsely populated.

Mural in one of the temples of Tsaparang (15th century). The unprepossessing sacred buildings here have proved to be real treasure troves of Tibetan art, of which this is one of the finest examples. It shows the mystic Buddha in the so-called yab-yum position, enfolding his "female embodiment," or female partner.

THE KARNALI AND THE GANGES

Swami Pranavananda's view of the Tibetan belief of how the four rivers start from Mount Kailas and the Raksas and Manasarowar lakes (taken from an oil painting by E. H. Brewer). His interpretation is that the Ganga (Ganges) starts from the elephant's mouth, the Sindu from the peacock's (and then it flows off to the west), the Pashku comes from the horse's mouth and then flows to the east as the Brahmaputra, while the Sita comes from the lion's mouth and becomes the Indus.

Following the Karnali enables us to make the acquaintance of a little-known part of Nepal. The river rises due south of the Kailas in the glaciers of the western Gurla Mandhata mountains. A second and equally large river arrives from the west, coming out of the hills to the southwest of the Raksas lake. Between Gurla Mandhata and the Himalayas the river flows southeast, past the little town of Taklakot (Purang), whose crumbled monastery lies on a high terrace, dominating the whole valley. Here a wide plain and many terraces provide evidence of the latest rise of the Gurla Mandhata massif. Toward the Nepalese border the plain narrows, near the sacred place called Kojarnath, and the Karnali begins to find its

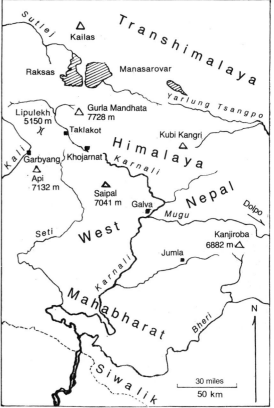

Left: The Karnali rises to the south of Lake Manasarowar and then flows between the Gurla Mandhata massif in the north and the Api Saipal massif in the south, on its way to west Bengal and then on to India to join the Ganges. The pilgrim town of Taklakot (Purang) lies on the Karnali.

The source area of the Karnali. The river is fed by the glaciers of Gurla Mandhata and cuts through the High Himalayas in deep gorges.

way through the Himalayas. Around the impassable gorges, most of them very deep and steep-sided, the vegetation increases, with conifers and rhododendrons first, then bamboo and, lower down, oak forests. Until now the Karnali has been flowing in an easterly direction, but here it makes a sudden turn to the south and is joined by the Mugu, a large tributary that is almost the equal of the Karnali itself. The source of the Mugu is far to the east, not far from the remote Dolpo region, which is inhabited by Tibetans, with Bon and Lamaism existing side by side. On its way south the Karnali passes through a jungle area, which is practically uninhabited. The old tribes that lived in central Nepal never reached this region, and it is only

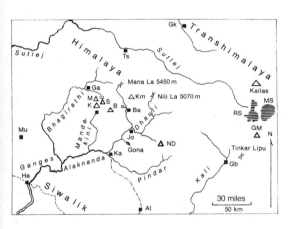

The source area of the holy Ganges:

Al = Almora, Ba = Badrinath, B = Badrinath peak (7,140 m), Ga = Gangotri temple, Gb = Garbyang, Gk = Gartok, GM = Gurla Mandhata, Ha = Hardwar, Jo = Josimath, Ka = Karnaprayag, K = Kedarnath peak (6,940 m), Km = Kamet peak (7,756 m), M = Meru, MS = Manasarowar lake, Mu = Mussoorie, ND = Nanda Devi peak (7,816 m), RS = Raksas lake, S = Shivling, Ts = Tsaparang.

farther to the south – really in the tropical belt – that we find a Nepalese tribe, the Tharu. The Karnali has now reached the last chain of hills, but it cannot find a way through this still geologically active part of the Mahabharat range and it has to make long west-east loops in order to reach the foothills. Here another major tributary flows into the Karnali, the Bheri, coming in from the northeast. It starts out from the north of the 8,000-meter-high [26,400-foot-high] peak Dhaulagiri and also drains part of the distant Dolpo area. The river diversions caused by the Mahabharat chain in southern Nepal would be ideal for obtaining hydroelectric power. If tunnels were bored between the loops of the river, which are close together but possess the necessary difference in water level, then no dams would have to be built. This is an important factor when the rivers involved carry so much silt and are subject to unpredictable fluctuations in water level. In full flow the level of the Karnali can rise by 7 meters (21 feet) in the gorges. Since Nepal itself would hardly need all the energy that could be generated, it could export its excess energy to nearby industrial centers in India.

The Karnali flows on through the once heavily forested, flat Terai zone, part of the jungle belt that forms the border with India, and as a wide flat river, it now enters the Ghaghara. Above Patna, the Ghaghara itself runs into the Ganges.

The Ganges, the most sacred of all the rivers of India, does not rise, like the other four Kailas rivers, on the north side of the main chain but in a range with several 7,000-meter-high (23,100-foot-high) peaks that is especially striking because of its steep white granite walls. Here we find leucogranites, the youngest of all the granite rocks that intruded into the Himalayas. Like all the other Kailas rivers, the Ganges, too, has many sources. According to religious tradition, three of these sources are most important, although their importance is not always related to the amount of water that they carry. The main source river is known as the Alaknanda, and its source is the site of the pilgrimage center of Badrinath, where the temple is built above a hot spring that delivers water at over 60° Celsius (140° Fahrenheit).

When we visited, the pilgrimage season was over, and so the high priest had time to show us the temple. Unexpectedly he showed a great interest in our geological research. We were able to explain to him that the large granite block outside his house had once been carried along by a glacier, but answering his question about whether there were rocks that grew proved to be no easy task, even with the best interpreter. We visited the hot springs, where the steaming water trickled down over the rocks and had formed thick deposits of travertine. So we were able to show him a "rock that grew," and this he seemed to understand. From the priest we learned that the most important source of the Ganges was the Satopanth glacier, watched over by the most sacred Satopanth lake. At the lower end of this glacier we found a cavern in the sheer black ice and out of this sprayed a milky stream – the Ganges! Several kilometers up the glacier, between the lateral moraine of the Satopanth glacier and another glacier on the right, lies the sacred lake, 4,400 meters (14,520 feet) above sea level, reflecting in its dark green water the glaciated 7,140-meter-high (23,562-foot-high) Bad-

rinath. The uncanny quiet of this spot is broken from time to time when an ice avalanche crashes down out of the high granite hills.

North of Badrinath a tributary of the Alaknanda rises from a small lake on the 5,450-meter-high (17,985-foot-high) Mana pass on the Tibetan border. According to old pilgrim stories, this lake led to the false conclusion that the Ganges started here at Lake Manasarowar.

From Badrinath, which is today an unattractive pilgrim center, with corrugated iron roofs and now even a military road, we follow the Alaknanda southward through a narrow 20-kilometer-long (12-mile-long) gorge, with steep quartzite walls. Caravans of sheep and goats, laden with salt and

Gaumukh, or "Cow's Mouth," is the name given to this spot, one of the most sacred places for pilgrims in the whole of India. The Baghirati – the most important source river of the Ganges – storms wildly out of a great glacier cave. Many pilgrims travel for years on the way from the mouth of the Ganges up to its source. For them Gaumukh is the highest goal of all earthly journeys, the gateway between earth and heaven.

wool, follow the gorge, and mountain dwellers, their herds loaded with their household goods, move down to winter quarters. At the end of the gorge the Alaknanda is joined by the Dhauli, a river of equal size that flows down from the glacier on the 7,770-meter-high (25,641-foot-high) Kamet.

An eastern tributary of the Dhauli, the Rishinganga, leads directly to the 7,820-meter-high (25,806-foot-high) Nanda Devi – the sacred mountain of the goddess Devi, the Shakti or holy consort of the god Shiva – the highest mountain in the central Himalayas. A lovely little temple in Lata, a small forgotten village in the Rishi gorge, is dedicated to this goddess.

At an altitude of 2,000 meters (6,600 feet), above the confluence of the

Alaknanda and Dhauli rivers, lies Joshimath, in contrast to Badrinath one of the handsomest villages in the whole Ganges region. The houses are made of wood and stone and all the roofs are covered with slabs of slate. Doors, windows and balconies are decorated with splendid wood carvings, those on the balconies often depicting elephants and stained dard red or brown. In many of the small Himalayan villages, even the most remote, these artistic buildings can be seen, from the Nepalese border in the east – including the trading center of Garbyang, which is important in summer – to the Sutlej. They differ, however, from the decorative buildings of Nepal, which are usually temples or palaces.

The pilgrim route leads on, southward along the Alaknanda, usually high up on the left flank, through splendid oak forests in which long-tailed monkeys with black faces can be seen swinging in the trees. High above the gorge, great vultures circle with never a wing beat, borne upward by thermal currents. The entire Alaknanda valley is full of wildlife, perhaps because it is a sacred region.

In a side valley off to the east lies one of the rare lakes on the south side of the Himalayas, the lake of Gona. It was formed by a great landslide, and 1,000 meters (3,300 feet) above the lake on the limestone cliff to the north a scar marks the area where the landslide started. According to an official

Gangotri, the last town on the upper Ganges. Today a temple houses the stone seat of the holy Baghirati. Here pilgrims come to pray to Shiva and to the goddess Ganga. Many gurus, yogis and swamis live here, some in monasteries, others in primitive huts. Their lives consist of meditation and asceticism.

Garhwali woman with typical gold jewelry inserted through the nose. She has come to Gangotri to celebrate the birthday of the god Shiva.

This pilgrim wears his hair, three meters [10 feet] long, like a scarf. His possessions consist entirely of his saffron yellow pilgrim's robe, a pilgrim's staff and a copper pan, which he fills with holy water from the Ganges river.

report, the landslide took place in September 1893, following the monsoon. It took almost a year for the river to fill up the basin behind the dam, forming a lake 4 kilometers (2.4 miles) long and 300 meters (990 feet) deep. On August 26, 1894 a great catastrophe occurred when the dam broke, the water flooding out and causing extensive damage far down into the valley. Because local officials promptly sounded a warning and most of the villages are high above the gorge anyway, only one person lost his life; he was a Sadhu who did not believe the warning and sat praying by the river. As the dam wall has been worn away, so the level of water has dropped and today the lake is only 120 meters (396 feet) deep.

Near Karnaprayag (we are now only 850 meters [2,805 feet] above sea level) the Alaknanda is joined by a tributary from the east, the Pindari, which drains the southeastern side of the Nanda-Devi massif. Here the pilgrim routes separate. One leads off to the southeast, climbs over several low passes, continues via the former Gurkha capital Almora into the final range of hills to the small town of Nainital, which has the extra attraction of a landslide lake. The other route follows the course of the Alaknanda through oak and pine forests in a southwesterly direction. Twenty-five kilometers (15 miles) farther on, the Alaknanda is met by the second source river of the Ganges, the Mandakini, whose origin is the wild glacier of the 7,000-meter-high (23,100-foot-high) Kedarnath. There is a temple of the same name at that spot. Another 50 kilometers (30 miles) downstream we meet the third tributary, the Bhagirathi, which in terms of sacredness is almost the equal of the Alaknanda. Its source lies on the west side of a granite mountain, and the river breaks through the western ridge in a rugged gorge. This leads to the holy temple of the goddess Ganga Mai, Gangotri. After 10 kilometers (6 miles), at the end of the great Gangotri glacier, we find the source. To the south the scene is dominated by the mighty Shivling, probably the most magnificent and wildest granite mountain in all of the central Himalayas, with its almost vertical white granite walls and its ice-covered summit cap of black slate. Fed by two additional sacred tributaries, the Alaknanda increases greatly in size and flows on through the foothills of the Himalayas until it reaches the pilgrim center of Hardwar, where it leaves the last hills of Siwalik and enters the wide plains of India as the Ganges. Hardwar has been a sacred site for over 3,000 years.

The story of the exploration of the source of the Ganges is also the story of the exploration of the central Himalayas and their northern borders. As far back as 3,000 years ago, Hindu pilgrims and yogis told tales of secret springs in the mountains. The first official exploration took place during the time of the Grand Mogul Akbar, who ruled the whole of northern India between 1556 and 1605 and was renowned for his tolerance of non-Islamic cultures. His main interest was directed toward the holy Ganges and its legends. The first expedition attempting to follow the river to its source labored under great difficulties. A mountain with the form of a cow's head was discovered, and a river flowing from this mountain was taken to be the source of the Ganges. The Grand Mogul also had an interest in learning about Christianity and invited Jesuit missionaries to his court. There they learned of a legendary city on a large lake to the north of the Himalayas, and in Latin texts the name "Mansaruor" (Manasarowar) turns up for the first

Next double page: *Nanda Devi (7816 meters [25,793 feet]), the "Divine Nanda," is the main peak of the Garhwal Himalayas. The mountain was first scaled in 1936, on its south face. The 2000-meter [6,600-foot] north face (our picture) has not yet been climbed.*

time. The legends also told of the remains of a Christian culture, which naturally aroused greater interest among the Jesuits than did finding the source of the Ganges. In 1624 an expedition was organized under the leadership of a Jesuit priest, Antonio de Andrade. Dressed as a Hindu pilgrim, he set off with a younger Portuguese companion, Manuel Marques, several Christian servants and native porters. This was the first official Himalayan expedition. The group followed the Alaknanda northward. When they reached the holy temple of Badrinath and the hot springs, they parted company with the pilgrims they had been traveling with and secretly tried to reach the Mana pass on the Tibetan border. The last ascent was a very

A bride receives delicately engraved gold or silver jewelry for her wedding from her husband and his family. The ring worn through the nose is the visible mark of a Garhwali woman's marrital status. Marriage partners are still selected by parents in the mountain villages of the Garhwal Himalayas. Girls are considered marriageable at 14 to 16 years of age; divorce is unusual.

strenuous climb. Only Andrade and two of his servants managed to cope with the deep snow and a howling blizzard; the rest of the party took ill. The struggle up to the 5,450-meter-high (17,985-foot-high) Mana pass lasted three days, and Andrade was snow-blind and suffering from severe frostbite when he got there. This was the end of the first known Himalayan expedition. Nonetheless, Andrade was the first to discover one of the source rivers of the Ganges and to determine that it originated from the little lake of Deo-Tal. A month later Andrade and Marques managed to cross the Mana pass, and by way of the wild Sutlej gorges they reached the kingdom of Guge.

The waterfall of Gangotri. According to Indian mythology, the Ganges here is flowing over Shiva's head. Bhagirathi moved the gods to save the earth and to feed all the people by sending Ganga down to earth. The force of the waters of Ganga falling from heaven was so strong that it would have destroyed all before it, so Shiva said he would allow the waters to flow through his locks to lessen the impact.

The 18th century saw the rise of the East India Company, which not only sent out armies to conquer the land but also expeditions to explore it. Even a special cartographic department, the Survey of India, was established. In the middle of the century it was under the control of Major James Rennell, the first European geographer to recognize the significance of the Himalayan chain. On his map of northern India we see for the first time a hint of a possible connection between the Yarlung Tsangpo and the Brahmaputra (the report that Desideri had written on this subject 100 years earlier having been temporarily lost). Yet the desire to find the source of the Ganges led to importance being attached to the old Hindu pilgrims' belief that the river

Many holy men have settled near the Gangotri waterfall. They live here isolated from the materially oriented world. During the course of the millennia, the river has scoured out meditation spots for these men from the stone; there, they endeavor to break away from all earthly values and attain new spiritual dimensions. The swami tries to explain his philosophy by means of the following comparison: "If I were to learn to enjoy tea, I would suffer if the habitual pleasures were missing. This suffering would dominate all other joys of life. Yet only after denying all pleasures of the material world does one experience the essential joys of life!"

rose high up in the mountains, and that its outlet was linked by a long tunnel to the holy Lake Manasarowar and that this lake was therefore the real source of the river. Determining the truth of the matter was taken as a challenge by two cousins, Henry and Robert Colebrooke. Henry, a thinker and a Sanskrit scholar, studied the Ganges legends. He also took part in the survey that first determined the altitudes of the distant Himalayas, the results of which showed heights of over 8,000 meters (26,400 feet) — regarded as absurd at the time. Robert had spent 20 years exploring the lower course of the Ganges. In 1807 the Governor-General of the East India Company granted the survey permission to explore the western Ganges sources as far as the legendary "cow's head." Robert Colebrooke organized the expedition, which was accompanied by two Army officers, Webb and Hearsey, who not only commanded the small troop assigned as a protective force but were also skilled in survey techniques. The expedition's first

The Garhwalis have journeyed from their villages to Gangotri for the birthday celebrations in honor of Shiva. They cleanse themselves of sin by ritual ablutions in the holy river. The monotone rhythms of old drums and tin horns accompany the ceremony. The water creates the contact between them and their gods, whom they revere intensely and piously. For the Hindus, the Ganges is synonomous with the eternally recurring cycle of life and death.

move was to climb to the top of a range of hills on which the summer resort of Mussoorie would later be established. From here they had a magnificent view of the mountains from which the Ganges rose, with the prominent peaks of Badrinath, Kedarnath and Gangotri. Unfortunately Robert Colebrooke suffered a severe bout of malaria and was unable to continue, so he waited at the foot of the mountains while Webb took over leadership of the expedition. The little party followed the course of the Bhagirathi as far as the last gorge, but surprisingly the group was not able to continue: true the trail was a difficult one, but it had been traversed by many a pilgrim. Thus the expedition never reached the temple of Gangotri but sent a Pundit to the source. He indeed reached the temple but the real source was not visible because of the great depth of snow in April 1808.

To compensate for this lack of success, Webb and his party now explored the Alaknanda valley to the north of Badrinath. Unfortunately, here too the

Swami Sundarananda doing his daily yoga and meditation exercises. Swami is a religious term meaning "master." Through yoga, the swami attempts to bring his body under complete control; in the process, some swamis develop astonishing abilities. They can influence the vegetative functions to such an extent that they can, for example, intentionally cause cardiac arrest. Not until they control their bodies are they able to push ahead into new spiritual dimensions.

Facing page: *The first ascent of the north ridge of Meru was made on September 1, 1981 by two Austrians, Sepp Friedhuber and Peter Haslinger. It took them three days to reach the summit from their base camp at 4,500 meters (14,850 feet). On the way down they were surprised by a turn in the weather and had to bivouac in the open at 6,000 meters (19,800 feet), not far from the safety of their camp.*

source river was covered with deep snow, but they had at least discovered one of the Ganges' sources. On their eventful trip back they were held captive for a week in the Gurkha fortress Almora. In the meantime the rainy season had begun, and it took a lot of effort to reach the little border town of Bareilli, south of Almora. Webb was now on a stretcher, and Robert Colebrooke, awaiting his arrival, was seriously ill. However, Colebrooke was satisfied with the results of the expedition, which had at least produced the first sketch map of the area, and wanted to return to England after 30 years in India. Because of his illness he decided to travel by river, rather than take the more strenuous overland route, but he did not get far – on September

Tapovan: This meadow lies below the north face of the Shivling and looks like a field in paradise. High above the Gangotri glacier, at 4,400 meters (14,520 feet), the most beautiful flowers can be found, such as the blue-violet aconites shown here. This lovely spot is ringed by the sacred mountains of the Ganges source.

Next double page: *Fishing boats on the Ganges in the early morning.*

19, 1808 he died from malaria on his beloved Ganges.

Nearly 10 years later, in June 1817, Captain John Hoggson of the Survey of India was the first European to visit the fabulous "cow's head" source, which he reached in the company of a large group of pilgrims. Arriving at the sacred Gangotri temple he was lucky not to be killed by a rockslide that had been set off by an earthquake – the revenge of the goddess Ganga Mai? He found the source at the end of a large glacier; instead of looking at the "cow's head," he saw a huge glacier cave from which the river splashed out. Fascinated, he looked up at the mountain that seemed to be keeping watch over the source – the Shivling!

BETWEEN MYTH AND REALITY

THE VARIETY AND UNITY OF RELIGIOUS TRADITIONS

Stone relief near Padum (in Zanskar) dating from about the 10th century. The first Buddhist pictures from Ladakh and Zanskar show the influence of Kashmir art. According to traditional lore, Buddha's teachings reached Zanskar as early as the second century A.D., during Emperor Kanishka's reign.

We can discover beautiful passages in old sources about the infinite variety, yet fundamental unity, of the religious traditions in the Himalayas, although they often seem to differ on the surface: Hark to the wisdom preached by Buddha,

Observe faithfully the law of the Jain,

Lead your lives according to the [Hindu] Vedas,

Strive for the supreme [salvation] in oblivion!

These are words attributed to Sarasvati, the Goddess of Learning, that reflect the Indian mind. The ancient meanings of these sayings were handed down from generation to generation and molded into stirring new form by Rabindranath Tagore, the Indian poet and philosopher. He was awarded the Nobel Prize in 1913 and also founded The House of Peace. He spoke of the world soul, of Jivan Devata, the deity of life, which is neither out of this world nor unattainable but rather reveals itself as joy, beauty and love, demanding devotion as expressed in participation in the tasks assigned to one.

Helmut von Glasenapp, Indologist and expert in the history of religions, has used Sarasvati's words to further our understanding of "Jainism as an Indian religion of salvation," just as he has explained the basic teachings of Hinduism, Brahmanism and Buddhism in his *Religions of the World*. The basic texts of the 50-volume *Sacred Books of the East* were edited in English by F. Max Müller over a period of decades. It would be preposterous to believe that more than limited information about Himalayan religions can be provided in the space of a few lines.

Facing page: *"Om ma ni pad me hum" are the aboriginal sacred syllables of the creatures of the six worlds. In the Himalayas, they have been chiseled into stone countless times and line the roads that lead to holy sites. They express the desire that the Most Sacred also manifest itself on earth. In Europe, they have been incorrectly interpreted as Sanskrit words and by relentlessly contracting the syllables, the meaning "Oh Jewel in the Lotus Flower" was squeezed out of them.*

Below: *The title page of an illuminated, block-printed book that is*

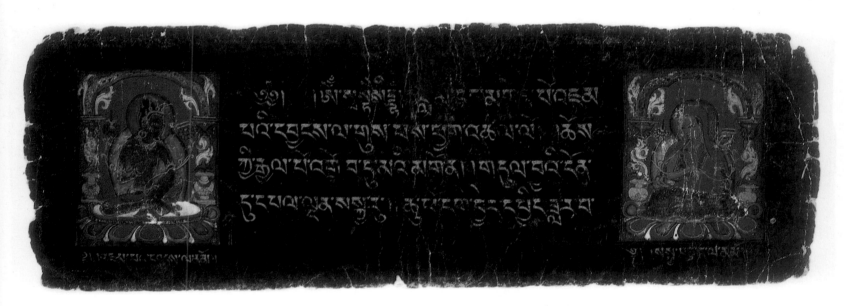

only a hand's breadth wide and a span long and contains calligraphy in golden letters on a black background. It comes from the Sakya school in Mustang. The book is a short biography of Sakya-Pandita, who founded the line of Tibetan lama-kings. He died in 1251 at 70 years of age. His picture is on the right and that of Manjushri, the Bodhisattva of Wisdom, is on the left.

Before we deal with the various religious traditions found in the Himalayas, it should be mentioned that the original forms of religious life and thought have survived, particularly in its hidden canyons and valleys. Tribes that wandered or were driven into these areas were able to maintain these practices nearly unchanged. Shamanistic religions drawing on archaic techniques of producing ecstasy and magical forces have been preserved, as have the "journeys" to heaven and hell by the shamans and oracle priests possessing supernatural powers. They persist in the background of the old Bon religion in the Himalayas, which later was to adapt to the wave of

The Great Masters

Right: *Buddha* Shakyamuni *(Tibetan miniature dating from around 1400).*

Below from left to right: Padma-sambhava: *Introduced Buddhism from India in Tibet (eighth century), worshiped as the founder and "second Buddha." All monastic orders of the "Red Hats" can be traced back to him.*

Damarupa: *A siddha, Tantrist and scholar of the early period of Tibetan Buddhism.*

Naropa: *Tibetan scholar of religion and one of the spiritual fathers of the Kagyupa ("Red Hat") school. Lived during the 10th century.*

Paintings that portray Illuminated Beings or saints symbolically indicate that the person represented walked in the footsteps of Buddha, the Tathagata, and thus followed the right path. From Padmasambhava, the great missionary of Himalayan legends, to the present reincarnation of the Dalai Lama, these holy people have embodied and proclaimed the Path of Buddhism and its goal: to attain "Serenity of the mind" free of spiritual poisons.

Padmasambhava

Damarupa

Naropa

Rinchenzangpo

Rinchenzangpo *(958 – 1055): Tibetan scholar of religion, whose most important achievement was the translation of Buddhist texts from Sanskrit into Tibetan. He and Atisha started the "Buddhist Renaissance" via west Tibet.*

Facing page from left to right: Atisha *(about 982 – 1054): Similar to Rinchenzangpo in western Tibet and Ladakh, Atisha was most active in west Tibet. He was born in east Bengal and was initially a great teacher at the famous monastery academies. In 1042, he came to the west Tibetan kingdom of Guge via Nepal and helped establish its cultural and artistic reputation.*

Buddhism that swept over it. Old customs also managed to survive in Mahayana Buddhism, which absolutely forbade bloody sacrifices and subjugated the old gods while at the same time converting and adopting them as patron gods of the new religion – an extremely clever piece of religious psychology. Thus, the old gods endured. The people are also very fond of the gods' frequently quite grim aspects, since their wrath and their weapons, having become merely symbolic, are directed only against enemies of the religion.

Indian tradition is based on the Vedas, the "Sacred Knowledge," which originated on the upper courses of the holy rivers of the Himalayas. Written down after being passed on orally for about 4000 years, the Vedas constitute the most ancient collection of Indian Sanskrit texts. The first Vedic hymns were composed by the Seven Wise Men, the Rishis, or "Hermits." According to the legends of Nepal, one of the hermits, Kaushika Vishwamitra, meditated on the banks of a river later named after him: the river now named Kosi, where his memory is still honored.

"In India, religious life forms the core and is the keynote of the entire music of national life," Swami Vivekananda has said. He has spread the Indian spirit throughout the modern world: "Ask him [any Indian] about spirituality, about religion, god and the soul, about infinity and spiritual freedom, and I will guarantee you that even the lowliest farmer in India is better informed about these things than some so-called philosophers in other countries."

In addition to the rudiments of high philosophy expressed in Indian mythology, the battles of the new gods against the old may also reflect the migration of new tribes into areas occupied by older, settled peoples. After the Vedic period, as of the sixth century B.C., Brahmanism began to develop, and in it rule by priests, the Brahmans, became more established. Their path to awareness of the world soul requires sacrifices, and virtuous behavior regulates the transmigration of souls – molded in earthly life by the caste system of priests, warriors, peasants, traders and servants.

Milarepa's favorite pupil, *who like Milarepa, cups his hand around his ear to listen to his inner voice. Fresco in Hemis monastery in Ladakh dating from the first half of the 17th century.*

Tsongkhapa *(1357 – 1419): Reformer of Tibetan Buddhism and founder of the Gelugpa ("Yellow Hat") school. Second to Padmasambhava, he was the most important religious figure in Tibet. Many of his writings are still among the most significant texts of Buddhist literature.*

Atisha

Milarepa

Pupil of Milarepa

Tsongkhapa

Milarepa *(about 1040 – 1123): The great poet, saint and one of the spiritual fathers of the "Red Hat" school. In a competition held on Mt. Kailas, he defeated the Bonpo representative. His religious and vivid poems about nature are among "The Jewels of Ancient Tibetan Literature."*

Right: Dalai Lama: *Today's Dalai Lama ("Great Ocean") is the 14th incarnation of the head of the Gelugpa school, who was posthumously declared the first Dalai Lama. Tsongkhapa had founded the Gelugpa school shortly before. Each Dalai Lama is also the living manifestation of Bodhisattva Avalokiteshvara, the "Enlightenment Being of All-Embracing Mercy."*

Panchen Lama: *Pictured is the present, seventh Panchen Lama (photo from 1985), who lives in Peking yet also visits Tibet occasionally. Out of gratitude, in 1650, the fifth Dalai Lama*

declared his spiritual teacher to be the incarnation of Buddha Amitabha (who thus became the first Panchen Lama).

Reformed Hinduism also is based on the revealed original truth and opposes false interpretations, such as the cremation of widows. The grandfather of modern India, Raja Rammohan Roy, who founded the Community of the Faithful/Society of God in Calcutta in 1828, led Hinduism into the present. Mahatma Gandhi, who considered himself an orthodox Hindu, wrote about tolerance in his magazine *Young India* in 1921: "I do not believe that the Vedas alone are of divine origin, but that the Bible, the Koran and Zend Avesta were equally divinely inspired. Hinduism is not an exclusive religion. There is room in it to honor all the prophets of the world. Hinduism enables everyone to worship God according to his own laws ..." Mahatma Gandhi was murdered by an Orthodox Hindu in 1948. There as elsewhere, fanatics bash one another's heads in and tolerant sages often remain lonely voices of admonition, who nevertheless have many followers in the Himalayan countries.

Brahman is the cosmic Self, emanating from itself, eternal, the One from which All Being originates and to whom All Being returns. It is unborn, invisible, all-fulfilling, yet only an object of abstract meditation for Hindu sages. What is revered and worshiped are the manifestations of the Supreme Divinity in being, becoming and passing away: they are personified in Brahma, the God of Creation; Vishnu, the Preserver; and Shiva, the Destroyer. However, each perishing also entails a new creation.

We shall encounter the tradition of the Jain school elsewhere in this book. It is thought to have been founded only 2500 years ago, i.e., during Buddha's time; however, its adherents insist that it is much older and point out that their first spiritual leaders meditated on the sacred Mt. Kailas. They refer to a mythological history analogous to that of Hinduism and they also follow the same ethical principles. Asceticism, however, is carried to the extreme in practice, for example, in a holy person's "fast until death." The soul appears as a being unto itself chained to the material body by 80,000 incarnations.

This Tantric double statue shows the Mystic Buddha in the yab-yum, *or father-mother, position, which is a symbol of the unity of all contrasts. It is one of the oldest statues in the Cylinder Temple in Paro (west Bhutan) and is attributed to the temple's founder, Thangtonggyalpo.*

Facing page: *This huge* thanka *is a scroll made in an exquisite appliqué technique by monks, who worked on it for years. It depicts Padmasambhava, the second Buddha and greatest Buddhist missionary, who traveled to Bhutan around 800 A.D. Each spring, the great* thanka *in Paro is unrolled for his birthday and honored by mystery plays and temple dances in which the entire population participates.*

Buddha opposed this belief and eliminated other, at that time specifically Indian, socioreligious elements, such as adherence to the caste system, the dominance of the priesthood, the sole validity of the Vedas and the custom of sacrifices. Nonetheless, important aspects of the old Indian world view were retained: the tenet of Karma, the law of actions and their consequences, that is, of fate, from which no one is exempt; the law of inevitable reincarnation, from which, however, one can be saved; traditional mythological and, above all, cosmological concepts that were further refined. At first, the type of Buddhism propagated was *Hinayana*, the "Lesser Vehicle"; as of Buddhism's second century it took the form of Mahayana, the "Greater Vehicle," which was particularly widespread in the Himalayan countries. Shakyamuni, the Enlightened One from the Shakya dynasty, preached his first sermon in Sarnath, near Benares, in 528 B.C. He followed a middle course, with which he spiritually won over not only India but also Sri Lanka (Ceylon), the gold cities and the islands of Indonesia, China and Japan. After Buddhism was driven out of India by Brahmanism and exterminated by the sword of Islam, it lived on in the

The four Guardians of the World are the Lokapalas, the Kings of the Earth's Regions, who protect Buddhism in all directions.

ཀྲ་མ་ཐོས་སྲ་ས་ལ་ནས་མོ།

Above: *The tutelary God of the North, Vaishravana. He is waving the round banner of Buddhism in his right hand and holds the jewel-spitting mongoose in his left. During the migration of the Tibetan peoples, he was transformed into the main tutelary god of Sikkim, where Kangchendzonga, the "Great Glacier of Five Treasures," became his seat. (Taken from the block print of* The Three Hundred Icons, *18th century).*

Above right: *Dhritarashtra, the Guardian of the East, with the lute that identifies him as the King of Celestial Musicians, whose food consists of sweet smells and who lives in the Paradise of the Gods on Mt. Kailas.*

Himalayan countries: even today in Ladakh and Sikkim and as the state religion in Bhutan. In Nepal, the Brahmans who fled from the arrival of Islam reduced Buddhism to the status of tolerated religion. Nevertheless, it flowered in Tibet after the seventh century A.D.; from there, Mongolia was converted to Buddhism af ter the 15th century A.D. The Dalai Lama's state of priests, which dates back to the time of the great reformer Tsongkhapa (1357 – 1419), became the center of the Buddhist faith. Its theocratic head has been revered as the incarnation of the Bodhisattva of Mercy, Avalokiteshvara, up to the present, 14th Dalai Lama, who was born in 1935 and

Above: *The Patron God of the West, Virupaksha. He is portrayed holding a small stupa/chorten. Virupaksha protects the doctrine of Buddhism in the countries west of Kailas, the holy mountain. (Taken from the block-print of "The Three Hundred Icons," 18th century).*

currently lives in exile in India. The emphasis placed on the impermanence of all existing things in Buddhism does not entail a sad or unrealistic philosophy of life by any means. The attempt to not merely suppress but entirely to banish all spiritual poisons (hate, which creates strife and war; insatiable greed; and, above all, the madness of prejudiced ignorance) in one's own interests creates a "Serenity of the Mind." This promotes a true tolerance that also respects the customs and laws suitable to the mentality of each people, and corresponds to the different natures of individual persons. In the "Lotus of Good Law" in the earliest Mahayana scripts, it is said of the

Above left: *The Guardian of the South with the flaming sword is Virudhaka, portrayed on a large thanka. Like the King of the East, he emphasizes the spread and protection of the doctrine in the south of Mt. Kailas.*

161

Bodhisattva of Mercy, Avalokiteshvara, that he brought salvation to several beings as Indra, Brahma or Shiva, and that he proclaimed in the shape of a universal emperor:

> The wise bodhisattvas assume
> Many guises in every form
> And preach in every tongue
> The eternal law's norm.
>
> They become the sun, the moon,
> The earth, water, fire, air, these all;
> Indra, Brahma and also God,
> Who being into existence will call.
>
> For whatever form of devotion
> Every being here does hold:
> Through them the way is shown
> For him to overcome this world.

Facing page: *In the kingdom of Bhutan,* thanka *painting of religious scrolls is zealously propagated in painting schools. This is an old* thanka *showing one of the holy men from the Nyinmapa school, who is identifiable as the incarnation of the Bodhisattva of Wisdom, Manjushri, by the Book of Transcendental Wisdom on the lotus flower. The flaming sword on the second lotus flower also indicates his identity.*

Above: *The lama portrayed on this* thanka *floats in a large rainbow circle above the eastern Himalaya mountains. The five-colored softly shining rainbow glory symbolically implies that the lama has already attained the state of nirvana.*

Above: *This fresco from Kyichu Lhakhang temple in Paro, west Bhutan, shows King Songtsengampo, who dispatched Buddhist missionaries as far away as the southeastern Himalayas in the middle of the seventh century* A.D. *Small stupa-chorten on the grounds of the temple commemorate this event.*

The Rainbow Circle

An awed admiration of the rainbow, traditionally honored as a lucky symbol of the bond between heaven and earth, dates from the oldest times and, indeed, still lives on today. In the well-settled alpine regions of the present, a rainbow is commonly believed to be merely a good omen; in the Himalayas and central Asia, on the other hand, it has remained a miracle in several versions of traditional explanations.

Facing page: *A life-size statue of Buddha Maitreya (17th century) in the city temple of Lhasa.*

The legendary first "Seven Divine Kings" of Tibet are said to have soared to heaven as rainbow bodies after their deaths. This belief was preserved in the Buddhist epoch as a symbol of the blessed fading away of saints. The miracle of the rainbow is most beautifully described in the biography of Tibet's great poet and yogi Milarepa, who died in 1123. W. Y. Evans-Wentz, who became the first popular Tibetologist in Sikkim, translated the block-printed biography, thus making it available to Western readers in 1917. The text helps the reader to understand the ceremony of cremation: Milarepa's

Above: *The head of an approximately 10-meter-tall [33-foot-tall], modern statue of Buddha Maitreya in Thiske monastery (Ladakh), evidence of Buddhism's vitality in the Himalayas. The "eye of wisdom" is a bundle of rays between the eyebrows and one of the outer marks of a Buddha. Here, its shape imitates that of an ammonite.*

165

This fresco shines from the wall in the Gonkhang, the secret temple of the tutelary deities in Tamzhing monastery in Bumthang (central Bhutan). It depicts the leading tutelary god of the earth, Rahu, mounted on horseback in a blazing circle of fire. Rahu's many-eyed body tapers into that of a snake and the powerful fangs of a scorpion project from his crown. A human skin flutters on his back. He gallops thus across the night sky as the lord of the earth's tutelary gods.

Rahula's retinue, painted in bright colors on a shining black background, fills the walls in the temple of omnipotent tutelary deities.

On the temple rooftop the Gonkhang is indicated by a Buddhist round banner crowned by a flame-like trident. It remains hidden from secular eyes and can only be visited by special permission. Unfortunately, from time to time the temple walls are painted over, a custom that is viewed as a mark of religious merit. The old paintings disappear and following generations have only pictures of them taken by marveling strangers, who photographed old religious art by official permission.

The dancers' and actors' valuable masks and costumes are stored in the upper rooms of the temple. They are only brought out for the mystery plays that take place in the large temple courtyards and are always announced with great ceremony.

disciples and followers, who had gathered in grief around his pyre, saw how his soul rose bodilessly toward heaven, like a brilliant rainbow in a radiant manifestation, and finally disappeared.

The appearance of a rainbow is also connected with the current incarnation of the Karmapa Lama, who belongs to the Karmapa branch of the Kagyupa school and presently lives in Rumtek monastery in Sikkim, his "expatriate" residence in emigration. During his missionary journeys he usually bestows his great blessing outdoors, in front of a temple; "blessing" ("*wangkur*") in this sense literally means "transmission of power." During the blessing, the temple trumpets are sounded to the highest descant, depending on the length of the ceremony for up to an hour. It may happen that it then suddenly starts to rain – out of a clear blue sky. When the brief shower is over, a faint rainbow appears in the sky. This has been seen and experienced by Western observers (including natural scientists, such as A. Gansser). Whereas it may be impossible for us to explain this phenomenon, the words of the Tibetologist Giuseppe Tucci should be called to mind. He said that one must silently and respectfully bow one's head wherever other people see and experience their most sacred objects and phenomena.

A rainbow is formed when water droplets from a rain cloud or a waterfall are illuminated by a strong, powerful source of light such as the sun. The center of the rainbow lies as far under the horizon as the light source is above it. However, according to one scientific explanation, when the droplets are illuminated by light reflected from a large water surface, the rainbow appears as a huge, complete circle above the horizon. This phenomenon is known in the Alps as the *"Specter of the Brocken,"* and seeing it supposedly depends on where the observer, whose own dark shadow appears in the middle of the rainbow circle, stands. This "Specter of the Brocken" is also described in English reference books and it is asserted that the name comes from the Brocken, the highest peak (1142 meters [3769 feet]) in the Harz mountains, where proto-Celtic-Druidic traditions have survived the longest. In pre-Christian rites, the prehistoric spring festival Walpurgis Night was celebrated here on the 1st of May. This rite, later called Witches' Sabbath, has been immortalized in a powerful scene in Goethe's *Faust*.

In 1850, the British natural scientist Joseph Dalton Hooker described this strange atmospheric phenomenon, which he had seen at Donkyala, the "Pass of Wild Yaks," in the north of Sikkim: "my own shadow being projected on a bank of thin mist that rose above the tremendous precipices on whose crest I stood. My head was surrounded with a brilliant circular glory or rainbow." The language of the original inhabitants of Sikkim also has a special name for this reflected shadow: *tungkung taklak*.

The mysterious shadow in the middle of the rainbow circle still sometimes appears today at the holy mountain Emei, which is located south of Chengdu, the capital of Sichuan province in China. In the Emei range, the 3099-meter-high [10,227-foot-high] main peak bears the honorary title of "Loveliest Mountain Under the Sky" and is one of the oldest pilgrimage sites. It has now become a favorite tourist attraction as one of the four sacred mountains of Chinese Buddhism and as the place where one can see the Shadow of Buddha in the rainbow glory. It is considered a symbol of

Above: *The stupa of Sungkhar, carved from rock near Samye monastery on the northern bank of the Yarlung Tsangpo river.*

Facing page: *Taktshang, the Tiger's Nest monastery, clings to the high rock walls above Paro valley (in west Bhutan). It was founded by Padmasambhava and his partner, the Tibetan cloud fairy Yeshe Khado, about 800 A.D.*

Nirvana, the completely closed circular light rays of one released from the chains of forcible rebirth, of a Buddha, of an Enlightened One. Thus is it described in the *thankas*, the scroll paintings of Tibet and the Himalayan countries. Surrounded by a rainbow aureola, the Enlightened One floats above the peaks of the mountains. The circular rainbow implies that the person depicted has attained the nirvana level of consciousness.

It is even possible to observe this phenomenon, so peculiar to us, from a plane. When the sun shines from behind, one can see the airplane's shadow in a rainbow halo, floating above the sea of clouds.

Below: *The 76-year-old lama of Samling monastery, the most important center of the Bonpo sect in Dolpo in Nepal. He is wearing the traditional peaked cap.*

Right: *The monastery of Dechenlabrang, the seat of the "Great Bliss," is located above the Nankhong river in Dolpo. The lay persons' houses are white; those of the monks, yellow. Barley is grown here. The chorten protect the inhabitants from evil spirits. A salt caravan from Tibet has pitched its tents here.*

Lightning in the Hands of the Gods

Especially noteworthy among the ritual objects and instruments with which we are acquainted through finds from prehistoric times are the sacrificial knives made of different ores, the thunderbolts, or *vajra* (*dorje* in Tibetan), and, above all, the *phurbu*, the strange ceremonial nails with which evil demons were symbolically nailed fast and banished. Even today, they are swung by dancers in mystery plays, thus exorcising the demons.

This chorten passageway, or chorten gate, photographed in the Zanskar valley, south of Ladakh, is typical in the Himalayas. The passage is often decorated with slate reliefs or stone drawings.

The rare and oldest material used for these tools is called *namdo* ("stone from heaven") in Tibetan. The ore is of meteoric origin, and it was certainly known at that time that it came out of the sky.

An American meteorologist, F. A. Paneth, noted that long before man had learned to smelt iron, he used meteorites to manufacture tools. We have evidence that he knew of the heavenly origin of this precious material: in many languages its name refers to the sky, and in some sources its origin is distinctly compared with that of earthly gold and silver. The awe-inspiring

Below Tiger's Nest monastery in Paro, a tiny meditation cell clings to the rock wall above a small bubbling rivulet. Yogis and saints used to meditate here in the solitude of the mountains. They could only be reached via a difficult path and often shut themselves off from worldly contacts for years at a time in order to come nearer to the truth in seclusion.

Devout worshipers brought them the necessary minimum of supplies from time to time, usually a small sack full of tsampa, the staple food of the Himalayan peoples. They shyly deposited the supplies near the cell and climbed back down without disturb-

Right: *This hermit's cell was built into a sheer rock wall and is only accessible by a ladder. It is located in a gorge on the way to Taktshang monastery in west Bhutan.*

Above: *This cliff monastery near Shergol lies on the Buddhist-Islamic "border" east of Kargil in Ladakh. The monastery and its meditation caves were built into a conglomerate cliff; formerly it was supposedly a convent.*

ing the sage in his spiritual quest ... The way the structure is adapted to the natural conditions, fits into them and adds to them without changing them is characteristic of the architecture here.

fall of the meteorites convinced primitive peoples throughout the entire world that meteorites must come from the gods. This is why they are also respected in various cultures ... At the same time in 18th-century Europe, the Académie française, the highest scientific authority at that time, declared that such an irregular phenomenon as a stone's falling from the sky was impossible.

Below: Ladakhi monks with censers and typical musical instruments at a solemn ceremony.

Above right: A lama in Pharo Dzong, Bhutan, studying a block print. His ritual objects are bells, a scepter and a standing drum.

Right: The Head Lama of Lamayuru monastery in Ladakh.

Far right: Gelugpa monk wearing the yellow hat characteristic of this religious school (Ganden monastery, Tibet, 1983).

Above: The Head Lama of Rumtek monastery in Sikkim murmuring the sacred syllables. He is wearing the five-leaved crown as a symbol of the five-fold wisdom.

When the Waters Receded

We are not the only ones to wonder just when and how the first settlers wandered into the rising Himalaya mountains, recently become inhabitable. The people themselves have conjectures that were passed on orally for millennia before being written down; they are still alive today. Following a prehistoric custom common the world over, important genealogies concerning the "Roof of the World" (as well as later historical accounts) began with at least allusions to the origins of the universe, the earth and mankind, and with references to older sources.

The Tibetans also have prehistoric accounts, as Padmakarpo, a 16th-century historian, points out: "One can read in the Manjushri Mulatantra that one hundred years after the death [of Buddha] the lakes in the Land of Snows [Tibet] had shrunk and a forest of sal trees was growing. According to the prophecy, this marked the end of the drying out of the great sea that had once covered the entire Land of Snows. In its claim that a forest grew, it agrees with the traditional story that the entire country was once covered

Left: *The frescoes in the Himalayan monasteries often depict and honor the most famous Tibetan monasteries, for example, Samye. This is a fresco in the main temple of Gangtok, the capital of Sikkim.*

Above: *By turning the prayer wheel, which is filled with small text scrolls, the Buddhist wish for "Luck and Happiness for all Creatures" is multiplied a thousandfold and disseminated in all directions.*

by a wood of juniper trees."

When one asks whether the world is surely not older than that and did not Buddha die only 2500 years ago, the reproachful answer, accompanied by a shaking of the head, is that, after all, "Buddha" can also mean one of the buddhas of past human ages, of whom Shakyamuni, the Buddha of the present epoch, is the seventh.

Mythological accounts of the earth's history were by no means unpopular and are mentioned in the *Blue Annals* dating from 1478. Tibet's most

Above: *A pilgrim in Ladakh during the monsoon rains. His only possessions: the umbrella is his house and he carries his food in the pitcher.*

Right: *Rock stairway to Toṅgsa Dzong, the ancestral castle of the Bhutanese royal family. The first fortifications were built under Shabdung in 1648 and enlarged over the centuries. The wooden balconies and verandas, built without nails, are typical in Bhutan, which has abundant supplies of wood. The strikingly beautiful painted decorations on the balconies are rich in Buddhist symbols.*

important block-printed work, the *Blue Annals*, describe the different phases of the introduction of Buddhist teachings in Tibet. Even Phadampa, an Indian sage, is mentioned here. He made several pilgrimages to Tibet and was over 100 years old when he died around 1117 A.D. He was one of the most popular Tantric sages in Tibet, probably also as a result of the many stories told about him. When at one point he was to be expelled, he related cheerfully in the first person how well he knew Tibet, which he had already visited several times in previous lives. He claimed to have been there seven times. During the first visit, the country was still completely

covered by water; during the second, the water had already receded somewhat; and finally, after other visits, he saw that only the two large Tibetan lakes remained of the great ocean: Nam Tso, the "Sky Lake," in the north and the Yamdrok Tso in the south.

Later historical works, such as that written by Sumpa Khanpo in 1784, also emphasize that the turquoise lakes of Tibet were much larger and more numerous at one time and that a small lake called Ozhang Tso, the "Lake of the Milk Plains," remained a long time on the plains of Lhasa. The main

Top: *Painted wooden ceilings in a chorten gate in Alchi monastery, dating from the 11th century.*

Above: *Chorten in Alchi monastery, Ladakh.*

temple of Lhasa was built above the rest of this lake during King Songtsengampo's life in the middle of the seventh century A.D.

The astonishing thing about these accounts of mythological earth history and their narrators is that the pedagogical methods then and now have remained almost identical. Professor Wilhelm Bölsche, for example, endeavored in 1913 to give his students his explanations of *Continents and Oceans in the Course of Time* in a manner similar to that used by the Indian Phadampa in the 12th century. In order to do so, he invented a fictitious rower in a small boat who experienced the continental drift and the disappearance of the geologic Mediterranean Sea, the Tethys. His tale engrosses his readers just as Phadampa fascinated his audience by describing the changes in the landscape he had experienced in his previous lives.

Potala Palace in Lhasa, residence of the Dalai Lama since 1650. A thousand years before, the Tibetan King Songtsengampo had the first residence built. Shortly before the mid-17th century, the time had come for a new Potala Palace. The head of the Gelugpa sect, the fifth Dalai Lama, had also been granted the political leadership by the Mongol Prince Gushri Khan, who at that time also had influence in Tibet. The Dalai Lama's political authority lasted until 1959, when the 14th Dalai Lama was forced to leave his home and go into exile in India.

Widely varying versions of lost geological facts, such as those concerning the vestiges of the Tethyan Ocean, have been preserved in traditional myths. Near Kathmandu, the exact spot is marked where Manjushri, the Bodhisattva of Wisdom, once hewed through a dam with his flaming sword when the entire valley was still covered by the Haga Hrad lake. As a result, the waters drained off and the land that emerged became fertile. This place, called Chovar, is located about 11 kilometers [6.6 miles] from Kathmandu

Left: *In Potala Palace, brilliant colors have been used to paint plant and flower borders on the finely carved columns. These borders also frame inscriptions of the holy syllables that bring good fortune and blessings; the syllables have been written in an ancient "divine alphabet."*

Below: *In the great hall of Drepung monastery, lamas meditate at the foot of temple columns hung with woven silk imported from China. Round temple banners made of precious brocades hang between the columns.*

Left: *Butter lamps (here, in the cathedral of Lhasa) are one of the "Seven Offerings": water, flowers, incense, light, food, scents and music (exalted tones).*

at famous Bagmati canyon, the gap supposedly formed by Manjushri's sword blow.

This legend may well represent the vague memory of a cultural hero who came from the northeast and created fertile land for cultivation out of the flooded valley of Kathmandu. Without further ado, he was then identified with the Bodhisattva of Wisdom because of his great deeds. He was supposed to come from "Cina," an assumption that would correspond to the geography of over 2500 years ago. At that time, the kingdom of Qin was the leading power politically and commercially. Its influence extended far westward and it controlled all traffic with the West many generations be-

The traditional art of mask making, common throughout the Himalayas, is displayed during the mystery plays, for example, here in Bhutan. The oldest masks of carved wood have only small eye-holes, through which the dancers can hardly see. Other masks are secured higher on the head so that the dancers can look through the

open mouths and bared teeth. The artistically painted masks are part of the temple's treasures. The death's-head masks, with their crowns of five skulls, are particularly striking. Their grim expressions are heightened by the long fangs, which emphasize the threatening opened mouth. This expression does not terrify the pious observer but rather reminds him of the transcience of all life and calls upon him to perform good deeds in this life. The red and blue masks of the guardian gods, crowned with death's heads, as well as the stylized animal masks, especially those of birds, worn by the companions of the guardians, also serve the same admonishing function in the dances.

fore the rise of Qin Shi Huangdi, who united all of China in the middle of the third century B.C.

Manjushri's stupa, the Manjushri Caitya, bears witness to the great reverence for him as the creator of Kathmandu valley. This is a Buddhist temple also known as the Sarasvati temple, named for Manjushri's female partner in wisdom. It is located west of Swayambhunath. The Hindus in this area worship Sarasvati as Shakti, the active power of Brahma, the God of Creation, and also as the Goddess of Learning.

Not only in Lamayuru but at several holy sites in the western Himalayas (present-day Ladakh) as well, the first missionaries of Buddhism are also

known as those who made the great waters disappear by means of their sacred powers. These missionaries were pilgrims who had come to the Karakorum region during either Buddha's time or the era of Emperor Ashoka, i.e., around 500 or 250 B.C. respectively. Questions pertaining to the inconsistency of dates would merely provoke yet another regretful shake of the head — these holy men of course were able to visit these sites in countless earlier incarnations. Even millions of years are irrelevant. The myths clearly state that every living being unconsciously carries the collected impact and experiences of the entire past within himself, from cosmic to earthly creation, existence and decline; this is a psychic fact recognizable

Below right: The entry of the companions of the dancers of death is breathtaking: the dancers march in with "Thunderbolt Steps" and crush the evil along their path with crisscross steps. They continually remind one that all factors of existence, everything that lives and exists, is void of absolute reality and will pass away.

Above: Special among the dances in Bhutan are the dances of chivalry. The actors appear in medieval knights' costumes with long skirts that twirl during the dance, and wear ring crowns on their heads. They dance the knights' round dance in honor of the temple and the saint celebrated on that particular holiday.

only to the enlightened who are capable of controlling the entire range of the unconscious. Our material relics are only a welcome confirmation of spiritually comprehended and inwardly seen facts.

The Ancient Indian Noah-Manu Lands on a Himalayan Cliff

The tribal progenitor who survived the Rising of the Great Waters is also known in Hindu mythology. In Sanskrit, the ancestors of mankind are called "manu," the "Thinking Ones," the Humans. There are 14 of them and each presides over a human age, a *manuantara*, which is a period comprising 4,320,000 years. The guide of the present epoch is the seventh Manu, called Vaivashwata, the "Sun-Born," who is connected to the Indian version of the saga of the Great Flood. Manu once caught a fish but let him

live. In return, the fish promised to save him from the coming catastrophic flood. Manu then built a safe ship, and when the deadly waters began to rise, he fled to the secure ark with the Seven Sages, the Rishis, and the sacred writings. He tied the ship to the horn of the fish, which in the meantime had grown into a giant fish. It guided the ship to the high peaks of the Himalayas. There, the fish advised Manu to secure the ship to a cliff so that it could slowly sink with the water. The following report is included in the Great Epic, the Mahabharata, which includes stories that date back over 3000 years according to Indian tradition and which is 220,000 lines long, thus probably the longest epic in the world:

It [the fish] bore the Lord of Men in the stately ship through dancing, tumbling waves on roaring waters over the ocean. Only Manu and the Seven Sages survived in the ship, which the fish finally pulled to a peak of the Himavan that rose above the waves. It spoke to Manu: "Now tie your ship to this high rock peak and recognize me as Brahma, the God of Creation, who has saved you in the guise of a fish ..."

The God and the Daughter of the Himalayas

In myths, the glacier-covered peaks of the Himalayas play a significant role even in the oldest names. *Devi*, "goddess," is a word that derives from *div*, "to shine." The goddess is in countless manifestations the Great Goddess Maha Devi; she is the wife and female power (*shakti*) of Shiva and inseparably bound to him. He without Her and She without Him – inconceivable. According to her genealogy, however, she is Haimavati, the "Daughter of the Himalayas," for the personification of Himachala and Himadri, as the mountains are called in Hindu sources, is named Himavat. Devi is often also addressed as Parvati, which means "the Mountaineer" or female mountain inhabitant; another name is Giri-Ja, "Mountain-Born." Shiva and Parvati, the God and the Daughter of the Himalayas, play leading roles in mythological dramas. In the myths, she eventually becomes Sati, a late classical term for the loving widow who voluntarily throws herself into the flames of the funeral pyre so that she might accompany her spouse into the next world – a rite that did not become a merciless obligation until the rule of the Brahman priests. In the oldest myth, Devi-Parvati flings herself into the flames in protest against her father, who had not invited her husband to the Feast of the Holy Sacrificial Fire – this was tantamount to a refusal to recognize him. Desperate, Shiva rushed in, gathered Parvati-Shiva into his arms and then he flew through the air scattering her dead body over the mountains. The spots where parts of her body fell are the holiest of places, *pitha-sthana*, on which temples were erected. On the spot in Kathmandu valley where her most divine sexual organ, the *yoni*, fell, her temple is still considered sacred, as is Shiva's holy site, where his stone phallus, the *lingam*, juts up from deep in the earth and is decorated with the face of the lovely Great Goddess. Various versions of this tale are told and immortalized in secret temple sites, where entrance is strictly forbidden to strangers.

Hindu pilgrims have wandered to these temples on the same path for millennia; they include the *sadhu*, holy men who go around naked and bare of all earthly trifles. The paths leading from the Indian plains to the Himalayas were always open to them and their followers up to the temples in Kathmandu valley. From there the path led north and then west to the Kailas, also called "Shiva's Paradise." The pilgrims' path remained accessible even

during the centuries when Nepal shut itself off completely to protect against the invasion of the Muhammadan army. Therefore, old traditions were preserved in Nepal and observed by the Brahmans who fled India.

The temple symbols *yoni* and *lingam* represent the most sacred Tantric unity of the contrasts between man and woman: cosmic-earthly, divine-humanly, inseparably bound to one another. Repeatedly, it is always Devi, the Great Goddess whose brilliant white glacial throne is revered in several Himalayan peaks. She is the omnipresent Devi, even when she is called upon in other languages, for example, as the "Mistress of the Divine

The monastery of Yangser lies on the Panzang river in Dolpo, Nepal. It was built about 600 or 700 years ago. Its religious name means "Island of Enlightenment."

Mountain," Jomolhari, in western Bhutan. She is the one honored in the Tibetan language as the "Great Tutelary Goddess of Religion," Paldan Lhamo, whose retinue, the "Five Sisters of Long Life," storm through the wild world of Labchi (Everest). Finally, Shri Devi and her partner, the chief tutelary deity, became Mahakala, the "Great Black One," in Buddhism. It is always Devi in her gracious as well as her wrathful manifestations, the latter of which, however, always calm the minds of the believers, since her wrath and symbolic weapons are directed only against enemies of the faith.

of importance from a distant region, and had to therefore seem eager for an interview. With mixed feelings I stood before the little door leading to the head lama's quarters. Paldin and one of the Bhotias accompanied me. Paldin, who was familiar with the ways of lamaseries, had given me an hour's private instruction, the best way to conduct myself in these unfamiliar circumstances. Barefooted, with folded hands and lowered head, I entered the dark chamber, which was lighted by only a few small butter lamps. Behind a long altar, which looked like the table of a medieval alchemist, squatted the high priest, in tailor fashion. Slowly and reverently I approached His Holiness. He had sharp features and an intelligent expression, very different from that of many lamas, who look like self-satisfied materialists. Paldin announced me as an extremely holy man from far, far away, and fortunately sanctity connotes the idea of a discreet silence. My head still devoutly lowered, I handed him two small colored goblets of mar-

Facing page: There are various "pilgrims' maps" for the path to sacred Mt. Kailas. Some are painted on plant-fiber paper, others appear as frescoes on the walls of the temples along the pilgrims' road; they are always executed in a naive style that is easily understood. This thanka *depicts the path to the Mountain of the Gods, painted by Tulku Tsewang in Tragyam Gompa in Dolpo, Nepal.*

Above: The summit of Mt. Kailas from the northeast. In the foreground is small Lake Gaurikund, which is reached after crossing the Dolma pass, located at an altitude of 5500 meters [18,150 feet]. To sprinkle oneself with its water is obligatory, particularly for the Hindu pilgrim.

bled vulcanite, a somewhat risky gift here, but we have found them effective and comparatively easy to transport. An attendant rummaged in a small chest, and then, with a solemn gesture, His Eminence handed me a strip of red ribbon, which, according to custom, was immediately hung around my neck. I was also given a little bag of tiny pills, that would prepare me from every possible mishap.

A glorious morning followed. I was up at the break of day and set off with my camera. Hidden behind a rock, I took what pictures I could of this

Below: *Gossul monastery on the western shore of sacred Lake Manasarowar (photo from 1985). Since then, the monastery, whose surroundings Sven Hedin described so vividly in 1907, has been partially rebuilt.*

Right: *Holy Lake Manasarowar; in the background Gurla Mandhata massif, 7700 meters [25,410 feet] high. For Buddhists and Hindus, this "Lake of Supreme Consciousness" is just as important for pilgrimages as Mt. Kailas and can be circled on foot in three days.*

194

Milarepa, the great yogi who wore only cotton, lived from 1024 to 1123 and was Tibet's most popular poet. For nine years, he meditated in the rock grottoes of Kyirong, the "Happy Village" on the Nepal border, and then wandererd to Mt. Kailas, where he defeated the Bonpo. This bronze statue is honored in an altar niche of the Cylinder Temple of Paro in west Bhutan.

Below: *Pilgrims on the strenuous path around sacred Mt. Kailas.*

unforgettable spectacle. Like a vision in the morning light Kailas stood between two dark granite peaks, with new snow powdered on rocks and glaciers. Slowly I made my way back to the lamasery. In the rays of the rising sun the head lama was standing on the flat roof, with folded hands, contemplating Kailas and bowing before the sublime view. Every morning throughout the year, summer and winter alike, he greets the sacred mountain, praying to his god and praying also to demons. In a granite cave beneath the monastery the gilded emblems of the gods are kept. They grinned at me meaninglessly, for their symbolism was beyond my power of comprehension. We entered this sanctum through a low doorway, after traversing a little library. Everyone who came in had to give the big prayer drum a turn. Now I stood before the holiest of all the images, that of Kailas. We prostrated ourselves in front of this divinity, who was draped in tulle. Each pilgrim must offer up a little butter lamp. All around were the strangest figures of demons, whose goggle eyes stared at us from every corner. Befitting the holiness of the place, on leaving I gave the great prayer drum an especially vigorous thrust. Drawing a deep breath of relief, I found myself once more in the sunshine. White prayer flags were fluttering, and Kailas shone down upon us.

Now we are on a pilgramage to Dolma La, a pass over 5,600 meters (18,000 feet) high, the highest on the circuit of Kailas. A forest of cairns indicates the holiness of the place. Great piles of human hair are encircled by little walls. A rock is covered with newly extracted teeth – religious sacrifices made by fanatical pilgrims. Huge wild granite crags border the pass, which is covered with newly fallen snow. My companions kneel at the tomb of a saint. Close by is a rock showing what are said to be the holy man's footprints.

Beside Dolma La is an enormous crag topped by a flag staff from which small multicolored prayer flags flutter. The abundance of cairns gives the place its peculiar character. Almost everyone who goes by erects his own cairn, for which he must often steal from previous structures since stones are scarce. A white stone usually crowns the little edifice. Although the summit of Kailas is not visible from this spot, it is of special importance. When we recall that many of the pilgrims are persons who have never before left the plains of India, we must conclude that a number of them fail to return home, perishing here from the hardships of the journey. The more fanatical of the pilgrims make the circuit of the mountain crawling on their bellies, thus achieving the highest degree of spiritual purification.

Here is a description of the actual process. With hands crossed, the pilgrim prostrates himself. Then, wearing gloves with metal plates, he makes a scratch as far ahead as he can reach. Rising erect at the point where his feet are, he strides to the scrach mark the length of the body with arms outstretched prostrates himself once more, and repeats the process.

A little below Dolma-La there is a small sacred lake where the pilgrims make their ablutions – as a rule. But this time the lake, which is at an altitude of 5,400 meters (18,000 feet), is frozen and thickly covered with snow. Near the shore we see piles of rock which the pilgrims have flung onto the ice in the vain hope of breaking it. It seems to be an unfavorable year for pilgrimages.

The eastern side of the pass descends steeply into a new, long valley, ending far to the north in a high pass, which is an important route over the chains of the Transhimalayas. But we turn southward, leaving the wild granite landscape to find ourselves once again amid imposing walls of conglomerate. Soon we will reach a new monastery, the Tsumtulphu Gompa ...

Night was close at hand when I finished my geological sketches, and dark storm clouds had gathered. Entering Tsumtulphu Gompa as pilgrims, we found it uninteresting. Relative disorder prevailed, for the head lama had

gone to Lhasa, so the inmates were somewhat disorganized. Still, I found it worthwhile to visit a number of caves in the cliffs, formerly the dwellings of famous ascetics that are now vacant. The valley widened here, and we had a good view of the broad plain that lies on the southern side of the Transhimalayas. We are only about 10 kilometers (6 miles) from Darchen, where we started on the circuit of Kailas. On the way to it, we passed huge heaps of inscribed Mani stones, on which the words "Om mani padme hum" had been chiselled. When I moved to pick one up, Kali cried: "No, no, Sahib, don't touch it; the gods will be angry."

Holy Lake Gosainkunda is located north of Kathmandu in Nepal at an altitude of 4298 meters [14,183 feet].

Still, Paldin sympathies with my collector's fever and would like me to have one of these stones. A storm is threatening, and it grows darker. I look cautiously around and then hide a particularly well-carved Mani stone beneath my caftan. There comes a loud clap of thunder, followed by a cloudburst, as if the Last Judgement was at hand. "Put down the stone, Sahib, put down the stone!" Paldin is pale from anxiety. Certainly all the commotion in the heaven is enough to make the poor fellow anxious and convince him that the gods are angered by my sacrilege. Still, the stone remains in my pouch, where I feel it will prove a goodluck charm. A pitch dark night

Ama Dablan (6856 meters [22,625 feet]) in the Khumbu region of the Himalayas is worshiped by the Sherpas as a sacred mountain.

has fallen. It is still raining heavily, with lightning flashes and peals of thunder. After an arduous trek, we reach Darchen, stumbling in one place over a lama who lies in the pouring rain, having fallen asleep exhausted after a long day of bellycrawling ...

The Unapproachable Mistress of the Mountain of the Gods

Pious Tibetans circumambulate sacred Mt. Kailas three or 13 times. The most devout carry out these ritual rounds in a prostrate position. They throw themselves flat on the ground and cover the length of the holy path with their bodies. Some complete this ritual, called *parikrama*, in only one day; older and ill pilgrims no longer able to bear the exertion "hire" beggars or carriers who circle the sacred lake or mountain in their stead. Formerly, a sheep was paid for such a proxy *parikrama*. It was believed that through

parikrama a contribution was made to the peace of the dead, and one hoped that one circumambulation would erase the bad deeds of one life and 10 rounds would erase the sins of an entire earth age, as Swami Pranavananda, the keenest explorer of Mt. Kailas in our time, reported in 1949.

The holy mountains are venerated as "Divine Ancestors" or the "Throne of the Gods"; it would be absolutely inconceivable to contemplate climbing and wandering about on them. The first expedition to climb Chomalhari (also Jomolhari), the "Mistress of the Divine Mountain," which

A huge Mani stone in Khumbu valley. The prayers have been chiseled out of the large granite block. The lettering is dark and corresponds to the former rock surface, whereas the carved-out areas show the fresh, snow-white granite.

started from Bhutan, shows how deep this belief runs in the Himalayan mountain peoples. In April 1970, an Indian-Bhutanese group set out to conquer the peak. This spelled an acute clash between ancient traditions and modern times, as reflected in the experience of a Bhutanese lieutenant named Chachu. He reports:

"For our people the 24,000 foot Chomolhari is a very holy mountain, since it is the abode of the Goddess *Jo-mo lHa-ri.* Most of the Bhutanese believe that the sacred peaks cannot be climbed. Such feelings are prevalent among all hill people. It is probably because mountains play such an important part in our lives. I, too, was brought up in such an atmosphere and always thought that Chomolhari was a sacred mountain, never to be trodden by men... We were moving together as a team, like a family moving to Chomolhari on a pilgrimage. The base camp was established on April 14th, at an altitude of 16,500 feet, just below the ice. The great sacred peak of Chomolhari could be seen, looming above us, calling to us with all its majesty. It was an awe-inspiring sight. A party of three managed to find a route up to 19,000 feet and Camp I was established there on April 18th."

Three days later Camp II was pitched at 23,000 feet, and on April 23rd, at 4.30 A. M., Lt. Chachu started out with his team of five:

"It was a clear day. I prayed for a while and then we all started moving up. Dangerous stretches had to be traversed over which we belayed each other. Steps had to be kicked or cut into snow and ice."

They reached the southwestern summit after some hours and, having rested a while, proceeded toward the main summit:

"After what appeared to be days we were near the summit, about a hundred feet below it. I looked up towards the seat of the Goddess Chomolhari and something happened to me. I felt that I would not go up to the top. I was too steeped in the traditions of my country to break with them so suddenly. I decided that I would stay where I was and it was with much reluctance and after great argument that the other members left me there after securing and anchoring me safely. They said there was nothing wrong with going to the abode of the Goddess Chomolhari to pray. We all had come there in utter humility on a pilgrimage. That is the way of mountaineers: they love and respect the mountains and do not climb them to desecrate them. A little later, the four members returned after planting our flags on the summit. They also left a holy urn with the image of Buddha, blessed by the holy Lamas, in the snow on the summit."

They returned to Camp II, where they met the second summit party, who proceeded in high spirits to achieve ther goal. But theirs was an unlucky attempt. An abrupt change of weather occurred, and the second party was lost and could not be traced despite the closest search.

The Original Home of Gods and Men

Nowhere else is the "genius loci" so overwhelming as in the Himalaya mountains. Perhaps this is because traditions here were able to survive uninterrupted despite tribal migrations and the storms of war, whereas elsewhere they lie buried under the debris of the past.

explains why the Ganga is also called the Jahnavi or the Bhagirathi, after the son and the grandson of King Bharata.

In this tradition, being so very old as the Jains believe, Sarasvati plays a starring role as the Source of the Holy Waters and of the first murmured words in the guise of Shruti-Devi, the leading Goddess of the Revealed Words. Her importance was expressed through the great Sarasvati movement that began in the second century B.C. and gave rise to a renaissance of Jain literature that was significant throughout India. When King Boja sought the truth among the teachings of all sects in the 11th century A.D., Sarasvati is supposed to have appeared in visions and uttered one of the most beautiful sayings about the source of equality among all religions.

Sarasvati and the so-called eight-footed sacred Mt. Kailas are not the only figures in Jain tradition; of course, their holiest lake, called Padma Hrada, "Lotus Springs," is also prominent. In old Hindu texts it is named *Manasarowar*, or Manasa Lake. It is said that the ocean once fell from heaven onto Meru mountain, whose earthly equivalent is Mt. Kailas. This heavenly ocean flowed four times around the mountain and then divided into four

Facing page: Hindus bathing in the holy Bagmati river at Pashupati temple east of Kathmandu. The platforms on the shore (ghats) are also used for the cremation of corpses, as in Benares on the sacred Ganges.

Above: In a small, sacred pond near Kathmandu rests the god Vishnu, here called Narayana (nara = water, ayana = resting place). He lies atop the snake Ananta, the symbol of never-ending time. The unusual figure was carved from a single stone block. The present King of Nepal, Birenda, an incarnation of Vishnu, is not allowed to visit the site.

rivers, which ran down the mountain and formed the sacred lakes.

Swami Pranavananda writes enthusiastically about Manasarowar: "She is majestically calm and dignified like a huge bluish-green emerald or a pure turquoise set between the two mighty and equally majestic silvery mountains, the Kailas on the north and the Gurla Mandhata on the south and between the sister-lake Rakshas Tal or Ravana Hrada (*Langak Tso* of the Tibetans) on the west and some hills on the east. There stand eight monasteries on the holy shores, wherein Buddhist monks strive all their lives to attain the sublimity of the eternal silence of Nirvana."

In pre-Buddhist times, the glacier-covered mountains were also venerated as the ancestors of the different peoples, a custom still remembered by the Laya people in northwest Bhutan. The peaks became the thrones and homes of the gods worshiped by the Bons, the Hindus and the Buddhists. It is thought that one can neither approach nor, above all, set foot on the homes of the gods. The tribes who live at the foot of these giant glaciers watch the desecration of the seats of their gods by modern mountaineers with reserve and horror.

The Layas, a small mountain people, live at the foot of Masang Kang and differ in many aspects from other Bhutanese. The women have long hair and wear peculiarly shaped plaited hats. They speak their own dialect and evidently are still strongly bound to the Bon religion. Strange wooden sculptures guard the entrance to the village of Laya and resemble the wood culture in east Afghanistan.

Homes of the Gods

"Armed with an ice-axe, the stranger from the West strives to conquer the divine magnificence, to defeat the peaks and pause awhile at the very top, where no one before him has ever stood. There he can enjoy the lonely beauty of nature at its most gigantic – and nearest to heaven. The local population of the East views the mountains in a different light. Many of them have probably been shocked at the presumptiousness of those who have dared to storm the seat of the gods. For the Hindus and the Buddhists, the Himalayas are highly sacred ground. There, atop the snow-covered peaks, they have located the paradise of the gods, the inaccessible homes of these superhuman beings. The gods of the original, Shamanist inhabitants also reigned there at one time. The pre-Buddhist believers in the Bon religion also considered the Himalaya Mountains to be sacred. All pilgrims go there in humility so that they can be near to the gods and, most important, attain spiritual heights at the foot of the glacier-capped mountains."

B. C. Olschak: *Sikkim – Himalayan Country between Jungles and Glaciers.*

Sacred Mt. Masang Kang (2700 meters [8,910 feet]). It is the symbol of the legendary Masang people, who came from southeast Tibet and settled in the western part of the eastern Himalayas. The Masang were supposedly the first inhabitants of Bhutan.

VARIETY OF HIMALAYAN BUILDINGS

Seldom are so many architectural styles to be found within the region of a single mountain range, as is the case in the Himalayas. This has come about because of the varying influences of climate and altitude, the availability of building materials, as well as the different races and religions. The eastern Himalayas alone provide a good example of this great variety. Here we find the most primitive bamboo huts – in the tropical regions often built on piles and occupied by tribes following animistic religions – as well as the simple stone houses with shingle roofs that the Monpas live in, and the mighty fortress-monasteries, or Dzongs, of the Bhutan Himalayas. Everything is possible here. The prototype of all the Dzongs is the Yumbu Lhakhang, the oldest fortress in Tibet. It lies in the legendary Yarlung Tsangpo valley and has recently been rebuilt, following its complete destruction during the Cultural Revolution.

The Bhutanese Dzongs show a pattern similar to the Dzongs in Tibet – a basic structure upon which are built tiers of walls that are more and more recent as one ascends. Thanks to the amount of timber available, the roofs of the Dzongs are usually composed of several layers of wood, expertly constructed without the use of nails and covered with large wooden shingles,

The Cylinder Temple, Dumtsi Lhakhang, built by Thangtong-gyalpo in Paro (west Bhutan) in the mid-15th century. It stands, modest and off to one side, frequently unnoticed, in the background of the huge castle grounds. Today, the cylinder is protected and partially hidden by a square temple addition. It is topped by a super-structure, the 13 levels of enlightenment.

weighted down with stones. Because of the potential fire risk, this type of roof construction was abandoned to some extent, and corrugated iron sheets were used instead of wood, but this practice is being replaced by the use of slabs of dark slate, which is locally available. In the oldest Dzongs we often see half-rounded towers, which were added for defense or lookout purposes at various points around the periphery of the building.

All Dzongs serve a double purpose – they are the seat of the local administrative body as well as being a monastery. In addition to these functions

Opposite page, right: *This statue, lavishly encrusted with turquoise stones and gems, is 45 centimeters [18 inches] tall and made of rock crystal. It portrays the Dhyani Buddha of Eternal Life. The idea and execution of this unique jeweled statue is attributed to brilliant Thangtonggyalpo.*

Right: *Not only has Nepalese architecture preserved and refined the ancient Indian art of wooden construction, but Nepalese architects and artists were among the builders who traveled farthest: they participated in the construction of Borobodur in Java (around 800 A.D.) and were also summoned to China as court architects in the 11th century. The towering roofs, decreasing in size with increasing height, of Nyatapola temple in Bhaktapur, near Kathmandu, are characteristic of the squares and streets of the capital city. The preservation of these architectural jewels, which are endangered by climatic conditions, is one of the foremost concerns of the king and the government.*

Right: *Bjakar Dzong in east Bhutan. It traces back to Zhabdung I, founder of the then theocratic kingdom of Bhutan. The Dzong dominates the high valley of Bhumtang, where white cranes spend the winter, often circling above the Dzong. Zhabdung named the Dzong "The Castle of the White Bird."*

Facing page: *Thikse monastery in Ladakh viewed from the north. It dominates the Indus valley. Thikse is a typical example of Tibetan monastery architecture; its flat roofs differ from those of the Dzongs in the Himalayas of Bhutan.*

Tongsa Dzong in central Bhutan is the royal family's ancestral seat. Twenty temples are included in its complicated structures. The Dzong rests on top of the steep canyon of the Mangde Chu, which has its source on the highest mountain in Bhutan, Kangkar Punsum.

they are also used as storehouses for foodstuffs, which are distributed to the local population in times of shortage. The great Dzong of the Bhutanese capital, Thimphu, also houses the state's administrative center as well as the headquarters of the Buddhist state religion. Twenty-five years ago the farsighted king of that time had the Dzong extended, in the original style and using traditional building methods. The walls are up to 2 meters [7 feet] thick and are usually filled with mud. It was interesting to observe the construction of the walls: as many as a hundred women and girls would stand on the walls, each with a tool for tamping down the mud. In time with a loud rhythmic song and moving in an almost dance-like fashion, they would beat down the mud, which the men brought up to them on ladders.

In the Bhutan Himalayas it is not only the Dzongs that make an impression, the houses are also worthy of note, built in a chalet style with colorfully painted wooden pergolas. Along the main caravan routes that lead from Sikkim through Bhutan and on to the East, we find countless chorten and little chapels, with their mill wheels driven by a diverted stream and connected to a prayer drum. In fact one could speak of a chorten pathway here, founded about 800 A.D. by Padmasambhava. It was along this route that the art of building stupas found its way into the eastern Himalayas. A particularly fine example of this skill is seen in the great "Chorten of Khora" in east Bhutan.

A splendid mixture of building styles can be seen in the Nepalese Himalayas, where Hinduism and Buddhism exist side by side. Next to the characteristic Hindu temples, often showing the emblem of a monkey, we can see large stupas, decorated with prayer flags. Only in the northern border regions, such as Mustang and Dolpo, are the building styles dictated by pure Lamaism. In the western Himalayas, too, a mixture of styles can be seen, but here the change is not from north to south, from Tibetan to Hindu influence; rather it varies between the Buddhist and the Islamic style and often quite sharply.

The colossal stupa constructions of Nepal, with the eyes of the mystical Buddha looking out over the shining dome toward all four points of the

BONANZA STREET
BOOKS

JACKIE MI

compass, have spread their message far and wide. Padmasambhava, who is revered as the second Buddha, not only founded the first temple in Tibet, Samye, south of Lhasa, but is also credited with having set up whole stupa routes as he traveled through Bhutan from east to west around 800 A.D.

The First Missionaries and Founders of the Stupas and Temples

According to Buddhist legends, some of the *arhats* were the first missionaries to spread Buddhist teachings in the Mt. Kailas area. These were pupils of Buddha who had already attained nirvana, the first level of emancipation, about 2500 years ago, and who had gained "Serenity of the Mind"

Below right: The opulent facade of the inner courtyard in Sakya monastery south of the Yarlung Tsangpo. Sakya preceded Potala as the main monastery in Tibet and is almost eerie with its gloomy, red-and-white-striped walls. Only the south monastery and its voluminous library have survived. The various buildings of the north monastery have been completely destroyed during the Cultural Revolution and later on were rebuilt.

The durable facade of a Thakali house in Kali Gandaki valley. The flat rock layers in this region make it possible to build solid stone walls held together by clay "cement." The extremely spare stock of trees in this dry valley are still ruthlessly cut down and stacked for winter fuel.

and were free of the "three spiritual poisons": the illusion of deliberate ignorance, insatiable greed and hatred. They supposedly not only came as far as Mt. Kailas but also taught the "Children of the Gods" Buddhist doctrine and saw to it that the lot of the poor nomads in the region was improved. Legends are still told about them in the area extending from present-day Ladakh to the sacred mountain, and in some places, such as Ladakh, their continually reborn incarnations are worshiped. The places where the missionaries were active are commemorated by stupas and temples.

The second great wave of pilgrims appeared during the rule of the great Buddhist Emperor Ashoka (272–231 B.C.). Initially, he supported all religions equally, as was typical of Indian kings. He is therefore also glorified by the Hindus and, especially, the old Jains as one of their own members. However, near the end of his life he turned completely to

Buddhism and actively propagated it throughout his huge empire. Each year, he would make a pilgrimage down the imperial roads he had had constructed. There were comfortable roadhouses under shade trees about every 5 kilometers [3 miles] along the way. The chronicles indicate that the transportation system of that time must have been extremely well-thought out, although it deteriorated over the following centuries. One can imagine how the imperial caravans, 1000 strong, slowly proceeded from the capital,

Pataliputra, (now called Patna), in central India to the distant pilgrimage sites. Sacred monuments – stupas (chorten in Tibetan) – were erected to mark the sites of imperial visits; their locations are still held in reverence from the far northwest of the Himalayas to Nepal.

The famous Chinese pilgrims who traveled during the sixth to eighth centuries, particularly Quanzang (Hsuan Tsang), relate how lively these places were; however, for the most part, the imperial inspections have been considered to be pious legends. Yet today, Ashoka's visit to Nepal is seen in

The gaily painted facade of one of the royal seats in Bumthang, east Bhutan. The typical Bhutanese windows, which can be closed with wooden shutters, are incorporated into all buildings in the kingdom, even military barracks.

213

a new light. In Kathmandu valley, not only did he supposedly establish one of the greatest stupa-temples, but his daughter, who accompanied him, married a high ranking Nepalese and founded monasteries and temples.

The conversion of the northwest (present-day Ladakh) has also been put at that time and is connected with the name of an entire group of monks, the *Madhyantika*, who are also individually venerated in various places. They originally lived in Benares, where the common people became envious of the privileged status of the Buddhist monks. General opinion held that they cost the people too much. Therefore, when a group of monks boarded a ship on the river, it was decided to drown them all. However, the monks rose in the air and flew toward the Himalayas to spread their teachings there. During that period levitation was considered a quite "normal" ability of certain yogis who possessed special spiritual powers and who physically practiced.

Facing page: The gate of the old royal palace in Patan, guarded by two stone lions. Kathmandu, Patan and Bhaktapur were small autonomous kingdoms until 1769, when the Rana dynasty united them.

The unique wood carvings in the royal palaces in Kathmandu valley reveal a mixture of Hindu, Buddhist and early animist influences. They trace back to the appreciation of art by the Newars, who appeared as the dominant ethnic group around 900 A.D. and whose origins are still obscure. It is said that a true Newar cannot let a piece of wood lie without first decorating it artistically.

The magnificent wood carvings in the former royal palaces in Bhaktapur, east of Kathmandu, are unequaled. Their dark coloring harmonizes with the red brick buildings. The art of wood carving was supposedly introduced by the Newars over 1000 years ago.

Another notable missionary journey was undertaken in 233 A.D., according to Tibetan tradition. At that time, the first tidings of Buddhism, i.e., sacred writings, were said to have fallen onto the palace of King Thothori in the Yarlung valley. Learned lamas of later generations interpreted this legend in a contemporary sense, as it is written in the *Blue Annals*. They thought that the ancient Bonpos, for whom all sacred things came from heaven, had told this story. What in fact had happened was that Indian missionaries had come to the Yarlung valley on their way through the eastern

part of modern-day Bhutan. Since neither the king nor anyone else could understand them, they moved on.

Pilgrims' roads, which also figured significantly as trade routes, were maintained throughout the centuries. Whole books could be written about the journeys of Chinese and Indian pilgrims. Guru Phadampa could be considered a characteristic case. The *Blue Annals* contain information about his five visits to Tibet in the 11th and 12th centuries. During his first visit he wandered from Dingthang to sacred Mt. Tsa-ri and then on to

Right: *Luntse Dzong in east Bhutan, one of the most impressive, although less-known, monastery-castles. The government and the religious authorities of the district rule here side by side. The Dzong also serves as a store-room for hard times.*

Three water-driven prayer wheels under one roof. In each of the small huts, a prayer wheel is turned by means of a horizontal mill wheel powered by a diverted stream, and it "prays" as long as the stream flows. The water emerging in front is "holy."

Kongyul and the district of Lower Kham in eastern Tibet. His second visit led him to Kashmir and western Tibet; his third to southern Tibet via Nepal. During his fourth visit he remained longer in Nepal and made a pilgrimage from there to central Tibet. When Phadampa set out for Tibet for the fifth time, he went as far as Chian, where he stayed for 12 years before returning to Dingri in southwest Tibet. There he founded Dingri Langgor monastery in the northeastern section of Labchi Glacier (near Mt. Everest), where he preached for 21 years before dying there.

Phadampa's pilgrimage to holy Mt. Tsa-ri seems especially interesting. This mountain is located in southeast Tibet, near the territory of the wild Lopa tribes, which were greatly feared at that time; the Lopas are probably related to the formerly head-hunting Nagas, who moved south to Assam. The site on Tsa-ri was dedicated to the Tantric deity Sambara Demchog, and amulets containing sacred earth from Tsa-ri were worn. Thangtong Gyalpo erected buildings, paths and bridges in the Tsa-ri area. This region was famous for the medicinal herbs that grew there. They were called *lalo tigtu* by the area's inhabitants. The herbs were used to treat yellow fever and diseases of the gall bladder. It is reported that in the mid-14th century bridges and paths were repaired, ferries established and rope and chain bridges constructed. Resthouses were also built to ease the pilgrims' journey to Mt. Kailas and Mt. Tsa-ri.

Right: *Paro Dzong in west Bhutan. It is known for its New Year's festivities, when the huge thanka of Guru Rimpoche is displayed; it is only unrolled for the duration of the heroic dances early in the morning. The splendid "Cosmic Mandala" strikes visitors in the front courtyard of the Dzong.*

The "Leonardo da Vinci" of the Himalayas

Thangtonggyalpo lived from 1385 to 1464, although in legends it is claimed that he reached 125 years of age. He was the greatest architect, artist, sculptor and, above all, pioneer of engineering in the Himalayan countries. After the focus of interest had shifted from all further technical developments to exclusively religious matters, he was worshiped as one of the "Ninety Great Miracle Workers," the Mahasiddhas. The Tibetans added

The elegant Gaza Dzong in the central Mo Chu valley in northwest Bhutan. It is famous for its medicinal hot springs as well as for being a marketplace for the yak caravans from the north. Gaza lies at the foot of Kang Bum, the "Great Mountain" (visible in the background).

six mahasiddhas to the original circle of 84 who were famous in India and Nepal. Thangtonggyalpo gained immortality as the "Builder of Iron-Chain Bridges," Cagzampa, since these bridges were the last great work of his life and vividly remembered by all. It is said that he erected over 58 chain bridges in an area from central Asia deep into eastern Bhutan. He himself supervised the production of iron and usually had the strongest chains made by smiths in Kongpo and Bhutan; these chains were then transported to the construction sites. When he was 73, he planned the buildings on

Below right: One of the picturesque old houses on Barkhor circle in Lhasa. Usually, the inhabitants of the Tibetan capital live in two-storied houses. The kitchen and storage rooms are located on the ground floor, the living space on the top story.

Above: The architectural style of Sakya monastery is based on the royal castles of the Yuan dynasty (1276 – 1368). The square complex is surrounded by walls with painted stripes, which symbolize the different directions within the Sakya ideas. The eaves of the roofs are decorated with cloth hangings of the same colors.

"Water Mountain," Chuwori, southwest of Lhasa: two monasteries, large stupa-chorten and his best-known chain bridge.

After completion of these works, he moved back to Bhutan and built his small, well-tended family monastery between Thimphu and Paro. His secret biography is guarded as a treasure there. It is a small block-print, only four fingers wide and a hand-length long, made of apparently blank, light-colored fiber paper without writing. Only when the pages are held under water do faint red letters appear. Thangtonggyalpo was born in Olkha

Lhatse, a small principality west of Shigatse on the White River. As a child he already displayed supernatural powers and soon knew more than the lamas who instructed him. As a youth, he traded with yak tails and musk, the costly Tibetan export product, in Dolkha in southern Tibet. When seven people were sentenced to death there, he gave all his wares to the prince, thus buying freedom for the condemned. Around 1427 he served for three years in the military in fulfillment of a type of family tax that required soldiers to be supplied for the defense of the country. During his

military duty he won an unbloody victory over a charging enemy that is still talked about today.

Princess Kalzang became his chief patron in Lhasa. She enabled him to realize his artistic and architectural plans. On "Iron Mountain," Cagri, a house was built for him, from which a famous college of medicine later developed. With the support of his patron, he was able to make a statue of the Protector of Wisdom, Manjushri, out of pure gold and also to carry out his idea for jeweled statues, which he created from imported mussel shells,

Tashilhunpo monastery in Shigatse, south Tibet. The mausoleum of the third Panchen Lama (d. 1737) is in the middle; in it lie the mortal remains of the deceased in a stupa reliquary, in imitation of the procedure used for the Dalai Lama in Potala Palace in Lhasa. The cylinders crowned by a trident on the rooftop are supposed to ward off all evil from the holy site.

219

coral and turquoise. Another work that became famous was his image of the patron saint of Tibet, Avalokiteshvara-Cenrezi, who had appeared to him in a vision and inspired him in his works.

Unique among his buildings is the "Cylinder Temple," Dumtsi Lhakhang, located in Paro valley in western Bhutan. True to its name, the building rises from the four-sided temple (a later addition) surrounding it. The cylinder has no windows and its several stories are connected only by ladders. It almost seems as if Thangtonggyalpo had projected the ancient many-storied structure of underground temple grottoes upward. The walls

have been covered with beautiful frescoes and four altar niches have been built into each story of the central part of the temple, which rises like a column. The holy statues are worshiped in these niches by the flickering light of butter lamps. The statues are attributed to Thangtonggyalpo, especially the Tantric representation of the mystic Buddha in the *yab-yum*, or mother-father, position and a large bronze statue of the poet Milarepa.

IN THE GORGES AND ON THE HEIGHTS

In this age of exotic journeys, whoever takes a stroll among the cheerful crowds mingling at the bazaar in Leh, the capital of Ladakh, can contemplate individual types that reveal much of the turbulent history of this country. The faces along Karakorum Road indicate the variety of their descent. The country is also called, rather justifiably, "Little Tibet," owing to the Tibetan troops who fought here when Tibet became a world power during the eighth century. At that time, Zhangzhung was finally annexed

The famous Chinese pilgrims spared no pains and fled from no dangers on their way to India in search of the original copies of holy Buddhist scripts, especially during the fifth to ninth centuries. Neither the Pamir mountains nor the Karakorum gorges kept them from their religiously motivated undertaking. Less known is how these pilgrim and trade routes developed and were promoted by dynastic marriages. For example, the first King of Great Tibet married a Nepalese princess and a Chinese princess and had residences built for each of them in Lhasa. They became a meeting place and crossroads for merchants, pilgrims and, in particular, Buddhist missionaries, who wandered from the heart of ancient China via Lhasa to Nepal and India, richly endowed with gifts from Brikuti, the Nepalese princess, and Wengcheng, the Chinese princess. Historical research is only gradually leading to a recognition of the extent of the peacemaking influence due to the union of peoples and cultures that resulted from these marriages.

Arhat Angara, who preached Buddhism, made a pilgrimage to sacred Mt. Kailas, where he explained Buddhist teachings to the Children of the Gods. Out of gratitude, they gave him a censer and a yak-tail fan to keep away the flies; he is waving the yak-tail as a symbol.

as West Tibet and battles were waged with China for Baltisan. In 740, the King of Brusha (Gilgit) married a Tibetan princess in order to strengthen the relationship between the two dynasties. His empire thus broke away from China and China embarked on an unsuccessful punitive expedition. Wakhan, the high plateau in northeast Afghanistan and south of the Pamirs, was ruled by the Arabs, whereas the Pamir area recognized Tibetan rule. Badakhshan, located south of Ferghana, was described by Islamic writers as the gateway to Tibet. Yet the tides of war turned like the winds.

At the beginning of the eighth century, Tibet fought with the Arabs against the Chinese in Ferghana; later, however, it was the other way around. In 791, Tibet emerged the victor and ruled over the Tarim basin for a few decades. A legend claims that Pehar, the main tutelary god of the Samye monastery, was converted and brought from there to central Tibet.

As of the 11th century, when the descendants of the Tibetan royal dynasty fled to the west and married into Ladakh, the Tibetan influence in

this area continually increased. The descendants of the Yarlung dynasty even dreamed of reconquering Tibet from Ladakh. Several dynasties pursued this goal by military means. They even enlisted the assistance of Moslem troops, although the effort was unsuccessful. A mosque in Leh dating from the mid-17th century bears witness to Moslem participation.

The local costumes of the women in northern Ladakh, with their heavy *perak* headware, indicate that it was probably for the most part Tibetan warriors who initially came to the country and married the female inhabi-

Caravans crossing Baga pass on the Grain Road. Painted by monk Kungya from Tarap monastery in Dolpo.

223

tants. Furthermore, the tall figures of the turbaned men are particularly striking. They have aquiline noses and, frequently, sparkling light-colored eyes, and they like to dye their beards bright yellow. They are descended from the Indo-European Dards, presumably a tribe split off from the yellow-haired Wusun peoples of Ferghana described by the Chinese. Their Indo-European facial features have often led to their description as the "sons of Alexander," since Alexander the Great's troops reached the Indus area 2300 years ago. As a matter of fact, "Iksander" is named as a forefather in various genealogies of minor royalty in this area. If one considers the function of royal weddings – demonstrated by the grand royalty and imitated by the small – this actually does not seem improbable. Alexander himself literally represented the marriage of the Orient to the Occident by wedding the

Facing page: In contrast to the black variety, white yaks are often considered sacred animals.

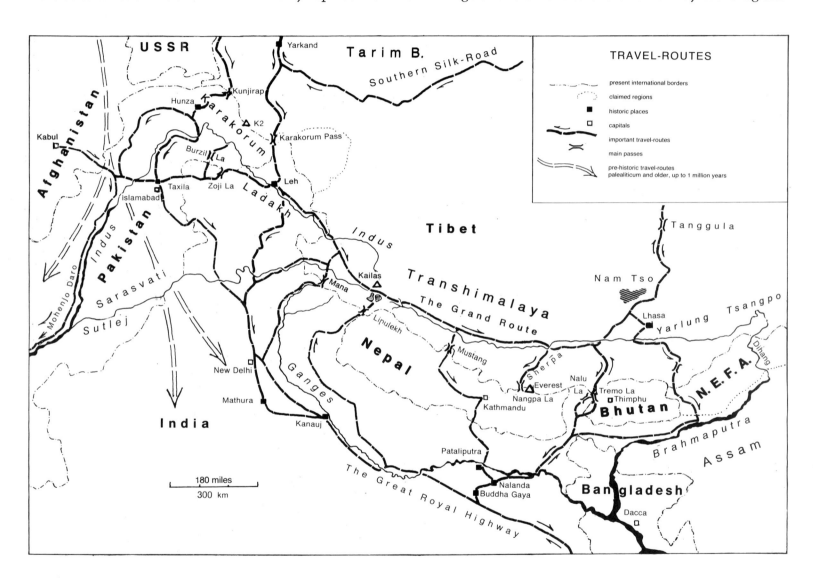

This map shows the traveling routes that have been used during the last 5,000 years. The migration routes (arrows) correspond to those of very early times. The old Indo-European trade routes spread eastward from the civilized area along the Indus. It was only possible to bypass the Himalayas to the north or to the south, and so the caravans followed the great depression between the Himalayas and the Transhimalayas to Lhasa, along what became known as "The Great Route." To the south travel was along the valley of the Ganges, "The Great Royal Highway." Links between these two main routes had to pass over high Himalayan passes and were very hard going. It was along these major and minor routes that the spread of Buddhism occurred. Then, pilgrims used to join the caravans, first the Hindus, later the Bonpo, the Jainists and the Buddhists. When the southern silk route became popular, links were formed via Yarkand and Kashgar to the southern migration routes.

Xuanzang (602 – 664) was a Chinese monk who translated important Buddhist texts. He was also an extremely well-traveled pilgrim. On his back is a case filled with Buddhist texts and illustrations.

Right: *A yak caravan, laden with Tibetan salt, makes its way through a mountain forest in a snowstorm. In the village of Ron-pa the salt will be exchanged for barley.*

A young Dolpo girl. A layer of grease and blue-black root extract protects her face from the rays of the sun while crossing the high passes. The facial markings can also have a ritual meaning.

daughter of the prince of his allies from Taxila near Rawalpindi in the Punjab. A thousand years later, when the Indian princedoms fell to the sword of Islam, the Indian princes fled. Not welcome in their own home (Greater India did not exist at that time), they sailed to the "Gold Countries" to seek their fortunes there. Thus, "Iksander" still appears as an ancestor today in the genealogies of Indonesian houses of princes.

The Hunza tribe, which has been rediscovered as a result of the opening of the plateau highway connecting Kashgar with Pakistan, even claims Gesar, the hero of the central Asian saga, as a tribal ancestor. As a matter of fact, a version of this saga exists in the old language of the Hunza people, Burushaski, which apparently is not related to any other language. The isolated Hunza people, who wear beards dyed reddish yellow, have tenaciously clung to life in their high valley. A curious story is told about how they managed to survive the advance of the victorious Moslem army. The clever prince of the Hunza dispatched scouts, who reported to him that resistance would be hopeless, but that people professing the Moslem faith would be acknowledged and spared. The prince dipped deeply into the treasury and sent out scouts with gold to invite a mufti to come to Hunza with an edition of the Koran. When the first Moslem warriors appeared, they were greeted by a prince calling out *Allah inshalla* and a mufti holding a Koran in his hands. Thus did a "Moslem flavor" enter the lives of the Hunza people, who have lived on a caravan route, recently rebuilt, for thousands of years — a route that is certainly one of the world's oldest. Here one is struck not only by Buddhist rock pictures but also by old drawings of animals and other figures, which demonstrate that people migrated and traded here millennia ago.

The Lepchas of Sikkim are a warrior people driven into the Himalayas by the endless turmoil of war, probably over 2000 years ago. As Rongpa, "Canyon Dwellers," they established a kingdom in Rongyul, "Canyon Land." At one time it covered an area that extended from present-day Darjeeling to the Chumbi valley in southern Tibet and also included parts of modern southwest Bhutan. Their "Tatar cast of features" was described by Joseph Hooker, one of the first to study the Himalayas. However, since 1900 almost one-half of their vocabulary has consisted of words borrowed from the Tibetan language. Today, there are only a few thousand Lepchas. They were able to preserve their uniqueness for a fairly long time because in the 15th century they became blood brothers to the victoriously advancing Bhutia people, who founded the kingdom of Sikkim. It was therefore possible for them to maintain their shamanist rites, with Jacob's ladders, rainbow fairies and mountain spirits, as well as to preserve their language. They lived alongside the Bhutia-Sikkimese for centuries at the foot of sacred Kangchendzonga, the "Great Glacier of Five Treasures."

The people of Mustang also live hidden away (though not in a gorge) in the far north of Nepal on a narrow plateau that juts into Tibet. Mustang is the sole Tibetan principality that has remained entirely medieval, and it also has ancient, scarcely studied tales. Tradition claims that Mustang was founded by a grandson of the Tibetan sovereign King Thisongdetsen, that

Next double page: *Tibetan ponies are small but hardy. Here they are carrying their loads along a steep cliff path in Zanskar, with the ever present danger of a rockslide.*

Facing page: *Protected by salt bags, a grandmother looks after a baby like a madonna, both inside a heavy woolen blanket.*

is, around 800 A.D. Since 1795 it has been annexed to Nepal as a small autonomous princedom.

The Sakya sect dominates in Mustang. Athough the rock-cave monasteries must have prospered in medieval glory at one time, nothing remains of their wooden framework and stairways. As Peter Aufschnaiter, a Tyrolean mountain climber and colleague of Heinrich Harrer, the Austrian explorer of *Seven Years in Tibet*, reported, the cave entrances yawning high up in the rock walls can now only be reached by climbing or being hoisted up in a basket on ropes.

A salt caravan camped for the night at Kianglapa resting place in the Dolpo area. The sacks of salt form a horseshoe barrier against the wind, while the animals forage for whatever food they can find. A girl is seen feeding one of the dogs, taken along to protect the sheep from wolves.

The Sherpas, whose name literally means "East People," belong to the groups that migrated into the Himalayan area later. They did not settle in northeast Nepal until about 500 years ago. The German ethnologist Friedrich W. Funke writes that there they were able, "protected by the highest walls in the world, [to] preserve a culture much older than the culture of Tibet, which had converted to Buddhism. On the Roof of the World, the ancient Bon religion, with its evil and protective spirits, bloody sacrifices, natural deities, wizards, fertility rites, black magic, miracle healing and

uncanny powers, was suppressed by a strict, powerful priesthood. The Sherpas, however, remained faithful to their original beliefs, left East Tibet and found a new home at the foot of the world's highest mountain range."

From the 16th century on, Tibetan peoples moved into the southeastern Himalayas. Together with the previously settled Lepchas, they founded the kingdom of Sikkim. Farther to the east, the kingdom of Bhutan, the "Land of the Thunder-Dragon," arose; its theocratic rulers first established a Buddhist culture that survived for centuries before it was replaced by the Bhutanese kings in the 20th century. Extremely ancient cultural elements

Below: *A nomad making tea in one of the black yak-hair tents.*

Right: *Mother and daughter look out of the window of a typical Dolpo house, watching the loading of salt and cereal.*

have survived in this "Land of Hidden Treasures," and a tradition reaching far back into the past is reflected in the languages of this country. *Dzong-kha*, the standard language, is spoken by the ethnic Tibetan immigrants as the high language; six dialects belonging to this language group are still used. An additional seven spoken languages, however, belong to separate language groups that have not yet been investigated. They reflect the country's history as a refuge for various peoples who came to this area thousands of years ago, at the time of the great Indian epic.

On the Backs of the Sherpas

The great classic Himalayan expeditions were all carried on the backs of the Sherpas. This astonishing tribe from northeastern Nepal, or more exactly from the Khumbu region south of the Everest group, originally came from the east Tibetan province of Kham. This in fact is the derivation of their name (Sher = east, Pa = origin). But why this east Tibetan tribe left its homeland in the middle ages and migrated over the 5,700-meter-high (18,810-foot-high) Nangpa La pass into the Khumbu valleys is still uncertain. Whatever the reason, after arriving, they constructed mountain mon-

Next double page: *After crossing the Kagmara La in the Dolpo area, a yak caravan goes down a steep cliff path toward the south. Laden yaks do not like going slowly downhill and often break out of the group.*

asteries, such as Tangboche at the foot of Ama Dablam, the wildest peak of the whole Everest group. The many local groups cultivated the hill regions and traded their products in the main market, Namche Bazar. When the Rana dynasty fell, and King Mahendra opened up Nepal to foreigners in 1950, a new occupation for the Sherpas began. They were men of the mountains who coped easily with great altitudes and were much sought after as companions, guides and porters for the many expeditions that would soon be coming to explore the world's highest mountains.

Barley is measured out using this bowl and is filled into sacks, to be exchanged for the salt that the caravan has brought.

Next double page:

The art of the suspension bridges:

Left: *A suspension bridge over the Kuru Chu in east Bhutan. Woven from lianas and split bamboo, it will support the weight of laden animals.*

Right: *A special kind of suspension bridge with lianas woven into rings is used to cross the Yarlung Tsangpo at this narrow point in the East Himalayas. Invention of the suspension bridge is credited to the Chinese. Interestingly enough, the Incas made similar bridges in the high Andes, where there are no trees, using woven mountain grass.*

Below: *Smaller rivers are spanned by this simple type of wooden bridge: overlapping layers of logs are set into the banks and the gap between them is closed with long beams.*

Both Nepal and Tibet were closed countries in 1921 when permission was granted by the Dalai Lama for a group to explore Everest from the Tibetan side. The request had been made by General Bruce. First, however, approach routes leading to the mountain had to be found, a problem that was neatly summed up by a young Englishman taking part in the expedition: "If you want to climb a mountain, first you've got fo find it."

Above: *Wooden bridges are also used for larger rivers or gorges, like this covered one in east Bhutan. The railings along the bridge are draped with small prayer flags.*

A year later the first attempt to climb Everest was in progress, and without oxygen the climbers reached a height of 8,170 meters (26,961 feet). Great hopes were pinned on the 1924 expedition. E. F. Norton reached the famous yellow band on his own but ran into great difficulties trying to climb the north-facing limestone slabs, which was a bit like a steep icy roof. At 8,580 meters (28,314 feet) he had to admit that he would not be able to reach the summit that day, even with the fine calm weather.

Following behind came a group of three climbers; the outstanding mountaineer George L. Mallory, the young and relatively inexperienced Andrew Irvine and the geologist Noel E. Odell. On June 8 Mallory and Irvine left the high-altitude camp at 8,145 meters (26,879 feet), in a light mist but with no wind. Toward midday, Odell saw two small dots just below the summit

ridge, then the mist closed in again. Odell, who still felt quite strong, continued to ascend, without oxygen. He felt quite safe in the knowledge that his companion was there to support him, but when he turned around there was no one. After a snow shower the weather cleared and the sun came out. Odell climbed on and had a view of the whole summit area, but there was no sign of the two dots he'd seen earlier.

Laden yaks don't care much for bridges either, preferring to ford the river, but this is often even more dangerous because of the load.

Left: *This drawing of Thangtong-gyalpo (1385 – 1466) depicts him as a long-haired yogi. He holds a vase with the water of life in his right hand and his mark of identification in the left: a piece of an iron chain, which he was the first to use in building iron-chain bridges. The illustration is taken from the 1982 reissue of the block print of his biography, produced by the Tibetan National Printing Office in Sikhron.*

Above: *Iron-chain bridge erected by Thangtonggyalpo in east Bhutan. Two to three percent arsenic was added to the iron so that the links of the chain could be joined: this decreased the melting point, while increasing the durability of the weld.*

Right: *A long suspension bridge over the Indus in Zanskar, made of lianas.*

246

The Dalai Lama then put a ban on all further Everest expeditions. It was maintained until a new attempt was made under Hugh Ruttledge. A Valaisan ice pick was found at 8,450 meters (27,885 feet) – Mallory's or Irvine's? The question of whether they ever reached the summit remains unanswered.

Famous guides on dangerous routes

Among the Sherpas, the men from northeast Nepal whose name has come to denote the quintessence of all Himalayan mountain guides, Tensing Norgay (1912 – 1986) is probably the most famous. He began his career as the companion and guide of the Tibetologist Giuseppe Tucci, then accompanied

Edmund Hillary; after five unsuccessful attempts between 1921 – 1938, he and Hillary were the first to conquer Mt. Everest, in 1953. Unable to write, he dictated his biography to Malcolm Barnes. He built a mountaineering and tourist center near Darjeeling and remained faithful to his beloved mountains for his entire life. This photo was taken in Zurich shortly before his death.

1951 saw the first British expedition to explore Chomolungma from Nepal, and in 1952 a Swiss expedition with Raymond Lambert and Sherpa Tensing reached the subpeak from Khumbu, having scaled the incredible Khumbu icefield on the way. In 1953 a second English expedition under John Hunt followed the Swiss route up and reached the summit. The New Zealander Edmund Hillary and the Sherpa Tensing Norgay reached the peak in fine weather on May 29.

After the Chinese invasion of Tibet, the north side of Chomolungma was closed to Western mountaineers. But the Chinese themselves made an attempt on the difficult north face and claimed to have reached their goal on May 25, 1960. According to a press report in *New China*, two Chinese, Wang Fu-chou and Chu Ying-hua, together with a Tibetan, Gonpa, reached the summit at 4:20 in the morning and left behind a Chinese flag and a bust of Mao Tse-tung. An American expedition that succeeded via the west and southeast ridges searched in vain for the Mao bust, as did the Indian expedition in 1965, the Japanese in 1970 and the Italian in 1973.

In the spring of 1975, 15 years after the disputed Chinese night ascent of Chomolungma, a large truck convoy reached the monastery of Rongbuk at the end of the glacier of the same name. The biggest Everest expedition ever to be mounted was under way, again via the north face. Hundreds of mountaineers made the base camp look like some kind of bazaar. The climb itself resembled a pyramid as the number continuing on decreased from one camp to the next. At 14:30 on May 27, a fine day with only a light breeze, a group reached the summit on two ropes. Eight Tibetans (including one woman) and one Chinese stood proudly at the top of the world, which they'd reached without oxygen.

The first successful ascent of the 8,597-meter-high (28,370-foot-high) Kanchenjunga was relatively late and followed a history of many unsuccessful attempts. This peak had caught the public's attention in the middle of the 19th century after the publication of Joseph Dalton Hooker's richly illustrated report on his travels and again after the serious attempts to climb Kanchenjunga by Dyrenfurth (1930) and Bauer (1931), who had not really found a route to the summit. In 1955, however, a small British expedition succeeded: from a last camp at 8,200 meters (27,060 feet) Joe Brown and George Band climbed to the top – almost: they stopped a few meters below the highest point, having promised the people of Sikkim that they would not desecrate the peak of Kanchenjunga, "The Five Treasures of the Eternal Snows."

Also worthy of note is the ascent of yet another sacred mountain, the Machapuchare, known as the "fishtail," which lies in Nepal, north of Pokhara. This imposing "Himalayan Matterhorn" appeared to be unclimbable. But "because it was there," Major James Roberts, a former

English military attaché in Kathmandu and "inventor" of "Himalayan trekking," would not give up trying. In 1957 he invited some climbing colleagues over from England, among them David Cox and Wilfried Noyce. The expedition almost did not get past the point of negotiating with the inhabitants of the two tiny villages that lay on the lower Modhi Khola, which drained the bowl northwest of the Machapuchare. The villagers were adamant that no foot should be set on the highest point of the mountain. After a climb of 15 hours from their final camp, the two mountaineers stood 50 meters (165 feet) below the peak, before them a sharp, glassy ridge of ice that looked as if it might easily give way. When the weather also took a turn for the worse, it was not too difficult for them to decide against desecrating the summit. And this last part will remain unclimbed for the foreseeable future – in 1964 the Nepalese government banned all further attempts.

Flying into the small airstrip in Lukla, which is on a slightly sloping terrace, passengers have a view of the whole Khumbu valley – home of the Sherpas.
On the left, Mount Everest; looking north.

Even far from their homeland of Solokhumbu, the Sherpas have been associated with the classic climbs of the Himalayas. The most tragic of all expeditions were those of the Germans attempting the 8,125-meter-high (26,813-foot-high) Nanga Parbat, a mountain that fate seemed to have decreed would be a scourge for Germany's climbers. This mountain lies near

249

the spot where the Indus passes through the Himalayas in Baltistan. Early reconnaissance was carried out in 1930, using information about the region that had been gathered a long time earlier, in 1856. Adolf Schlaginweit had come from Astor at that time and explored these regions, producing excellent maps and an estimate of the height of the mountain that was less than a meter away from today's figure.

In 1934 a German expedition set off to climb Nanga Parbat, with 500 porters, under the command of Willy Merkl, an experienced climber. Good weather allowed rapid progress as far as Camp VIII at 7,480 meters (24,684 feet), and the summit attempt was planned for the next day. But in the night a storm began and lasted for nearly a week. Contact with the main camps was broken, and after six days an exhausted Sherpa staggered into Camp IV with the terrible news that six Sherpas and three Germans, Merkl among them, had perished in the storm.

Three years later, Karl Wien led the next attempt on this seemingly unlucky mountain. After a heavy snowfall all the climbers and nine Sherpas were holed up in Camp IV, which had been erected in a spot that was apparently sheltered from avalanches and icefalls. The weather began to improve and hopes were high for the next day. Then, ominously, back in the base camp no word came through from Camp IV for four days, and no movement could be seen higher up the mountain. After a week the expedition's doctor, Uli Luft, climbed up to Camp IV with a Sherpa. As he reached the basin where Camp IV was supposed to be, he was astonished to see the whole area covered by an enormous avalanche of ice and snow — of the seven climbers and the nine Sherpas there was absolutely no trace. Back in the Khumbu region other Sherpas supposedly learned of the disaster from their lamas on the same day that it occurred.

In April 1953 Nanga Parbat was climbed for the first time by Hermann Buhl, a very independent climber. At 2 A.M. he set off from the high camp, leaving his less-trained companion, Kurt Diemberger, behind, and after a 17-hour climb he reached the summit, totally exhausted. By a miracle he survived the night at over 8,000 meters (26,400 feet), and sometimes climbing down, sometimes just standing, he got back to the lower camp. In 1957, Buhl and Diemberger were climbing together again, in fact coming down after an attempt on Chogolisa in the Karakorum, which they'd had to break off just below the peak on account of bad weather. Unroped, they were proceeding along a snow-blown ridge, with Diemberger leading, Buhl behind. Feeling a sudden movement behind him, Diemberger looked back to see that a large part of the snowdrift was gone — and with it Hermann Buhl!

The most recent remeasurements of Himalayan heights have confirmed K 2, which lies on the border between Pakistan and Tibet, as the world's second highest mountain, and it has perhaps seen a greater variety of climbing expeditions than any other — from huge parties dependent on Sherpa porters to the rapid "alpine" style with the lightest possible modern equipment. The early climber's equipment was about three times as heavy as that used today, and far less efficient as well. If Nanga Parbat is the German mountain, then K 2 is the sphere of the Italians. The sterile name, just a survey designation, says nothing about the majestic beauty of this peak,

Left: *Toughened by the weather and marked by hardship, a Sherpa.* Below: *A Sherpa musician with a typical wooden instrument.*

which stands alone and towers above all else in the Karakorum. The Baltis call it Chogori, the "Great Mountain."

The first research party in the K 2 region was a large Italian expedition under the leadership of Luigi Amadeo of Savoy, Duke of Abruzzi. The party brought back some accurate maps and some fascinating pictures. These were obtained by the well-known photographer Vittorio Sella from Biella, and his equipment can be seen today in his hometown of Biella in northern Italy, where there is a little Sella museum. One stands amazed before the display of equipment that he took to the Himalayas: a huge camera with a heavy stand and hundreds of photographic glass plates – it took several porters to carry the whole load. With this material transported to the most difficult spots to reach, he took pictures in the entire Baltoro glacier region that have not been surpassed even today. The incredible clarity of his photographs made it possible to plan the ascent of K 2 in the comfort of a warm conference room.

Facing page: *The praises of the lucky "Five Sisters of Long Life" have often been sung, notably by the poet Milarepa. Their region is located at the "Mistress of the White Glacier," Jomo Kangkar or Lapchi, on Mt. Everest. The "Five Sisters" belong to the retinue of the great tutelary goddess Devi-Paldan Lhamo. They are led by the "Life-Giving Mother of Happiness." Brightly shining, she rides on a snow leopard (second picture from the top), holds a vase with the water of life and swings a thunderbolt in her right hand.*

After the First World War ended, another Italian duke led an expedition to the Himalayas; this was in 1929 and the leader was Aimone of Savoy, Duke of Spoleto. His group was mainly interested in scientific research and consisted of 10 scientists and two mountain guides. One member of the party was a young geologist named Ardito Desio, now over 90 years old, and he carried out the first geological survey of this wide region. His maps, which are on a scale of 1:25,000, cover not only the whole of K2 but also the regions of Shakhsam and Sarpo Laggo to the north.

The Americans also attempted the ascent of K2 – three times in fact –

Namche Bazar, the Sherpa center in the Khumbu valley, south of Chomolungma (Everest). Here Sherpas are hired for expeditions and their provisions purchased. It is also a bartering center for various goods.

the last group under the leadership of Charles Houston in 1953, one year before the Italians finally made it. This time Ardito Desio was in charge. Over 500 Balti porters carried 16 tons of material, including two small winches, each with 150 meters (495 feet) of cable, for hauling equipment in difficult places. This time the mountain was conquered, and on July 31 at 6 P.M. Lino Lacedelli and Achille Compagnoni stood at the summit of K2. After that expedition, groups with ever more modern equipment pitted them-

252

selves against the mountain – with no Sherpas. The Pakistani government had forbidden the "importation" of these outstanding mountain men. Hunzas or Balti porters could be used, but in fact there was no longer a need for Sherpas. Modern alpinists were excellent climbers and the latest equipment was much lighter and more efficient. What was now necessary was governmental permission, and this became steadily more expensive to obtain, in fact providing a steady source of state income, as more and more permits were granted, often without much responsibility on the part of the government. Himalayan ascents began to be regarded as sensations, and the

press showed a great deal of interest – especially in the accidents. However, the press respected the real achievements, too, such as Reinhold Messner's ascent of 8,000-meter (26,400-foot) peaks without an oxygen mask. In 1986 alone there were 13 K2 expeditions, of which only a few reached the summit. But 12 climbers died in tragic circumstances – either perishing in snow storms, falling to their deaths or freezing to death exhausted in their tents.

Sherpa women are often seen alone in the trading center of Namche Bazar. Most of the men are either away on a journey or have joined an expedition, but in this matriarchal society brothers assume responsibility for the support and protection of the family.

The Saga of Yeti

It is strange how the Sherpas' memories of the creature called Yeti (*ye* = rock, cliff; *the* = animal) have stayed alive in remote areas of the mountains. In Tibet, this "cliff animal" is called *Migo* ("Wild Man") or *Gang Mi* ("Glacier Man").

The Lepchas, the original inhabitants of the gorges in Sikkim, have kept alive many stories about Yeti. They call him *Lomung* ("Mountain Spirit") or *Chumung* ("Snow Spirit") and worship him as a god of the hunt and lord

A Sherpa awaits the adventures and dangers of a new day.

Right: *"The Sherpas of the Mahalangur region describe the yeti as having a pointed head, a hairless face and widely-separated long toes, which footprints confirm." From: H. Tichy, Himalayas, 1968.*

Facing page: *The face of the high mountains.*

of all deer. The Lepchas and Tibetans describe him as a huge, dark brown, ape-like animal with an egg-shaped, rather pointed skull and sparse reddish body hair. His standing height is supposedly over 2 meters [6 feet, 7 inches]. He is said to live in highest mountain regions and to leave them only when he craves the salty mosses that thrive in the moraines. When searching for them, he sometimes crosses snowfields. His footprints reportedly resemble those of a bear, which is called *midé* by the Tibetans. This word actually means "bear-man," for the large *dé* is the Isabell brown bear (*Ursus isabellinus*) of the Himalayas. Native Lepcha hunters claim that the snow spirit, whom many have sought but none have found, is ratherharmless and shy, and probably already extinct. Many expeditions have looked for him. Only somewhat distinct tracks up to 30 centimeters [12 inches] long and 15 centimeters]6 inches] wide have been found, nothing else.

Russian and Chinese scientists are now inclined to consider Yeti a primitive human species, of which only a few individuals – or none at all – have survived.

254

Danger on every trail

Danger lurks on every side:
during an ascent of the
northwest ridge of the 7,100-
meter-high (23,430-foot-high)
Tilicho in the Annapurna
chain, a huge avalanche sud-
denly came down from the
glacier cap on the peak and
crashed 2,000 meters (6,600
feet) to the Tilicho lake be-
low. The weather was superb.
The climbers on the ridge,
among them the photographer
Giovanni Kappenberger, luck-
ily were not directly threat-
ened by the avalanche. But it
must have been a similar oc-
currence on Nanga Parbat in
1937 that swept away a camp
that lay in its path, and with it
seven German climbers and
nine Sherpas.

The Blessing of the Earth

This little bronze statue is the Bodhisattva of Wisdom, Manjushri. According to legend, he drained the valley of Kathmandu with a single stroke of his sword and created fertile soil, as fertile as that on the south side of the Himalayas, which is blessed by the monsoon rains.
Facing page: *This Bhutanese man carries the blessing of the earth on his head: splendid sheaves of barley.*

The inhabitants of high mountain regions have to fight for their existence, and even those living in subtropical regions who seem to have been blessed by the gods do not have an easy life. Many of the domesticated plants of today originated in these regions; for example, maize and potatoes come from the Andes and only reached Asia in the 17th century, where they are now grown very successfully in those Himalayan regions with the right climate.

High altitudes and the monsoon require a fine touch on the part of the would-be farmer. In the rainy and thickly forested East Himalayas different techniques are required from those used in the dry regions of the West Himalayas, where the need for irrigation is the main factor. Here the efforts of man are obvious, with water channels running through the most difficult terrain, often along the faces of vertical cliffs.

The construction of terraces along steep mountain sides has been going on for a very long time: and today it is particularly evident in Nepal. There it has proved to be the only way of preventing further erosion after the once-wooded slopes have been cleared. However, it has been only partly successful, and without reforestation the process of erosion can only be slowed down, not stopped. The soil in a forest acts as a sort of sponge for the heavy monsoon rains, which otherwise just carry the soil down to the Ganges. No other river on earth carries as much silt as the Ganges. Since Nepal was opened to foreigners in 1950, the urgent need for reforestation there has been a topic at a number of international conferences. But 30 years have passed, and little has been done. After all the irresponsible and unchecked deforestation, the need for replanting trees and controlled exploitation of the mountain regions is a pressing problem in the Himalayas. One shining example is provided by Bhutan, where a modern law protecting the forest was accepted by the people and is rigorously enforced.

Above the forests and below the glaciers is a region of meadows, often between 4,000 and 5,000 meters [13,200 and 16,500 feet]. This is the territory of the yak and the mountain sheep. In earlier times caravans of yaks could often be seen carrying salt down from the north and rice and other cereals on the way back. Now they are mainly used for ploughing and for threshing the tough mountain barley, which grows up as high as the meadow lands. Roasted barley and butter tea form the staple diet of the Tibetan tribes. Yaks and dzos (a cross between a yak and a cow) provide a fatty milk, which can be used locally to make butter for the butter tea or made into a very hard cheese that is cut into small cubes and threaded on a string. Today better use is made of the milk, and a good "Emmenthal" cheese is produced in the high meadows of Nepal and sent down to the lowlands, where it is very highly regarded.

Less spectacular perhaps but also vital for these mountain dwellers are medicinal plants. Although they grow at all levels, the most effective are those taken from the meadow levels. The local people are astonishingly knowledgeable about the applications of these plants, and a visit to one of their herbal pharmacy shops is most impressive. Seldom cultivated, the herbal plants of the Himalayas are usually picked from their natural habitat by local collectors. So much importance was attached to these herbs that

schools of natural medicine were founded, mainly in Tibet, and associated with a monastery. The most famous of these stood on the Iron Mountain in Lhasa, opposite the Potala, but today nothing is left of it.

After a hard day's work in the mountain fields or after crossing a pass with a yak caravan, to sit around a camp fire is a well-earned pleasure. Now there is time to discuss the events of the day, and when the fire casts great ghostly shadows on the cliff wall and the mood is right, tales are told about how the land was settled.

The Divine Monkey and the Heavenly Kings

Buton, a famous Tibetan historian (1290 – 1364), refers to prehistoric times with a classic brevity: "As to the manner in which human generations first appeared in Tibet, we read in a commentary on the Tanjur that at the time the five Pandava princes fought against the twelve armies of Kaurava, King Rupati, disguised as a woman, fled with a thousand warriors into the rocky areas of the Himalayas. The Tibetans are supposedly derived from these refugees. However, the Tibetan legends claim that they are the descendants of a monkey and a mountain demoness. Detailed descriptions about this [legend] can be found elsewhere."

Buton's first statement refers to the period of the Mahabharata, the Great Epic, which, according to Indian tradition, took place in the middle of the second millennium B.C. During that time, surviving members of the defeated Kaurava, including a woman, are said to have fled to the Himalayas.

Buton's reference to the descent from a monkey is intriguing. One can actually read about this "elsewhere," namely, in a medieval Tibetan compendium. This work not only portrays "The Divine Monkey and the Heavenly Kings" as the primeval parentage, but it also describes the landscape of Tibet before it was settled by man: "In the Middle Country [present-day Tsang, that is, Central Tibet], there were stony fields and boggy meadows. Apes and rock demons lived here, as well as deer and wild animals. The Highlands [sTod, that is, West Tibet] were like a pond. Here there were glaciers, iron mountains and cliffs, and wild yaks, snow leopards and other wild animals lived there. The Lowlands [Amdo and Khams] resembled a field. There were lakes and forests, also elephants and bears, as well as wild ape-men."

How these wild apes developed into humans is then recounted explicitly. The tale is based on traditional lore handed down from prehistoric Shamanism and lightly tinged by Buddhism, which is revealed in the subsequent declaration of the primitive man-ape to be holy. The Tibetan historian of religion, Padmakarpo, also mentions this version of the descent of the Tibetans: "A short time after the land had been formed in this manner [by the receding of the water], Avalokiteshvara, the Buddhist tutelary god of the land, and Tara, the savior and tutelary goddess of Tibet, mated in the guises of an ape and a rock demon and initially had ape children. Human beings then gradually developed from them."

Bananas are grown around Meito and Chayu in southeastern Tibet. In the almost tropical climate, rice is the main crop, but bananas grow well, too.

Facing page: *Terraced fields in Trisuli valley, Nepal. The main crop here is barley. The terraces often have support walls one meter (3.3 feet) high and are artificially watered. The farmhouses here have their own characteristic style, with shingle roofs weighted down with stone, quite different from the thatched roofs of houses in the rice areas.*

The first village they established is proverbially known as "The Monkey Place" and is located in the country of Kongpo, the area in east Tibet where the first humans appeared.

The Tibetan compendium also relates how the monkey, who had been seduced by the rock demon, eventually was given five sorts of grain and legumes by the tutelary god of Tibet for his many starving descendants; he sowed them in the present-day Yarlung valley. Grandfather Ape was then finally able to invite his descendants to the "Playground of the Monkeys," also called the "Field of Nourishment," Tse Thang. The different Tibetan peoples arose from the monkey children who had been supplied with food.

It is remarkable that the wondrous tale of the introduction of grain grow-

Harrowing with yaks before the onset of winter, in what was once the small Nepalese kingdom of Mustang.

ing and cultivation of land takes place in an area where modern Swedish researchers have discovered wild grain plants. One must also bear in mind that this legend was widespread among the peoples on the western edge of old China. These groups belonged to the tribe of original Tibetans, who were called Kiang (Quiang) by the ancient Chinese and whose descendants created a stir until the Tang era (618–907). They attracted attention not only because of their multistoried buildings but also particularly because of the high standing of their women, which seemed absurd to Confucian China. The appearance of a queen, accompanied by her humble prince consort, at the imperial court created a sensation. This was downright shock-

Above: *Threshing barley at 3,800 meters (12,540 feet) in Lunana, north Bhutan.*

Left: *A Ladakhi woman sowing seeds at over 4,000 meters (13,200 feet).*

263

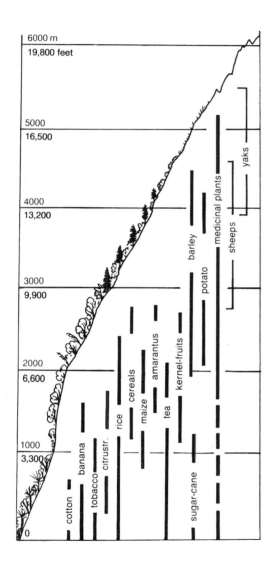

Agricultural products at different altitudes in the Himalayas.

Facing page: *A Bhutanese girl wearing a leafy protection against the sun as she works in a barley field.*

grain — depending on the altitude — has been used to produce *chang*, the national fermented drink, which ranges from a very light "beer" to the most exquisite, clear-as-water distilled liquor, or arrack. In Tibet, there are many types and blends of alcoholic drinks: grain beer; barley beer; rice wine; beer made from sugarcane syrup; mead; wine made from flowers, such as elderberry and woodruff wine; and slow bark wine, for which trees are tapped. Ground animal bones are added to bone liquor as a tonic. Of course, there are also numerous herbal and medicinal wines. In Sikkim, the local "beer" is drunk from large bamboo mugs through small canes. The beer consists of a sort of millet mash to which hot water can be added several times.

When we traveled through Bhutan on horseback, like the caravans of old, before the highway was completed, we saw that strong *chang* is also used to prevent altitude sickness. If several high passes had to be crossed in one day, a nourishing *thugpa* soup was served with a generous shot of *chang* early in the morning, and *tsampa* balls soaked in *chang* were taken along as well. *Tsampa* is the staple food of the inhabitants of the Himalayas and the oldest Tibetan concentrated food. It consists of roasted ground barley, a very practical provision that can be carried in small leather bags. When needed, it is mixed with butter tea in the wooden teacups that everyone carries.

The famous Tibetan butter tea, which is also a typical foodstuff, consists of tea usually imported from Yunnan and supplied in pressed brick form. It is churned with yak butter and salt in tall tube-like wooden kegs and is therefore also called "churned tea," *ja suma*. The butter is kept in small leather bags and stays fresh for a long time at high altitudes. Actually, the term "butter tea" is rather misleading, since it is rather more like a nutritious bouillon. Doctors point out that it is a very healthy folk food, because the caffeine in the tea neutralizes the effects of the cholesterol in the butter.

Guru Rimpoche, the "Precious Teacher," as Padmasambhava is admiringly called in the Himalayas, was one of the first to oppose the misuse of substances that affect the consciousness. In a block print dating from around 800 A.D., he vigorously protests against not only the vice of alcohol consumption but also that of smoking; he mentions the foreign word "tabaco" in his protest. In later times, tobacco was mixed with rhubarb leaves before smoking.

The praises of the popular butter tea are also sung in the "Tea Song," which is included in the cycle of the central Asian saga of Gesar. It is still heard when tea is churned, and contains some good advice for pilgrims and wanderers.

Lu ale thála thála re:
Homage to Bodhgaya, birthplace of the Holy Bird [Symbol of Buddha]!
if the eagle is hungry small birds will become its prey —
if you make business, handle it out on lotos-ground —
if you buy goods, buy them by the [known] uncle merchant —
if you have to pack luggage, let it do by [trustworthy] soldiers —
if the route is conquered, be sure that the pass is too. —
Tea-leaves should be used [liberally] like by Gesar's wife herself —

salt should be added [sparingly] from a hungry man –
tea has to be beaten [strongly] by a furious man –
tea has to be drunk like by King Gesar himself!

Ancient Trade Goods and the Treasures of the Earth

Among the oldest goods transported from the "Roof of the World" via the Himalaya passes to the Indian basin is the yak tail. The yak, this primordial animal of the high mountains, provides not only nearly everything essential to the highland people, including wool, milk and butter, but also

An old Tibetan farm in the lower Yarlung valley near Tsethang. Fine crops of different sorts of barley are grown on the lower terraces, which are artificially irrigated. Today these fields are controlled by a Kolchosa-type organization centered in Tsethang.

one of their most precious export articles.

Yak tails were so expensive and important in ancient India that the countries from which they were imported, such as Bhutan, were simply called "Yak-Tail Countries." The *camara*, called *ngayab* in Tibetan, was used as a fan to drive away flies and as such was a royal emblem. It is portrayed in statues of kings and in the hands of the prehistoric *yakshas*. The latter also appear as mythological fan-waving female companions in the retinue of Kuvera, the God of Wealth. They were probably among the first inhabitants of old India. The *camara* is also mentioned in the Mahabharata, the great Indian epic, which is said to have taken place in the middle of the second millennium B.C., according to Indian tradition.

Left: *In the lee of high stone walls, these women from Charka in the Dolpo region are weaving colorful blankets, a type of weaving done throughout the Himalayas. The wool used is spun by the men while they are on their journeys, usually as they walk.*

Left: *Typical farmhouses in the Nepalese village of Langtang, with their large wooden shingles weighted down with stones.*

269

Above: *Primitive bamboo huts in the mountain jungle of the East Himalayas.*

Above right: *Decorative mountain houses in the Bhutan Himalayas, lived in year-round. They are made of stone and wood, with stone-weighted shingle roofs.*

Below: *The village of Laya at 3,900 meters (12,870 feet) at the foot of Masang Kang.*

The precious counterpart of the yak tail is the conch shell imported from India, which was delivered from Tamralipta, the harbor of present-day Calcutta, up to our time. It represents one of the eight religious "Symbols of Good Fortune" and proclaims the fame of the saints. Prehistoric Tibetan sagas mention it as an important emblem of the founder of the royal family. White conch shells with a spiral to the right were worth a fortune and, when set in silver and inlaid with precious gems, adorned the edges of altars. They were also worn by women as wide bracelets and thought to

Above right: *Farmhouse in Zanskar. The method of construction used here, with the Tibetan flat roof, is quite different from that in the East Himalayas.*

Typical wooden house of the Balti tribe in the West Himalayas. The animals are kept below, the living area is on top, with a large terrace.

possess preventive powers against disease.

Among the most popular semiprecious stones in Tibet, Ladakh, Mustang, Nepal, Sikkim and Bhutan are turquoise and red coral. Since ancient times they were believed to be good-luck charms. They always had ritual significance and were valued as precious imports in Tibet. A turquoise chip cost up to one gold pound or 100 to 1000 *tamkha* (Tibetan silver coins), according to its quality. Turquoise from Tibet, called *po yu*, was especially expensive. The rest of the turquoise probably came from Persia on long caravan routes. Red coral was supposedly procured via Calcutta. Turquoise jewelry worn around the neck was thought to preserve life energy. It is thus blessed in a rite and worn for a lifetime.

Gesar, the hero of the central Asian epic, reportedly conquered the Turquoise Mountain and all its riches in the Far West. These included the mysterious *zhi*, or *dzi*, stones, agates with "eyes" treated by a primitive method. The value of the stone increases with the number of eyes. The stones are still worn by Himalayan women from Ladakh to east Bhutan as

270

their most precious, inalienable family treasure. These "eye stones" have supposedly been found in old graves. Because of their price, imitations were produced very early. A cheap plastic version is sold at Himalayan bazaars today.

Musk oil, the aromatic contents of the scent gland of the male musk deer, was another important Himalayan export article. Thangtonggyalpo, the "Leonardo da Vinci of the Himalayas," traded with this article in his youth and exported it from trading centers in southern Tibet to India.

Only one trade article, popular in Tibet since ancient times, remained

largely unknown in the West up to the present. This was the Tibetan carpet, essential as a saddle blanket for a people who were riders and nomadic tent dwellers, a cushion for sitting and a throne rug. Only since 1960 has the West known about the Tibetan art of hooking rugs. The art was brought to the West by Tibetan refugees who founded carpet-making centers in Nepal.

THE HIMALAYAS

PORTRAITS OF COUNTRIES

BHUTAN

Kingdom of Bhutan – Druk Yul (Tibetan "Land of the Dragons")

Area: 46,500 sq. km [18,600 sq. mi.]
Population: 1.29 million
(uncertain estimate from 1985,
including Indian advisers and military)
Capital city: Thimphu
(ca. 10,000 inhabitants)
Form of government: constitutional
monarchy

The Himalayan kingdom of Bhutan encompasses an area not much larger than Switzerland. It is separated from Tibet in the north by the mountain ranges of the relatively narrow part of the High Himalayas, with several peaks of 7000 meters [23,100 feet], and in the west by the watershed of the Tibetan Chumbi valley. The largest part of the land is taken up by the middle Himalayan chain, with heights ranging from 1600 to 5000 meters [5280 to 16,500 feet], extending to the east into the Indian constituent state of Arunachal Pradesh. The southern landscape of the foothills area ends in the jungles of the Duars, whose border also runs into India. The mountain range zone is subdivided by seven main valleys running from north to south and by their surrounding mountain ridges. The rivers in the eastern part of the country join the Manas before they flow out of the mountain range. The most important rivers in the west – the Amo-chu, Wang-chu and Sankosh – break through on their own in steep channel valleys into the lowlands. The middle portions of these river valleys are connected by mountain passes, which are mostly just under 3500 meters [11,550 feet], shaping the economic as well as cultural central area of Bhutan.

The country's climate and vegetation are largely influenced by the rainfall of the South Asian summer monsoon, beginning in June. This lasts until the first part of October and brings approximately 85 % of the annual precipitation. Because of the backup effect of the mountains most of the precipitation falls onto the southern mountain slopes. The wet, subtropical climate there allows the lush forest vegeta-

tion to flourish, with ferns, bamboo, hanging plants and orchids on giant sal, banyan and teak trees. A large number of animals can be found in these forests – mostly snakes, monkeys, birds, butterflies, deer and buffalo but also leopards, tigers and, particularly in the royal wildlife preserve of Manas, elephants, bears and white rhinoceros.

In the higher regions, the primeval forests thin out, although there is still a wide variety of poplars, ash, aspens, magnolias, oaks, conifers and multicolored rhododendrons. Above 3000 meters [9900 feet] bamboo and conifer forests (fir, larch, cypress, pine) take over; at 4000 meters [13,200 feet] birch, pine and rhododendron dominate before finally giving way to juniper and other bushes. The climate within the mountains themselves is very highly differentiated by the varying degrees of sunshine, precipitation and wind conditions, yet it is basically similar to the moderate middle European climate.

The daily air mass exchange between the highlands and lowlands causes often stormy, valley-upward-directed winds. These force the moisture of the weakened monsoon precipitation from the inside of the mountains onto the slopes, so that corresponding down currents above the middle of the valley disperse clouds, preventing rain. Therefore, the middle portions of big cross valleys 900 to 1800 meters [2970 to 5940 feet] above sea level are often extraordinarily dry and bleak in contrast to the lush growth of the mountain slopes. They require irrigation for farming.

At the height of the Himalayan main mountain ridge in northern Bhutan, alpine vegetation thrives as a result of the cold winter and the short cool summer. Shrubs, rhododendron and juniper grow up to the snow line at over 4000 meters [13,200 feet] on the southern slopes. Moss and lichen can occasionally be found between cliffs on the drier, north side. Only in the canyons of eastern Bhutan does the forest reach the otherwise bleak north side of the Himalayan main ridge.

History

After Bhutan had come under the influence of the Tibetan kingdom of Songtsengampo, a wave of immigration began at the start of the ninth century. Shabdung Ngawang Namgyal is considered the founder of the unified Bhutan. A lama of the Drukpa sect, founded in 1200, he ruled the country as spiritual and secular leader at the beginning of the 17th century and successfully repelled Tibetan and Mongolian attacks.

His successors were believed to be reincarnations of his person. Spiritual power and secular power, however, were separated, falling into the hands of a Dharma Raja and a Deb Raja. The various valley districts were ruled by governors, the Penlops, who resided in fortified monasteries, called Dzongs.

After the Mongolian invasion in 1697 under Lhazang Khan, Bhutan had to pay tribute to Tibet, while making several assaults itself in the south on Assam and West Bengal. When the Bhutanese attacked the Indian principality of Kuch Behar in 1772, its raja called upon the East India

Company for aid. Bhutan's relations with Britain began with the peace treaty of 1774 and strengthened after repeated military conflicts and the annexation of the Duars by Britain, when in 1904 the British expedition to Tibet under Younghusband found Bhutanese support.

After power struggles among the various governors, the Penlops of Tongsa, Urgyen Wangchuk, emerged as victor in 1884–85. He became the sole ruler, with the title "Druk Gyalpo" ("Dragon King") in 1907, three years after the death of the last Dharma Raja.

The presence of the Chinese in Tibet in 1910 troubled the Gyalpo. He therefore regulated the voting of Bhutanese foreign policy in a contract with the British. After India gained independence from Britain, the Indian government took over this duty. When the Chinese "People's Liberation Army" marched into Tibet in 1950, Bhutan gradually gave up its isolationist policy. This led to rioting, climaxing with the murder of Prime Minister Jigme Palden Dorji in 1964. Sovereignty was transferred to the national assembly with the proclamation of constitutional monarchy in 1968. At the king's suggestion, the assembly could even dethrone him with a two-thirds majority vote, if he should act against the people's welfare or to the country's disadvantage. Bhutan has been a member of the United Nations since 1971. The present state leader is Jigme Singhye Wangchuk, crowned in 1974.

People, Language, Religion

The majority of the Bhutanese people belong to the Tibetan-Burmese language family. Next to the Bhutias in central Bhutan, who emigrated in the ninth century and are related to the Tibetans, the most important tribes are the Dagpas and Sarchops in the east, the Doyas in the southwest, the Ngalong and Lepchas in the west and the Tibetan Lopas in the north. Their language, Dzongkha, is very similar to Tibetan in both the written and spoken form, its dialect changing considerably from valley to valley.

Estimates of the Indo-European Nepalese portion of the population who settled in Bhutan after having come to work on military road construction projects vary between 15% and one-third – significant in any case. They are restricted to the country's south and have practically not mixed in at all with the Bhutia population, mainly because of their completely different language and Hindu religion.

The Tibetan-related population practices Lamaism (Tantric Buddhism) almost exclusively. In contrast to the predominating Gelugpa sects in Tibet, however, the Drukpa school, a mid-12th century split-off from the Kagyupa – one of the red-capped sects – is dominant in Bhutan. As in all branches of the Buddhist faith, the religious goal of the Drukpa is redemption from the cycle of rebirth, entering into Nirvana; in Lamaism, this is thought to be achieved by castigation and magic deeds and formulas. The major differences between the various sects lie in the meaning they attribute to a certain kind of incantation.

Economy

Over 93 % of the population of Bhutan depends on agriculture for its livelihood. The most important fields lie in the Duars and in the middle sections of the large river valleys, where rice is cultivated on the valley floors and on the more level slopes up to 2400 meters [7290 feet] in irrigated terraces. In the lowest valleys and in the south, there are orange and banana trees, and at higher levels other fruit trees (apple, pear, peach). Above the rice tillage area, corn, millet, wheat, red pepper, and up 4000 meters [13,200 feet] even potatoes are grown on terraced fields and in crop rotation. The extensive forests are utilized within the framework of a modern forestry law but are nonetheless damaged by shifting cultivation, particularly in the southern foothills. The alpine meadows above the forest line are used as pastures, where herds of yak and sheep graze. A considerable part of the population travels back and forth between winter and summer residences. The development of the alpine agriculture is supported by the Swiss aid to underdeveloped countries. The most important milk products are yak butter and cheese.

Farming in Bhutan is essentially subsistence level, although in some years (1961, 1966) rice surpluses were exported. Because of the cessation of trade with Tibet in 1959, Bhutan has since come to depend on the exchange of goods with India, contributing substantially to its economic development: military road construction, small industries (fruit processing) and, most importantly, the construction of hydroelectric power plants, which deliver electricity to India. The traditional handicrafts encompass the working of textiles, metals and wood, paper manufacture, weaving and embroidery. The mining of slate has gained importance.

Tourism activities, although on a small scale, nonetheless provide excellent opportunities thanks to the amiability of the people, the charisma of the Lamaistic-Bhutanese culture, and the remarkably beautiful landscape and mountain world.

NEPAL

Kingdom of Nepal – Nepal Adhirajya/Sri Nepala Sarkar

Area: 147,181 sq. km [54,362 sq. mi.]
Population: 16.48 million (1985)
Capital city: Kathmandu
(395,000 inhabitants)
Form of government: constitutional Hindu-monarchy

This Himalayan state, the largest and for a long time completely independent, takes in the southern slopes of the Central Himalayas. Nepal extends 800 kilometers [480 miles] from the wet, monsoon-dominated East Himalayas to the drier, west side and

has an average north-south extension of 200 kilometers [120 miles] from the glacial main Himalayan ridge down to the lowlands of the hot, wet Terai. A basic north-south division is provided by the mountain ranges in the northern part of the High Himalayas, of whose 14 peaks of 8000 meters [26,400 feet], eight are in Nepal. In the south, the foothills reach up sporadically to 3500 meters [11,550 feet] in the Mahabharat chain. Between these mountain ranges lies the central landscape of true Nepal – the high valley of Kathmandu and a number of basins connecting in the east and west. This mostly open midland landscape of central Nepal is situated at an elevation of 2000 meters [6600 feet], lying in a 40- to 60-kilometer-wide [24- to 36-mile-wide] depression that stretches through the Himalayas. Its rivers flow together here before they break through the outer mountain range and the lower Siwalik and Churia chains to the Terai region. This southernmost region of Nepal lies at only 75 to 280 meters [248 to 924 feet] above sea level. Its climate is hot and humid because of the heavy rains during the summer monsoon. Thus, it is covered by dense forests (sal trees). The swamp and jungle areas are among the last big-game regions of Asia, with tigers, leopards, bears, rhinoceros, elephants and buffalos.

The land is further subdivided from the east to the west by the great rivers of the Ganges system. East Nepal is drained by the Kosi river system, the Kathmandu valley and central Nepal by the sacred Bagmati river and the Gandaki, and west Nepal by the Karnali river system. Although west Nepal receives less precipitation in the summer than the eastern regions, it is nonetheless affected by the west wind circulation in winter, which brings considerable rainfall. At an elevation of 1000 to 2000 meters [3300 to 6600 feet], sparse forests of *Pinus roxburghii* (pine) dominate. Farther in the north, on the other side of the Himalayan main ridge, west Nepal encompasses part of the dry Tibetan Himalayas. The rain shadow of the mountains causes long cold winters and rather dry summers. Here, under the glacial world of the mountain giants, one can find steppes where only grasses and thornbushes grow, or rocky deserts partly covered with moss.

The subalpine forest level in west Nepal consists of firs and cedar. In the central and eastern part of the country, oaks and rhododendrons are found up to an elevation of 2900 meters [9570 feet]. Above that level grow hemlock, white spruce and weeping pines. Up to the tree line at 4000 meters [13,200 feet] one can find juniper and rhododendron trees, as well as birch and white spruce forests. There live bears, Muntjak deer, gorals, musk animals, monkeys, leopards and a large variety of bird species (eagles, vultures, pheasants, ravens, etc.). The central part of the country is characterized by the greatest differences in altitude in the world. The gorge through which the Kali Gandaki forces itself between the 8000-meter-high [26,400-foot-high] Dhaulagiri and Annapurna has its base almost 7000 meters [23,100 feet] below their summits. The area encompassed by these

mountain giants is the region of Nepal most heavily covered by glaciers. Yet, the adjacent regions to the east have a very pleasant climate that is conducive to agriculture. The economy thrives here in the valley basin of Kathmandu, about 25 kilometers [15 miles] long and 15 kilometers [9 miles] wide, and the Pokhara basin, and the area is the most densely populated in Nepal. At elevation of approximately 1400 meters [4620 feet], it is neither too hot in summer (July average, 25 ° C [77 ° F]) nor too cold in winter (January average, 10° C [50° F]). About 90 % of the annual precipitation falls between May and September. As a result, one of the most facinating rice terrace landscapes has evolved, no longer allowing room for the natural vegetation.

East Nepal is marked by deep and narrow gorges and wide, high lying valleys, out of which steep mountain ridges arise, especially in the massif of the Kangchendzonga and in the Khumbu Himal, with four summits rising over 8000 meters [26,400 feet] and seven over 7000 meters [23,100 feet].

History

The Kathmandu valley seems to have already been settled by the first century B.C. The Mahabharata epic contains an account of the Kiranti ruling clan (700 – 100 B.C.). In 563 B.C. Prince Siddharta, later the Gautama Buddha, was born in Lumbini in the Nepalese Terai. Three hundred years later, the Indian Emperor Ashoka went on a pilgrimage there, thus promoting the spread of Buddhism.

Hinduism, on the other hand, reached Nepal through Indian immigrants. From 350 to 750 A.D. it attained its first high point, along with Buddhism, under the Lichhavi sovereigns, especially after the end of the Gupta dynasty in India (466 – 467), when many artists went to Nepal in exile. Weakened by attacks from Kashmir in the eighth century and the growing power of the Pali dynasty in Bengal, the Lichhavi empire gradually fell into ruin. The Thakuri dynasty reigned from the ninth century into the 12th century, when it is supposed to have been closely linked with Tibet.

Around 1200, under Ari Malla, who was of Indian descent, another kingdom emerged in the Kathmandu valley in which Hindu culture flourished as never before. Jayasthiti Malla (1382 – 1395) and Yaksha Malla (1428 – 1482) were the rulers most responsible for this extraordinary artistic activity.

After Yaksha's death in 1482, the Malla empire was divided into three city-states: Kantipur (Kathmandu), Lalitpur (Patan) and Bhaktapur. Until their ultimate downfall in 1768, they produced great artistic achievements, even when their power weakened – as under Pratap Mall (1641 to 1674) in Kathmandu, Siddhi Narsingh (1618 to 1661) in Patan, and Jagatpraksha Malla (1664 – 1673), Jitamitra Malla (1678 to 1696) and Bhupatindra Malla (1696 to 1723) in Bhaktapur.

When northwest India fell to the Islamic conquerors in the 13th century, the Rajputans had moved to the north, having conquered parts of the mountain country west of Kathmandu until the 16th century. In 1559 they established themselves in their new capital city, Gurkha. Under King Prithvi Narayan Shah († 1755), the "Gurkhas" began military campaigns into the Kathmandu valley, which they ultimately conquered in 1768. Based in the new capital city of Kathmandu, they succeeded during the next decade in a series of military campaigns against Kashmir, Sikkim and Tibet. Under attack the Tibetans called upon the Chinese for help. In 1792 the Chinese army marched up to Nawokot, approximately 50 kilometers [30 miles] from Kathmandu, and defeated the Gurkhas. Thereafter, the Nepali fought the British, who likewise defeated them in 1815. Under the Treaty of Sagauli (1816), a British administration was established in Kathmandu.

The empire that outwardly appeared strong became weakened from within by political intrigues and family disputes. In 1646 Jang Bahadur Rana appointed himself minister president and forced the Gurkha king to relinquish his family's inherited rights to this office. The kings thus became no more than puppets in the hands of the Rana family. They were supported by the English, and retained power in Nepal until 1951.

Soon after King Tribhuvan succeeded in fleeing to India from his Rana captors in 1950, he stripped the Ranas of their power and restored the kingdom. Under his successor, Mahendra, the first parliamentary elections took place in 1959. One year later, however, the king dissolved the parliament, forbade political parties and in 1962 instituted the so-called Panchayat community council system. King Birendra (b. 1944) has been ruling since the death of Mahendra in 1972. He set up a constitutional monarchy based on a new constitution and achieved support of the Panchayat system in a referendum in 1980.

People, Language, Religion

With immigrants from the Tibetan central Asian region as well as from the outlying Indian lowland, Nepal has become a melting pot of races of the entire Himalayan area during its history. The natural boundaries, which are barely surmountable, and major differences in living conditions of various regions have contributed to the considerable ethnic variety characterized by the physiognomy of the people, their language, and their religion as well as their material culture.

Basically four large ethnic groups can be distinguished: Old Nepali, Indo-Nepali, Indian and Tibeto-Nepali. The Indian population lives mostly in the lowland of the Terai, which is the home of over 40 % of the Nepali people. It has already surpassed the population density of the Kathmandu valley.

The most important cultural and economic and perhaps oldest ethnic group of Nepal, however, is the Newar. Settling mainly in the Kathmandu valley, this group has developed the country's building style with carved wood beams and temple pagodas. Newari are somewhat smaller than Indians and have light Mongoloid features. They have their own script and speak Tibetan-Burmese – or Newari – which is spoken by 4% of Nepal's population. The Newari are followers of the Hindu-influenced Shiva cult, to some extent also part of a strongly Hindu-influenced Buddhism. Both lines are partly mixed and have remained friendly toward one another. They follow the rules and ranks of the caste system.

The Indo-Nepalese immigrants from India (fifth – seventh century) known as "Gurkhas" are politically dominant. As Hindus, they strictly divide themselves into separate castes: the Brahmans, or priest caste (Bahun); the Dhetris; and the Khas. The term "Gurkhas" traces back to the town of the same name in central Nepal, which was the first capital. It was expanded, however, to include a series of old Nepalese native mountain tribes who, under the name "Gurkhas," achieved widespread fame as soldiers in Nepal as well as in the British-Indian army. They then broke up into numerous tribes, the largest being the Magar and Gurung in central Nepal and Limbu and Rai in eastern Nepal. The Limbu, Rai and part of the Gurung are similar to the Mongolian Thamang Lamaists, who also live in eastern Nepal. Some of them, however, are followers of the Bon faith as well as other cults. The languages of these peoples belong to the Tibeto-Burmese language group.

While the Old Nepali tribes have set up their living quarters at heights of 1000 to 2500 meters [3300 to 8250 feet], the regions above that level are occupied almost exclusively by the Tibeto-Nepali tribal groups, whose culture and religion are purely Tibetan. Referred to as Bhotias in Nepal, the Sherpas living in the northeast of the country are the Nepal Tibetans best known for their work as bearers and mountain guides for tourists and expeditions. In terms of cultural history, however, more importance is ascribed to the Tibetan Dolpos and Lhopas at the northern border of Nepal. Their small kingdom of Mustang lays claim to a rather long history.

The mosaic formed by the ethnic and cultural diversity of the people of Nepal makes it hard to believe a unified government is possible. Nevertheless, common history, mutual cultural influence and economic interdependence have managed to make the national language – Nepali, or Pahari, the mother tongue of only about 55 % of the population – understood by almost everyone. The national religion is Hinduism, its various forms of Shiva, Vishnu, Shakti and Ganesh worship accounting for about 90 % of the Nepali. Seven to eight percent are Buddhists and only 2 to 3 % are Moslems. The statistics of course do not reveal that Buddhism and Hinduism are often so strongly intertwined (many sanctums are claimed by both religions) that a clear distinction is frequently no longer possible.

Economy

Nepal is an agrarian state, with 93 % of the work force employed in agriculture and 80 % of the agricultural products exported. It is not surprising that with the wide diversity of landscape and strong ethnic cultural differentiation, the agriculture has developed rather complex structures due to the high rate of population growth and the adaptation to, in some cases, extreme national-spatial conditions.

The Himalaya foreland, constantly threatened by flooding, has developed into the most important agricultural area of Nepal. Sixty percent of the country's annual grain production comes from the Terai. Here, the rice is generally harvested two times a year, so that despite the dense settlement in the southern Terai of east Nepal, food surpluses can be exported to India. Also the large amount of livestock – zebu, water buffalo – are very significant.

In the barely accessible wider sections of the Dun valley of the Churia foothills, very few people have settled to date. Consequently, this densely wooded region contains few clearings. The southern slopes of the Mahabharat mountain chains are similarly covered with tropical, green mountain forests.

The midlands between the chains of the frontal and High Himalayas give a completely different picture. Because the wet central and eastern sections of Nepal are so densely populated, the midlands, particularly Kathmandu valley, have for the most part been transformed into a deforested, closed-culture landscape whose valley terrain and more level slopes have been transformed into irrigated rice terraces. Corn, millet, taro and winter wheat are cultivated on the steeper slopes. In addition, cotton, jute, sugar cane, spice and tobacco cultivation provide the basis for a small processing industry.

The rice tillage area ends at about 2000 meters [6600 feet]; in higher areas the cultivation of corn, buckwheat, millet, potatoes, oil seeds, winter wheat and barley becomes more significant. Water buffalo and other cattle are left to graze on harvested and abandoned fields and on depleted forest areas. They provide milk, meat and fertilizer and are used as draught animals.

The food production of most of the farmers goes barely beyond the subsistence level, which in some cases is not even guaranteed; especially since only one-fifth of the small-farm operators own their own land, all the others being tenants. In the higher regions, cultivation is further constrained by the seasons; the people in these regions therefore have to migrate during certain periods in order to find work; to some extent they work in other countries as soldiers (the Gurkhas for instance), servants, bearers, street workers, and tea plantation workers, for example, in India. Others bridge the gap as craftsmen working on house and agricultural machinery, a kind of small-village industry.

In areas far from settlements, particularly in the higher regions of east Nepal, shifting cultivation is still practiced. After centuries of reckless forest utilization (until 1957 there was an annual auction of the utilization rights) and forest clearing to obtain additional land to farm, the country can no longer afford these practices. The ecological damage – erosion, floods, depleted soil, landslides – resulting from the shrinking forest reserves (less than 30% of the entire surface) has increased threateningly. Reforestation has become one of the government's most important tasks.

Cultivation is limited for the Tibeto-Nepali people living in the High Himalayas: corn grows up to an elevation of 2900 meters [9570 feet]. Above that, buckwheat, barley and vegetables are cultivated. The highest elevation at which barley fields can be found – 4400 meters [14,520 feet] – is in the east Nepali Khumbu area. Since the potato was introduced in that area during the 19th century, (growing as high as 4690 meters [15,477 feet], the amount of food production has increased considerably. The population's main income, though, comes from cattle breeding. The people move with their yak herds to regular seasonal settlements near the high summer pastures. Since the Swiss founded the first modern yak milk cheese factory in the Langtang valley at the foot of the Shisha Pengmar in 1953, the milk industry has developed substantially.

Because of minimal precipitation in the northern area of west Nepal, farming is only possible in irrigated oases. The highest permanent settlements of the entire Himalayas are situated in the Dolpo district: Phidjorgaon at 4100 meters [13,530 feet] and Phopagaon at 4300 meters [14,190 feet] above sea level. The raising of livestock (sheep, yak) is very important as well.

Since tourism began in the fifties, its importance has grown very fast. Although its impact on the local culture can be criticized, certain positive effects are undeniable. New areas of employment have been created exactly in the fragile high mountain regions (for example, those of the Sherpas). The capital flowing into the country is used for the establishment of a still very modest infrastructure (road construction, hydroelectric powerplants) and for the development of industry (sugar, cigarette and textile factories, jute processing, woodworking and food industry; in 1982 approximately 2% of the population was industrially employed), which has not existed very long. Certainly the improvement of the infrastructure greatly serves the promotion of tourism.

MUSTANG

Former Small Kingdom of Lo

Area: 3017 sq. km [1207 sq. mi.]
Population: ca. 28,000
Capital city: Jomosom, or Lo Manthang
Form of government: Nepalese district
with certain autonomy

Mustang has an average elevation of 4000 meters [13,200 feet] above sea level. It is located north of the mountain giants Dhaulagiri and Annapurna, thus north of the Himalayan main ridge, geographically belonging to the highlands of Tibet. Situated beyond the rain barrier of the mountains, only winter-dry, mostly barren desert steppes can be found in this vast high valley, where thornbushes survive sporadically. The Photu pass lies at 4600 meters [15,180 feet], only 75 meters [248 feet] above the Tibetan Tsangpo plain. It presents an easily accessible border crossing into Tibet. While the Kali Gandaki, originating here, flows farther out of the wide valley in Mustang 60 kilometers [48 miles] south of the Thakko La. At first, it flows in a narrow valley and then breaks through the mountains in one of the wildest gorges of the Himalayas, its course thus characterized by many difficult passages.

History

The kingdom of Lo is said to have existed as an independent state as early as the fifth century A.D. With the expansion of the Tibetan empire under Songtsengampo, Lo was also incorporated into Tibet in the seventh century. After its disintegration it came under the rule of the Gungthang principality. At this time, Lo became an important center of the Lamaistic Sakyapa sect. After the division of Gungthang in 1430, Gayalpo Ame Pal founded a dynasty that is still in existence today.

After the Mongolian invasions in the 17th century, the small kingdom was conquered in 1760 by the Raja of Jumla, who in turn was defeated the Gurkhas in 1790. Since that time Mustang remained under Nepalese sovereignty. Its actual downfall began in the late 19th century with the loss of fiscal law and Tibet's loss of control of the Salt Straight to the Thakalis, who were neighbors to the south.

Population

The inhabitants of the former kingdom of Lo are exclusively Bhutias or Tibetans of Lamaistic faith. The south of Mustang is the home of the Magars and particularly the Thakali, the only tribe that wholly bridges the clear cultural boundary between the Nepali highlands and midlands: their tribal religion, Jhangrism, once suppressed by Buddhism, stems from the old Bon faith and has increasingly had to fight the influence of Hinduism.

Trade has always been important to Mustang because a main carrier and caravan route, the Salt Straight, led to Tibet through the kingdom's territory. The decline of the small kingdom came as a result of the shift of importance of trade in the adjacent Thakkhola. The Tibetans in Mustang are nomadic sheep and goat breeders. In addition they raise yaks, horses and mules. Due to the arid climate, farming (barley) is only possible in small irrigated oases fed by the Kali Gandaki or its tributaries.

TIBET

Bod-Yul (Tibetan), "Tibet," from the Mongolian "Tubet" or "Tobot"
Autonomous Region of Tibet (Chinese: "Xizang Zizhiqu")

Area: 1,220,600 sq. km [488,240 sq. mi.)
Population: 1.89 million (1982)
Capital city: Lhasa (ca. 120,000 inhabitants)
Form of government: autonomous region of
the People's Republic of China

The term "Tibet" in its geographical meaning describes the largest and most extreme highland of the world, extending in the heart of Asia over 2 million square kilometers [800 square miles]. The Autonomous Region of Tibet comprises approximately 60% of this area. Crossed by more than 20 mountain chains, the highland, lying for the most part 3500 to 5000 meters [11,550 to 16,500 feet] above sea level, is nicknamed "Roof of the World." It is enclosed on three sides by enormous mountain ranges: the Kunlun in the north, the Karakorum in the west and the Himalayas in the south, the last of which has peaks over 8000 meters [26,400 feet] high. The mountains crossing central Tibet unite in the east to the Tibetan outer ridges. They are among the world's most insurmountable mountain ranges.

In terms of landscape, Tibet can be divided into three parts. In the north and northwest there is a highland of cold deserts and steppes with sparse vegetation that extends at an average elevation of 4800 meters [15,840 feet], sloping to the north. Because of the lack of natural drainage to the sea, giant salt lakes occur. East Tibet is dominated by the mountains turning increasingly to the south, deeply cut up by large rivers and reaching to heights of over 7000 meters [23,100 feet]. The third region, Tibet's most densely populated area, lies between the Transhimalayas in the north and the Himalaya main chain in the south in the valleys of the Yarlung Tsangpo river and its tributaries. Its elevation is 3700 meters [12,210 feet].

In the far western section of south Tibet lies the watershed between the rivers Sutlej and Yarlung Tsangpo, both breaking through the Himalayas to India. It is near the "sacred lakes" Rakas (Langak Tsha) and Manasarowar (Mapham Tsho), at the foot of the sacred Mt. Kailas, or Kang Ripoche (6714 meters [22,156 feet]), identified with the mythological mountain Meru – the center of the Buddhist world and paradise of the Hindu gods.

The climate of the highland is characterized by great temperature changes, particularly during the course of the day. Nevertheless, it is not as cold as one might expect at this high level because of the pronounced clear weather conditions that dominate as a result of the modest precipitation and humidity in the rain shadow of the Himalayas. Another result of the high altitude are the powerful air currents, particularly on the far, flat Changtang plateau, often leading to extreme heavy and cold storms in the fall and winter.

In east and southeast Tibet, the climate is tempered considerably by the low elevation (Lhasa, 3675 meters [12,128 feet] above sea level) and by the influence of the monsoon. Thus, tree steppes in the Tsangpo valley turn into deciduous and conifer forests in the lower lying valleys of east Tibet. These are haunts for big game, which are becoming rare: the horse-ibex Takin, the cliff antelope Serai, Goral mountain antelope, the crowned deer Muntjak and the great deer Sambur, the white-lipped deer, the Argali blue sheep and even the great pandas can still be found there. In the bird world vultures and griffin vultures, golden eagles, ravens and pheasants are represented, on the highland lakes, there are also wild geese and ducks, seagulls and heron.

History

The ancestors of the present Tibetans probably settled this large area, coming from the east as nomadic shepherds. In the seventh century under King Songtsengampo, the first unified Tibetan empire, Tubo or Tufan, came into being. As a powerful military state, it established relations with Nepal and Tang China. When the two princesses came from China and Nepal to Lhasa in order to be wedded to Songtsengampo, Buddhism also came to Tibet. In the eighth century, this empire expanded to include central Asia, Kashmir, northern India and the western Chinese mainland. In 763, even the Chinese capital city Chang'an was conquered. In the following centuries, power struggles between the nobility and the king's court led to the downfall of the empire. Buddhism also suffered a fate full of changes. The Bon religion dominated for a time around 840 and many Buddhist monasteries were destroyed. Tibet broke up into small principalities. Originating in westernmost (Guge) and easternmost (Kham) Tibet, a renaissance of Buddhism began at the turn of the century. The formerly persecuted sects became strong again; they incorporated elements of the old Bon faith into their own religion and converted, as it were, all of Tibet. Nonetheless a reunited kingdom did not result. The Mongolian assault reached Tibet only indirectly. The confirmation of the Lama King Phagpa, the leader of the Sakyapa sects, as spiritual and secular leader by Kublai Khan in 1260 brought about the Tibetan theocracy.

The ruin of the Mongolian empire gave Tibet renewed independence under a restrengthened secular aristocracy. The various Buddhist sects battled one another. In the 14th–15th century, the reformer Tsongkhapa founded the Gelugpa sect. When the sect's leader, Sonam Gelugpa, converted the Mongolian ruler Altan Khan to Tibetan Buddhism in 1578, he was given the title "Dalai Lama" ("Ocean of Wisdom"). The expansion of Lamaism

under the Mongolians and their military support made it ultimately possible for the Gelugpa sect and the fifth Dalai Lama, Ngawang Losang Gyamtsho, to dominate politically and to rule the Tibetan church state into the 20th century. In response to an invasion by the Oirat Mongolians the Qing Emperor Kangxi sent troops to Lhasa in 1720. Tibet became a protectorate of Manchu China, which entrusted two imperial "ambans" to gain influence in Lhasa.

At the end of the 19th century, England and Russia tried to gain influence over Tibet. An English expedition led by Younghusband pushed up to Lhasa in 1904. As a result of the ruin of the Qing empire, Tibet was left to itself. At the Simla conference in 1914, Tibet declared independence, and the border between Tibet and India was set at the McMahon line. The consolidation of communist power in Peking in 1949 brought the "People's Liberation Army" to Tibet in 1950–51. With a mandate to reform the Tibetan social system by itself, the theocratic state of the Dalai Lama was outwardly at first left intact. After the abortive revolt in 1959 and the escape of the Dalai Lama to India, the troubles and destruction of the Chinese Cultural Revolution (1966–76) have gone by without effect in Tibet. In 1965 it received the status of an autonomous region. Since the beginning of the liberalization of the People's Republic of China in 1980, it is once gain possible for the Tibetans to maintain their cultural values and religious traditions, although with certain restrictions (e. g., a limited number of monks).

Religion, Population, Language

The life of the Tibetan is centered around the Buddhist religion in its special form of Lamaism, which has evolved from the Mahayana ("Great Vehicle") form of Buddhism. Whereas in Hinayana ("Small Vehicle") Buddhism it is only possible for those who follow the strict rules of monastic life to enter into Nirvana, thereby being freed from the cycle of reincarnation, Mahayana Buddhism is accessible to the laity. It offers everyone the opportunity to reach the holy objective, namely through certain rituals, temple ceremonies and consecrations. Along this path, one may count on help from "another world." In order to be able to help others to achieve redemption, those redeemed from the earthly desires of greed, hate and delusion do not enter immediately into Nirvana. In this way, Mahayana has created during the course of time a giant pantheon of gods and demons, reaching China and Tibet in this form. In the century-long conflicts with Tibet's Bon religion, Tibetan Buddhism had to adopt many elements from it in order to be able to gain acceptance; for example, the winning over of gods and spirits through magic and demonic appeasement rights and through mystery plays with dance, trance, ecstasy and cleansing. This special form of Mahayana is called the Vajrayana ("Diamond Vehicle"), or Tantrism. Its followers try to attain salvation by getting help from the other world either through practicing magic formulas, phrases and rights or through meditation, trance

and ecstasy. Engaging in sexual activities to the point of utter exhaustion was another attempt to bring the body to the concentration of the spirit and to free the soul from the body.

In reaction to these practices, Tsongkhapa wanted to reinstate righteousness, discipline and spiritualism through his reform movements in the 14th century.

Because the monks of the Gelupka sect, which he founded, wore yellow caps, they are known as the "yellow-(capped) sect." Before his death in 1419 Tsongkhapa prophesied to his most distinguished students, Kadubdsche and Gedun Drupba, that they would be continually reincarnated as high priests, thereby establishing the incarnation-succession of the later Dalai Lama and Panchen Lama, called god-kings. The title "Dalai Lama" was first given by the Mongolian Prince Altan Khan to Sonam Gyamtsho in 1578; he was later referred to as the third Dalai Lama, the title of the first and second Dalai posthumously given to Gedun Drupba and his successor. Losang Chogkyi Gyaltsen, high priest of the Tashilhunpo monastery and teacher of the fifth Dalai Lama, was awarded by the Dalai Lama the title "Panchen Lama" (Panchen Rinpoche = Jewel of the Scholars). As the incarnation of the Buddha Amitabha, the Panchen Lama stands hierarchically above the Dalai Lama, known as the reincarnation of Bodhisattva Avalokiteshvara, whose political office, however, had developed into the much more significant one.

During the Old Stone Age, people of the Paleo-Mongolian race were already supposed to have lived in Tibet. Later, tribes of the Turan race came from the north and settled in Tibet; they were called "Tanguts" by the Mongolians. The present-day Tibetans speak a language belonging to the Sino-Tibetan language family and have their own script, which is derived from Kashmir. They call themselves "Bodpa" and their country "Bod-Yul." They can be divided into two main categories: the heavily mixed, mostly farming population in the south, who are of medium height, with broad, strongly Mongolian faces; and the tall shepherd nomads in the west and northeast and in Kham. The latter have high, sharp features, hooked noses and reddish brown skin color, very similar to North American Indians. Approximately 3.9 million Tibetans (1982) live in the People's Republic of China; of that ca. 1.89 million in the Autonomous Region of Tibet.

Economy

The majority of the Tibetans in the highlands live in the farming areas in south Tibet. The north – the uninhabitable Changtang plateau – is only suitable as grazing land for cattle. Generally, though, both groups have always been closely, almost symbiotically, bound together. Cattle is raised in a nomadic way, with alpine grazing and small-scale livestock breeding. The nomadic shepherds living in square, yak hair woven tents, breed sheep and goats in the cold, dry west. The yak herds graze in the south and east at altitudes of 3500 to 5500 meters [11,550 to 18,150 feet]; the highest shepherd settlement is in the

Xainza at an elevation of about 5000 meters [16,500 feet].

The main agricultural product of the farmers in south Tibet dating back to ancient times has been a special highland barley. It is roasted with butter tea and mixed into *tsampa*, the typical Tibetan barley gruel and basic food of the Tibetans. The cultivated fields scattered about the pasture land gradually become solely farming areas around the cities of Shigatse, Gyantse, and Lhasa and farther east of the Tsangpo valley as the effects of the Indian summer monsoon increase. Its moisture is carried in the Tsangpo gap through the Himalayas up to southeast Tibet. There, in addition to the highland barley and buckwheat, which is cultivated in the Saka district up to 3700 meters [12,210 feet], various vegetables and fruit (apricots) grow as well.

Since the construction of the large roads from Chengdu in Sichuan and from Xining in Qinghai through Gomud to Lhasa, a modest industrialization (metal and wood processing, textile and food industries) has begun. A prerequisite for this industrialization was the expansion of electricity production. Not far from Lhasa, China's first geothermal powerplant is already operating. The public showers in the capital city are solar-heated. Ancient times have finally come to an end; the people nonetheless have remained kind, their traditional handicrafts and religiosity still very much alive. With the influx of portable radios, cars and factories into the "City of Gods," a certain amount of romanticism has surely been lost. But most of Lhasa's present visitors do not seem to miss the wild, romantic horseback rides or the weeklong hikes at frosty temperatures over 5000-meter-high [16,500-foot-high] passes along the many unclimbed peaks ...

THE N.E.F.A.

North-East Frontier Agency – Arunachal Pradesh ("Land of the Rising Sun")

Area: 81,426 sq. km [32,570 sq. mi.]
Population: 628,000 (1981)
Capital city: Itanagar
Form of government: union territory directly subject to the president of the Indian Union (as of Jan. 21, 1972)

The southern side of the Himalayan mountains is often referred to as Assam Himalaya in geographical literature. With its height of 7060 meters [23,298 feet] in Kangto, yet relatively low parts cut up into blocks by steep, south-sloping gorges, it incorporates almost all of the area of the present-day Indian constituent state of Arunachal Pradesh (formerly N.E.F.A.). The Himalayas are influenced in winter by the outer tropical west wind drift. Although its main effects are felt much farther west in the Kashmir Himalaya, the summit regions of the entire

range extend into zones subject to extremely high wind speeds of the subtropical jet stream at this time of the year. The often weeklong periods of fair weather open the view to the mountain giants. The mountains, however, remain unclimbable due to extreme wind speeds, up to 144 kilometers [86 miles] per hour. Under the rather weakly developed zone of the Assam Himalayas, with its perpetual snow and glacial-mountain slopes, the southern side regularly receives precipitation (even in winter), which, with the summer monsoon rainfall, adds up to the highest precipitation in Asia. Under such conditions a thick, tropical, evergreen rain forest vegetation has developed in the extended lowlands and on the mountain slopes up to high altitudes. In lower areas there are only deciduous forests, above that rhododendron-conifer (pine) forests, which are taken over by alpine shrubs and meadows. Such a lush forested area as this is naturally also rich in animal life, particularly in the oak and bamboo forests under the 1000-meter [3300-foot] level, which is home to monkeys, snakes, elephants and tigers. Above and beyond one can find takin, ibex, musk deer and bear.

History

Among the numerous ethnic groups that settled in Arunachal Pradesh, the Tibetan Monpa in the Kameng district – the westernmost part of the territory – are the only ones of historical significance. Because of them, the first Buddhist influences are supposed to have reached Tawang by the 11th century. Tawang was a small principality bordered in the east by the Kangto massif and otherwise surrounded by Bhutan and Tibet. While the fifth Dalai Lama (1617 – 1682) ruled in Tibet, the teachings of the reformed Gelugpa sect of Lodre Gyatso, the "Mera Lama," were circulated in Tawang. The great Gelugpa monastery Tawang Ganden Namgyal Lhatse Ling ("Heavenly Paradise, the Divine Site Chosen by a Horse") dates back to this time. It is where throughout two centuries all of the government's authority originated.

Like all eastern connecting districts, Tawang also came under the control of the British. After the Simla conference in 1914, the border between Tibet and the British Indies was set at the so-called McMahon line, the water divide of the Himalaya main ridge, which formed there the North-East Frontier Agency. Its purpose at the beginning was to protect the tea plantations in Assam against the raids of the region's mountain tribes, over which the British had not been able to gain any control.

After India gained independence and the communists took power in China, several border skirmishes ensued along the McMahon line, which China did not recognize. This conflict escalated, leading to open war in October – November 1962, during the course of which Chinese troops advanced to the Brahmaputra. Soon thereafter they withdrew voluntarily back to their initial positions. However, they regarded the entire Assam Himalayas as their national territory. In 1972 India granted N.E.F.A. the status of a union territory with the name

Arunachal Pradesh. The "map war" over the final setting of the border has continued up to now without resolution.

People, Language, Religion

The Monpa and Lhopa, coming from Tibet, are Lamaistic Buddhists. There are also said to be followers of the old Bon religion among them. At the foot of the mountains, a few Hindus can be found, while the so-called animistic religions are common in the largest part of the territory. The adherents of some of these religions, as well as those of the Bon faith and the Khik worship (Sherdukpas), follow the practices of the Shamanists.

The mountain world of Arunachal Pradesh is India's most sparsely populated area (on the average six people per square kilometer, or less than four per square mile) and least accessible and explored. Only in the north and in the higher mountain levels in the western part can one find ethnic groups of Tibetan ancestry, to which the Monpa (30,000) and the Sherdukpas (approximately 2000) belong. Clearly separate from them live the numerous, mostly small mountain races in the south and in the lower levels but particularly in the eastern districts (which are distinctly lower). The tribes (approximately 100,000 people) combined under the collective name "Adi" (earlier, Abor), to which belong the Gallong, Minyong and Padam. They populate the central Siang district. The most important groups of the Subansiri district and the Himalayan foothills are the Nishi and Miri (earlier, Dafla; together 70,000), Mishmi (23,000), Tagin (20,000) and Apa Tani (15,000). They all speak Tibetan-Burmese dialects that differ quite strongly from one another, indicating an origin in the north Burmese border area. Their manner of colonization in lake dwellings indicates a cultural link to the life-styles of Southeast Asia.

Economy

The Monpas living on the border area of Bhutan cultivate barley, corn, buckwheat and rice on fields that to some extent are fertilized and ploughed. They use the alpine meadows above their villages as pasture for their cattle. In contrast to their eastern neighbors, they use the milk to produce butter.

For the majority of the north Assam peoples the economy is based on shifting cultivation, which involves the clearing of forests by burning and the planting of rice, corn and millet as the most important indigenous plants, complemented by such tropical bulbous plants as yams and taro. In gardens near the villages, they cultivate vegetables, fruit and spice plants. Hunting, fishing and the gathering of wild plants play a much greater role as farming becomes more limited by higher altitudes.

As usual in economically self-sufficient societies, handicrafts among the individual members are well developed. Yet their manufactured objects (woven fabrics, woodcuttings, etc.) are not traded, but rather used for personal needs.

SIKKIM

Former Kingdom of Sikkim

Area: 7298 sq. km [2919 sq. mi.]
Population: 320,000 (1981)
Capital city: Gangtok
(36,000 inhabitants)
Form of government: 22nd federal state
of the Indian Union (May 1975)

The area of the present Indian federal state of Sikkim encompasses solely the upper valley of the Brahmaputra tributary Tista and the region of its source. The watershed ridges form the border in the east and in the north with Tibet/People's Republic of China and in the west with Nepal. The southern border with West Bengal is formed by the mountain rivers Rangit and Rangpo. Sikkim proper begins at the foot of the mountains, however, originally encompassing the areas in West Bengal around Darjeeling and Kalimpong. Sikkim's landscape is dominated by the 8597-meter-high [28,370-foot-high] massif of the Kangchendzonga and its 31-kilometer-long [18.6-mile-long] Zemu glacier on the western border. The long Tista valley, transversing the whole country from north to south, allows the summer monsoon rain to push extremely far to the north at its highest level of intensity. As a result of these large amounts of rainwater many narrow valleys were deeply cut into the rather soft stone (Daling slate) in the south. Level surfaces can be found only in the most extreme north (High Sikkim), where the dryness has created a treeless alpine steppe. Its barren high surfaces and mountains covered with rubble and boulder formations form the transition to the highlands of Tibet.

Because of the heavy precipitation the mountainous landscapes of upper and lower Sikkim encompass all gradations of vegetation: from the wet sal-tree forest with 660 species of orchids at the foot of the mountains to, the tropical evergreen mountain and rain forests (tree ferns, epiphytes, bamboo, oak, beech, chestnut, giant magnolia rhododendron trees and conifers [pines, firs]) up to the tree line – from 3600 to 4200 meters [11,880 to 13,860 feet] above sea level. In Sikkim tropical plants of different climatic regions mix together as nowhere else in the Himalayas all the way into the middle of the mountains. Sikkim has a corresponding variety in the animal world. It claims over 500 species of birds in this small area alone. Antelope, wild sheep and goats as well as wild asses and yaks can be found in the north. In the forested valleys live bears, lesser (red) pandas, silver foxes and leopards, and in the south macaques, langurs and other monkey species.

History

The original inhabitants of Sikkim are the Lepchas, who call themselves Rongpas. In the 13th century Tibetans began to im-migrate to Sikkim. In the 15th century the Namgyal family migrated from east Tibet (Kham) and settled in the Chumbi valley. From there the family won increasing political influence over Sikkim. In 1642 Chogyal or Gyalpo (king) Phuntsog Namgyal (1604 – 70) was placed at the top of a strong ruling system based on Lamaistic Buddhism. He divided the land into 12 Dzongs (fortified districts).

In the 18th century, armies from Bhutan and the Gurkha empire (Nepal) invaded. Sikkim lost considerable amounts of territory to its neighboring kingdoms. When the Gurkhas were defeated by the Chinese army in a campaign against Tibet in 1791 – 92, Sikkim won back its northern sections. Yet from then on the Chumbi valley was to belong to Tibet.

After the British victory over Nepal in 1917, the southern part of the country was given back to Sikkim. However, as soon as the next conflict with Nepal in 1827, Dorjeling (the present-day Darjeeling) had to be relinquished to the British to gain their support. In 1848 the entire Terai lowlands and the mountain periphery were annexed by British India. Within a single century Sikkim was reduced to a fraction of its former territory.

Since the beginning of the 19th century, the Nepali had increasingly immigrated to Sikkim, eventually surpassing the number of natives. This led to internal tension. After the British who refused to help stop the influx of the Nepali, the Gyalpos supported a Tibetan military plan during which Tibet seized a stretch of land near Darjeeling with a small unit of troops. In ensuing battles the British retained the upper hand and Sikkim became a British protectorate in 1890. The British had won their long sought-after easy entrance way into Tibet.

The state was controlled for years by the British "political officer" Claude White, who in effect stripped the Gyalpos of their power. Not until Sidkeong Tulku and Tashi Namgyal reigned was the king's power gradually restored.

The Indian Union took over the protectorate in 1950 and intervened between representatives of different Sikkim ethnic groups in 1973 after long lasting political conflicts. The Gyalpos lost their power as a result of the new democratic constitution. Consequently, the pro-Indian Nepali population became more influential. A law introduced into the parliament made Sikkim, by annexation, an "associated" Indian partial state. It became the 22nd federal state of the Indian Union in 1975 through an amendment to the constitution.

People, Language, Religion

In contrast to the native Lepchas, the Bhutias, who immigrated early, are of Tibetan origin. They speak a dialect that comes closer to Old Tibet than to the Lhasa dialect, and their culture is influenced by Lamaism. Among the Tsong [Nepali immigrants] there are Buddhists as well, even followers of the Bon faith and animists. The majority of Tsong, however, who make up 60% of the population, are of Hindu faith. Eastpahari, or Nepali, an Indo-Aryan language, has been generally adopted in lower Sikkim as well. On the other hand, the Tibeto-Burmese languages, including, Lepcha, which possesses its own alphabet, have lost importance.

Economy

The steep slopes and the heavy rains necessitate the terracing of fields almost everywhere. The Lepchas' original mode of cultivation, shifting cultivation, which was complemented by hunting, has become impossible due to the agricultural exploitation of the forest by the large number of Tsong (Nepali immigrants). It has since been prohibited. The high areas from 1100 to 2000 meters [3630 to 6600 feet] are almost completely deforested. Corn is grown in terraces and rice is cultivated where water is available. Wheat and barley are planted at higher levels. Potatoes, oranges and tea cultures (those in the Himalayan foothills near Darjeeling that no longer belong to Sikkim have attained great fame) and the spice cardamom are important export products. Fruit farming has led to the development of a small canned fruit industry.

At higher altitudes the importance of cattle breeding increases, forming the main economic base in upper Sikkim. In the summer sheep and yak are driven to pastures, which in some areas lie above 4000 meters [14,200 feet]. A large part of the cattle- breeding population there settles in the nearby summer villages.

For centuries the most important trade route led from India to Tibet through Sikkim. Its mountain passes on the southeast national border – Natu La, at 3310 meters [10,923 feet], and Jelep La, at 4374 meters [14,434 feet] above sea level – are relatively low for Himalayan passes. They form the shortest routes to Lhasa through the Chumbi valley. The bad relations between India and China have blocked this trade route for a long time. The immigration of the Nepali has made the original population of Sikkim a minority in its own land.

Indian Federal States and Areas of Pakistan

Himachal Pradesh

Area: 55,673 sq. km [22,269 sq. mi.]
Population: 4,288 million (1984)
Capital city: Simla (60,000 inhabitants)
Form of government: Indian federal state

Uttar Pradesh

Area: 294,413 sq. km [17,765 sq. mi.]
Population: 111 million (1981)
Capital city: Lucknow
(825,000 inhabitants)
Form of government: Indian federal state

Jammu and Kashmir

Area: 137,000 sq. km [54,800 sq. mi.];
100,569 sq. km [400,228 sq. mi.]
Population: 5.98 million (1981)
Capital city: Srinagar (520,000 inhabitants)
Form of government: Indian federal state

Azad Kashmir

Area: 83,806 sq. km [33,522 sq. mi.]
Population: approximately 1.3 million
Capital city: Muzaffarabad
Form of government: as of 1949, it belongs
to Pakistan

Baltistan and Gilgit

Baltistan (main city, Skardu) and the district of Gilgit including Hunza (main city, Baltit) are directly under the control of the Pakistani government.

Kashmir, Himachal Pradesh and the northern part of the federal state of Uttar Pradesh are crossed by three almost parallel mountain chains of the Himalayas and the Karakorum, which frame the high plateaus and valleys, as in the Kashmir valley. Their summits rank with the highest in the world, towering above the fertile foothills, called Siwalik. At its base the farming regions of the Doabs in Punjab and the jungle areas of the Terai extend into the great plain fed by the Indus and Ganges rivers as well as their tributaries.

The great differences in altitude and their corresponding temperature variations at relatively short distances cause a pronounced transformation in climate from the foot of the mountains to the top, affecting the vegetation.

The monsoon brings extremely plentiful rainfall to the Assam Himalayas for almost the entire year, even winter, as well as to the central Himalayas in the summer. Its influence diminishes from east to west. The tropical monsoon forests and grass forest marshes of the Terai, the subtropical mountain forests and tea cultures of the southern slope of the Himalaya and Siwalik chains and the rhododendron groves above them are transformed into a comparable steppe landscape in the western Himalayas by the meager precipitation which moreover falls in Kashmir in the winter months. To the north, the rainfall decreases even more, the steppe vegetation visibly making room for desert, allowing only sporadic farming in irrigated oases.

In the northernmost part of Kashmir, the so-called Gilgit Agency and Azad Kashmir, which belong to Pakistan (area 88,000 square kilometers [35,200 square miles], 1.35 million inhabitants), the largest connecting glacial area outside of the polar regions can be found in the Karakorum, towering above on the world's second highest mountain: the 8,611-meter-high [28,416-feet-high] K2 or Mt. Godwin Austen.

The mountains, sparsely covered with vegetation, and their valleys form a refuge for old ethnic groups and cultures in which influences from Iran as well as from India and Tibet combine. The strong geographic subdivision by steep slopes and narrow valleys has led to the formation of several principalities of the predominantly Islamic population. They earn their living by farming and raising cattle, and in recent times increasingly through tourism, especially in the Hunza valley. The Hunza and Nagar speak an isolated language, the Pathans an Afghanistan dialect, the Ladakhis and the inhabitants of Baltistan speak Tibetan dialects. The Balti are the only Tibetans professing the Islamic faith.

The part of Kashmir belonging to India carries the federal state name Jammu and Kashmir. This area's landscape is distinctly marked by the Himalaya main chain as well as by the Ladakh range and the Zanskar mountains, yet the main part of the country lies in the southwest in the province of Jammu at the foot of the mountains and at the 1500- to 1900-meter-high [4950- to 6270-foot-high] Kashmir basin. Both of these central areas make up only about one-fourth of the surface area of the federal state, although almost 92% of its population lives here. The 130-kilometer-long [78-mile-long] and 40-kilometer-wide [24-mile-wide] Kashmir basin is a tectonic depression. Since the Ice Age the river Jhelum has filled it with sediment. The large river, rich in suspended matter, creates an environment very favorable to rice cultivation on both sides of its course as well as on the irrigated terraces and alluvial fans. The rice farming, however, is threatened by flooding. In the area northwest of the basin, the Jhelum flows through Lake Wular before it breaks through the 4,700-meter-high [15,510-foot-high] Pir-Punjal chain in a narrow canyon. This is the only exit from the Kashmir valley. Its outer chains are mostly covered by hardwoods (holly) and thornbush forests, and at higher levels also mixed forests of conifer (cedar) and oaks. Also, in the upper slope levels of the Kashmir valley and its adjoining valleys, natural conifer forests grow, that is, those that have not already been deforested by settlers. Above that, there are high mountain meadows abundant in herbs; these are replaced in the north by steppes. The animal world has adapted to this change. Even here in the unfavorable climate of the West Himalayas, a variety of species of birds exist, e.g., ravens, bearded and snow vultures, pheasants and wild ducks. In addition, this area forms an important flight path for migratory birds between the USSR and India. Up to here, European as well as Far Eastern bird species exist.

In the high mountains, bears (the red-brown Tibetan bear, the black-collar bear) and wolves can be found all over. Snow leopards are more rare. Most rare are wild sheep and goats: pamir, or Marco Polo sheep; urial; blue sheep; Siberian ibex with horns 1 meter [3.3 feet] long; and the markhor, or screw goat. Aside from those, various deer and antelope species can be found, e.g., the graceful Tibetan gazelles and the famous musk animals.

History and Religion

The western Himalaya was probably already settled in the Old Stone Age, as shown by excavations in caves of the Swat region west of the Indus. Neolithic evidence (megaliths) was found in Zanskar (Kashmir) as well as in Spiti (Himachal Pradesh). Prehistoric rock paintings with hunting scenes and ibex suggest a hunting people. This group was related to Indo-European ethnic peoples, possibly to the Dards described by Herodotus.

Since the seventh century Kashmir had gradually come under the influence of the Tibetan kingdom of Tubo, and like the entire Himalaya chain it belonged to the Tibetan empire in the middle of the eighth century. Its monarchy broke down into several principalities 150 years later. In the 14th century these small Buddhist and Hindu empires gradually came under the political power of Islam (Srinagar became the summer residence of the Mogul emperor). Mogul rule ended in 1819 when the Sikhs of the Punjab conquered Kashmir and united it with the Hindu Jammu. The Dogra princes of Jammu also conquered Ladakh and the Karakorum areas in 1842 for the Maharaja principality, which from 1885 on (under British control) was only partially independent. When Kashmir did not become part of the newly created Moslem state of Pakistan after the breakup of British India in 1947 despite the Muhammadan majority (77%), an Islamic revolt erupted in the Punjab. At the same time, plundering Pathan tribes invaded from the northwest province of Pakistan. As a result, the Hindu Maharaja of Kashmir called upon the Indians for help, subsequently signing a treaty on Oct. 26, 1947, which united Kashmir with the Indian unions. The Pathans were forced back by Indian troops. However, regular Pakistani regiments attacked in the spring of 1948. The fighting was ended by the intervention of the United Nations at the year's end (1948 – 49).

The front, as it stood at this time, was set as the cease-fire line, with approximately two-thirds of the entire area falling to the Indian Union. It was annexed as a federal state of the Indian Union in 1957, five years after the monarchy was abolished. The remaining third went to Pakistan. A referendum was supposed to decide on the final affiliation, but it was never held. The Kashmir conflict continued. After frequent incidences along the demarcation line, the Indian- Pakistani War broke out in 1965, ending with the peace treaty of Tashkent in 1966. India's entry into the already ensuing civil war in what was then East Pakistan in 1977 resulted in renewed fighting in Kashmir. During the fighting, the Indians gained back the more favorable military positions on the passes at the demarcation line, which they had to give up in the Tashkent agreement. The Pakistani part of Jammu (Punch) was incorporated as the so-called Free (Azad) Kashmir, the fifth province, into the Pakistan Federal Union in 1974. The strategically important areas of Baltistan and Gilgit, however, were not left under the control of the administrative authorities of this "Free Kashmir" but were placed directly under the control of the Pakistani government.

With the creation of federal-state districts in Kashmir on both the Indian side and the Pakistani side, an adjustment was made to the de facto situation. A certain easing of the conflict was thus accepted. Nevertheless, inner political troubles, especially in the Indian part of Kashmir, have not yet been quelled despite the concession of certain autonomous rights. There are still pro-Pakistan Moslems there. The majority of the population of Ladakh, situated to the north of the Himalayan main ridge, is Lamaistic. They are demanding the direct incorporation of Ladakh under the Indian central government.

People and Language

Although Jammu and Kashmir are among the most sparsely populated areas of India, an enormous ethnic and linguistic variety can be found there. The Causasian Indians living in the plains at the foot of the mountains and in the foothills speak Indo-Aryan languages and in the Pakistan part Urdu which, in contrast to Hindu, has borrowed several words from Arabic, Persian and Turkish languages. In Jammu, Dogri is spoken; in the Kashmir valley, Kashmiri, belonging to the Dardic languages, is spoken. The written language of the Hindus is Devanagari, and the Moslems use an Arabic script.

On the other side of the Himalayan main ridge – from Baltistan across Ladakh to Spiti and Lahul – the inhabitants belong to the Tibetan culture, as evidenced by their Mongolian appearance as well as their language.

LADAKH

Former Kingdom of Ladakh

Area: 58,321 sq. km [23,328 sq. mi.]
(excluding the Chinese –
occupied Aksai Chin)
Population: 120,000 (1979)
Main City: Leh (6,200 inhabitants)
Form of government: Indian administrative
union at the district level

Ladakh lies embedded in the mountain world of the Karakorum in the northwest, the Himalayas in the southwest and the Transhimalayas at its core. Its position at the upper course of the Indus makes it the important connecting point of the trade route from northwest India to Tibet and to Turkestan. The main chain of the Himalayas prevents the Indian summer monsoon from advancing this far. Likewise the extended cold winter has little snow due to the position of the mountains in the rain shadow. Winter is followed by a short, dry and relatively warm summer. All year-round, however, there are great daily changes of temperature, with strong winds blowing in winter. As a result of the dry and harsh climate, only sporadic high steppes are covered with grass, and arid and semi-arid deserts dominate a nonetheless grandiose mountain world.

History and Religion

After the demise of the first Tibetan empire, it was divided among three brothers in 1020. One of them moved to Ladakh and founded the first royal dynasty there. When Tibetan Buddhism in the eastern neighboring kingdom of Guge experienced a new high point, this rejuvenation affected Ladakh. Its temple monasteries and the manner in which religion sharply pervaded the people's way of life gave clear evidence of this. In many cases, old shrines of the earlier Bon religion were transformed into Buddhist monasteries. In the following centuries, the Ladakhic kings extended their ruling territory. Lhachen Utpala (1080 to 1110) expanded his kingdom up to the realm of the related dynasties of Purang and Mustang (in present-day Nepal). New importance was attached to the culture of the Ladakhic monks when the reform sect of the Gelugpa created by Tsongkhapa led to the reestablishment of monasteries in the 15th century. Family fueds had ended at the beginning of the 15th century with the division of the empire. Lhachen Bhagan unified Ladakh in 1470 and founded a new dynasty, Namgyal. His successor was able to stand ground against an invasion from East Turkestan. Yet over the years Ladakh was to be plagued repeatedly by plundering, ravaging Islamic armies. During the reign of the powerful kings Sengge Namgyal (ca. 1570 to 1620) and Deldan Namgyal (ca. 1620 – 1660) the empire was not only further extended but blossomed anew culturally in Ladakh. It came to an end when the great fifth Dalai Lama of Tibet (Nawang Lobsang Gyatso,

1617 – 82) convinced the Mongolians, whom he had converted to Lamaism, to enter a military campaign against West Tibet and Ladakh. Their king, Delegs Namgyal, turned to Kashmir for help. In the Battle of Basgo (ca. 1685) the Tibetan-Mongolian army was stopped. Yet, from then on Ladakh remained under the rule of the Islamic empire of the great Moguls. Its history remained unalterably tied with the history of Jammu and Kashmir, but the country did not forfeit its Lamaistic tradition.

People and Language

The Ladakhi's features reveal a mixture of Tibetan-Mongolian and Indo-Aryan elements. They are still for the most part (Lamaistic) Buddhists, even though the Buddhist portion of the entire population of the district is only 52%. Among the followers of Islam, making up 47% of the population, immigrant Kashmiri and Dards (Shin), who also speak their own Indo-Aryan languages, predominate. Ladakhi belongs to the Tibetan-Burmese language group and differs significantly in pronunciation from the Lhasa dialect.

Economy and Tourism

The only areas where larger stretches of land are suited for settlement and agriculture are the adjoining valleys. They are enclosed by the mountain chains running northwest to southeast mainly at altitudes from 3000 to 4000 meters [9900 to 13,200 feet]. The extreme lack of precipitation here can be offset by irrigation, which has enabled the creation of fertile oases in the Indus and Zanskar valleys and in the adjoining valleys of the Suru, Dras, Nubra and Shyok. There highland barley, wheat, buckwheat and various kinds of vegetables grow in terraces, and in the lower and protected areas even apricot and walnut trees, cedars, poplars and willows thrive.

The region above 4000 meters [13,200 feet] is the world of the nomads, who wander about with their sheep and goat herds, especially in the southeast – in Rupshu – and above the foothills of the Changtang plateau. The wool of the Pashmina goats has achieved fame as "Kashmir wool," or cashmere, and has been one of the Ladakhi's main articles of trade for quite some time. It is transported on the backs of donkeys, mules or yaks to the valley because there are very few roads. The most important road – especially for military use (there are approximately 200,000 soldiers in Ladakh) – is that running from Srinagar to Leh. This is the only route out of Ladakh, and it is used mainly by truck convoys.

Since the Indian government has opened Ladakh to foreign visitors, albeit with many restrictions (before, it was completely sealed off), tourism has increasingly become a source of income for the Ladakhi people (1974: 500 tourists; 1979: about 11,000 tourists). Their cheerfulness and cordiality charm the visitors. The wonderful natural backdrop of narrow river valleys, high plateaus and blue sky above snow-covered peaks, the unusual Tibetan temple architecture, and in general the charisma of the people and their land of Lamaistic culture contribute to the visitors' fascination for Ladakh.

The isolation of the country and its location, with extreme hindrances to transportation, have prevented the development of mining and industry up to the present. Art handicrafts rank highly in the country's trade, which should grow through tourism.

In the more densely populated part of Kashmir and in the neighboring provinces of Himachal and Uttar Pradesh, handicrafts and the textile industry have expanded considerably. South of the Himalayan main ridge, commercial timber is cut in the forests (deodar, fir, silver fir). A conscientious forest protection policy is needed. For a long time the forests have been severely thinned out by the population in order to gain new land for farming. The effects can be seen in the loss of vegetation cover, erosion, and increasingly frequent and severe flooding. The people in the mountains are finding it more difficult to make a living by farming. Thus, work in the lumber industry and ranching has developed to provide additional means of income. In some of the isolated regions, tourism is beginning to play an increasingly important role. Alpine climbing could also offer opportunities here, as in Nepal, for example, whose Sherpas work as bearers and mountain guides. Mountain climbing, after all, has unquestionably made history.

SUGGESTIONS FOR FURTHER READING ON THE HIMALAYAS

General Reading

Atkinson, E.T. *Himalayan Gazetteer, Historical, Ethnological, Geographical & Scientific*, 3 vols. Sevenoaks, Kent: Coronet, 1974.
Commander, A.K. *Himalayan Diplomacy*. Dover, New Hampshire: Longwood, 1988.
Downs, H.R. *Rhythms of a Himalayan Village*. New York: Harper & Row, 1980.
Dracott, Alice E. *Simla Village Tales, or, Folk Tales from the Himalayas*. New York: Gordon Press, 1976.
Fisher, James F., editor. *Himalayan Anthropology: The Indo-Tibetan Interface*. (World Anthropology Ser.) Berlin: Mouton De Gruyter, 1979.
Gibbons, Bob & Ashford, Bob. *The Himalayan Kingdoms*. New York: Hippocrene, 1987.
Gupta, H.K. & Delany, F.M. *Zagros, Hindu Kush, Himalaya: Geodynamic Evolution*. (Geodynamics Series: Vol. 3) Washington, D.C.: American Geophysical Union, 1981.

Gupta, Rk. *Bibliography of the Himalayas*. Columbia, Missouri: South Asia Books, 1981.
Hooker, J.D. *Himalayan Journal*, 2 vols. in 1; reprint of 1854 ed. Houston: Scholarly Publications, 1975.
Kelly, Thomas L., photographer. *The Hidden Himalayas*, with text by V. Carroll Dunham. New York: Abbeville, 1987.
Lall, J.S. & Moddie, A.D., editors. *The Himalaya: Aspects of Change*. New York: Oxford University Press, 1981.
Mason, Kenneth. *Abode of Snow*, with foreword by Doug Scott; reprint of the 1955 edition. Seattle: Mountaineers Books, 1987.
Mehta, Ashvin., editor. *Himalaya: Encounters with Eternity*, illustrated by Maurice Herzog. New York: Thames & Hudson, 1985.
Pal, Saroj K. *Geomorphology of River Terraces along: Alaknanda Valley, Garhwal Himalaya*. New York: Apt Books, 1986.
Saklani, P.S., editor. *Structural Geology of the Himalayas*. (Current Trends in Geology Ser.: Vol. II) Houston: Scholarly Publications, 1980.
Saklani, P.S., editor. *Tectonic Geology of the Himalayas*. (Current Trends in Geology Ser.: Vol. I) Houston: Scholarly Publications, 1978.
Shirakawa, Yoshikazu, photographer. *Himalayas*, with preface by Arnold Toynbee, introduction by Edmund Hillary, contribution by Kyuya Fukada. New York: Harry N. Abrams, 1986.
Srivastava, R.A., editor. *Sedimentary Geology of the Himalaya*. (Current Trends in Geology Ser.: Vol. 5) Houston: Scholarly Publications, 1985.
Von Furer-Haimendorf, Christopher. *A Himalayan Tribe: From Cattle to Cash*. Berkeley: University of California Press, 1980.

The Indian Himalayas: Kashmir and Ladakh

Dogra, Ramesh C. *Jammu & Kashmir: A Selected & Annotated Bibliography*. Columbia, Missouri: South Asia Books, 1986.
Harvey, Andrew. *A Journey in Ladakh*. Boston: Houghton Mifflin Company, 1983.
Snellgrove, D.L. & Skorupski, T. *The Cultural Heritage of Ladakh: Zangskar & the Cave Temples of Ladakh*, vol. 2. Atlantic Highlands, New Jersey: Humanities Press International, 1981.
Singh, Raghubir. *Kashmir*, with preface by Jawaharlal Nehru; rev. ed. New York: Thames & Hudson, 1987.
Tsering, Nawang. *Buddhism in Ladakh*. Livingston, New Jersey: Orient Book Distributors, 1979.

Sikkim

Das, B.S. *The Sikkim Saga*. New York: Advent Books, 1983.
Kotturan, G. *The Himalayan Gateway-History & Culture of Sikkim*. Atlantic Highlands, New Jersey: Humanities International, 1983.
Risley, H.H. *The Gazetteer of Sikkim*; reprint of 1894 ed. New York: Apt Books, 1986.
Sengupta, N. *State Government & Politics: Sikkim*. New York: Apt Books, 1985.

Bhutan

Aris, M. *Bhutan: The Early History of a Himalayan Kindgom*. Atlantic Highlands, New Jersey: Humanities Press International, 1979.
Eavas. *The Dragon Kingdom Journeys Through Bhutan*. Columbia, Missouri: South Asia Books, 1986.
Rose, Leo E. *The Politics of Bhutan*. Ithaca, New York: Cornell University Press, 1977.
World Bank. *Bhutan: Development in a Himalayan Kingdom*. Washington, D.C.: The World Bank, 1984.

Nepal

Amatya, D.B. *Perspectives in Regional Problems & Development in Nepal*. New York: Apt Books, 1987.
Amatya, D.B. *Nepal's Fiscal Issues: New Challenges*. New York: Apt Books, 1986.
Baral, Lok R. *Nepal's Politics of Referendum: A Study of Groups, Personalities & Trends*. New York: Advent Books, 1984.
Bezruchka, Stephen. *A Guide to Trekking in Nepal*, 5th ed. Seattle: Mountaineers Books, 1985.
Blair, Katherine D. *Four Villages-Architecture in Nepal: Studies of Village Life*. Chicago: University of Chicago Press, 1975.
Caplan, Lionel. *Administration & Politics in a Nepalese Town*. New York: Oxford University Press, 1975.
Dharamdasani, M.D., editor. *Political Participation & Change in South Asia: In the Context of Nepal*. Columbia, Missouri: South Asia Books, 1985.
Dor Bahadur Bista. *People of Nepal*, 5th ed. Queens Village, New York: Asia Corporation of America, 1986.
Gaige, Frederick H. *Regionalism & National Unity in Nepal*. Berkeley: University of California Press, 1975.
Hitchcock, John T. *A Mountain Village in Nepal*. New York: Holt, Rinehart & Winston, 1980.
Prentice Hall. *Nepal*. (Insight Guides) Englewood Cliffs, New Jersey: Prentice Hall, 1983.

Tibet

Karan, Pradyumna P. *The Changing Face of Tibet: The Impact of Chinese Communist Ideology on the Landscape*. Lexington: University Press of Kentucky, 1976.
Kling, Kevin. *Tibet*. New York: Thames & Hudson, 1985.
Stein, R.A. *Tibetan Civilization*, translated by J.E. Driver; rev. ed. Stanford, California: Stanford University Press, 1972.
John Wiley & Sons. *Tibet: A Dreamt of Image*. New York: John Wiley & Sons, 1986.
Timpanelli, Gioi. *Tales from the Roof of the World: Folktales of Tibet*, illustrated by Elizabeth Lockwood. New York: Viking Penguin, 1984.
Van Praag, Michael G. *The Status of Tibet: History, Rights, & Prospects in International Law*. Boulder, Colorado: Westview Press, 1986.
Waddell, Austine. *Tibetan Buddhism with Its Mystic Cults, Symbolism & Mythology, & in Its Relation to Indian Buddhism*; reprint of 1939 ed. New York: Dover, 1972.

INDEX

Abor tribe, 60, 61, 70, 71
Academia-Sinica (Chinese Academy), 15
Aimone, 252
Akbar (Grand Mogul), 140
Alexander the Great, 224, 228
Amadeo, Luigi, 251
Andrade, Antonio de, 122, 128, 129, 141, 144
Angara, Arhat, 222
Ashoka (Emperor), 116, 212 – 214
Atisha, 123
Auden, J. B., 14
Aufschnaiter, Peter, 232

Bakula, Arhat, 88
Band, George, 248
Barnes, Malcolm, 248
Bauer, 248
Bell, Charles, 202
Bhutan, 35, 72, 74, 77, 200, 208, 210, 236, 278 – 279
    economy, 279
    history, 278
    people, language, religion, 278
Blue Annals, 175, 177, 214, 216
Boelsche, Wilhelm, 178
Boja (King), 204
Bon religion, 76, 154, 156, 232, 236
Bower (General), 70 – 71
Brahman, 158
Brahmanism, 41, 157
Brahmaputra, see Yarlung Tsangpo
Brewer, E. H., 134
Bridges, 117, 218, 242, 246
    suspension, 242, 246
Brikuti (Nepalese Princess), 58, 222
British Indian Survey, 60 – 61, 70
Brown, Joe, 248
Bruce, Charles Granville (General), 240, 242
Buddha, 84, 97, 98, 102, 116, 158
Buddha's Life, 8
Buddhism, 43 – 44, 77, 98, 100, 116, 122, 128, 156, 158, 160, 161, 165, 168, 170, 177, 180, 182, 210, 214, 216
Buddhist legends, 212 – 216
Buhl, Hermann, 114, 250
Buildings, 208 – 220, 270
Buston, 8
Buton, 260
Butter tea, 266

Chachu, 200
China, 222, 262
Chinese pilgrims, 213 – 214
Chinese troops, 51, 54, 55, 248
Chou En-lai (Chinese Premier), 51
Christian missionaries, 122, 129
Chu Ying-hua, 248
Colebrook, Henry, 146
Colebrook, Robert, 146, 148
Compagnoni, Achille, 252
Conch shells, 270
Continents and Oceans in the Course of Time, 178
Cosmology, 8, 10
Cox, David, 249
Cremation, 165, 168
Cretaceos period, 14
Curzon (Lord), 70

Dalai Lama, 60, 157, 160 – 161, 178
Darbela dam, 117 – 118
Denpas tribe, 60
Desideri, Ippolito (Father), 129 – 130
Desio, Ardito, 17, 251
Detsan, Thongson (Tibetan King), 228
Devi, 184, 186
Diemberger, Kurt, 250
Dihang, see Yarlung Tsangpo
Drummond, Robert, 188
Dyrenfurth, 248
Dzongs, 51, 176, 208, 210

East India Company, 144, 146
Eliade, Mircea, 10
Evans-Wentz, W. Y., 165
Everest, George (Sir), 240
Everest, Mount, 240, 242, 243, 248
Exploration of Ganges' source, 140, 141, 144

Farming, 258
    grains, 265 – 268
Flood waters, recession of, 19, 174 – 182
    Noah-Manu, 182 – 184
Flora and fauna, 28, 30
    medicinal plants, 258, 260
Fortresses, 74, 208
Fossils, 17, 122, 124
Freyre, Emanoel, 129 – 130
Friedhuber, Sepp, 148
Funke, Friedrich W., 232

Gandhi, Mahatma, 158
Ganges river, 136 – 148
    source, 140, 141, 144
Gansser, A., 14, 168, 188
Garhwali tribe, 140, 141, 146
Gaumukh ("Cow's Mouth"), 138

Geological Survey of India, 14
Geology
    map, 30 – 31
    origin of Himalayas, 6, 12, 14 – 32
Geotraverse of the Royal Society, 15
Glaciers, 136
Glasenapp, Helmut von, 154
Gondwanaland, 12
Gonpa, 248
Govinda, Anagarika (Lama), 127 – 128
Grains, 265 – 268
Granite, 16 – 17
Guge, kingdom of, 6, 127 – 128
Gurkhas, 70, 71, 279 – 280
Gushri Khan, 178

Hagen, Toni, 17
Harrer, Heinrich, 232
Haslinger, Peter, 148
Hearsey, 146, 148
Hedin, Sven, 40 – 41, 80, 87, 188
Heim, A., 14, 188
Herodotus, 28
Hiebeler, Toni, 48
Hillary, Edmund, 48, 248
Himalaya and Karakorum, 48
Hinduism, 158
Hindus, 146, 180, 182
    pilgrims, 184, 186
Hoffmann, H., 188, 202
Hoggson, John (Captain), 148
Holy mountains, 199 – 200
Hooker, Joseph Dalton, 168, 248
Hot springs, 56
Houston, Charles, 252
Hunt, John, 248
Hunza tribe, 106, 228

Ice Ages, 18 – 19
India, 51, 54, 55, 122, 144, 157, 202, 270
Indian Federal States, 285 – 286
Indian Ocean, 14
Indian troops, 60
Indus river, 80 – 119
Indus-Yarlung suture, 15, 81, 85, 86
Irvine, Andrew, 243
Islam, 98, 100

Jainism tradition, 158, 203 – 204
Jomolhari, see Devi
Juliana (Dona), 129

Kailas, Mount, 188 – 198
Kailas range, 38
Kaimavati ("Daughter of the Himalayas"), see Devi
Kalidasa, 10
Kalzang (Princess), 219
Kappenberger, Giovanni, 256
Karakorum, 16 – 17
Karmapa Lama, 168
Karnali river, 134 – 136
Khanpo, Sumpa, 177
Kinthub, 60 – 61, 70
Konegger, Kaspar, 98

Lacedelli, Lino, 252
Ladakh, 85 – 97, 103, 104, 116, 223 – 224, 286 – 287
Lakes, 19, 28, 188 – 220
Lambert, Raymond, 248
Langdarma (King of Tibet), 96
Laya tribe, 206
Lepcha tribe, 228
Lhasa, 43, 58, 61
Li Gotami, 128
Lopas tribe, 60
Lydekker, 17

Mahabharata (Great Epic), 260
Mahakala, see Devi
Mahendra (King), 237
Mallory, George L., 243
Marques, Manuel, 129, 141, 144
Mask making, 180
McMahon line, 51, 54
Medicinal plants, 258
Merkl, Willy, 250
Messner, Reinhold, 253
Meteorites, 171 – 174
Milarepa, 157, 165, 168, 196
Mishmi tribe, 60
Moguls, 122
Monasteries, 17, 26, 35, 44, 51, 104, 208, 218, 219
    cave, 122 – 123, 127 – 128
Mongolia, 160
Monpas tribe, 60
Mueller, F. Max, 154
Mustang, 281
    people, 228, 232

Naga warriors, 70
Namgyel, Sengge (King), 90
Nepal, 134, 136, 156, 160, 186, 200, 209, 210, 212, 258, 279 – 281
    economy, 280 – 281
    history, 279 – 280
    people, language, religion, 280
Noah-Manu, 182 – 184
North-East Frontier Agency (NEFA), 54 – 55, 283
Norton, E. F., 242
Noyce, Wilfred, 249
Nyathitsenpo, 65

Oceanic ridges, 12
Odell, Noel E., 243
Olschak, B. C., 72, 74, 207
Origin of the world, 7 – 8, 10

Padmakarpo, 175, 260
Padmasambhava, 44, 158, 220
Pakistan, 80, 253, 285 – 286
Paldan Lhamo, see Devi
Panchen Lama, 157
Paneth, F. A., 171
Parvati ("The Mountaineer"), see Devi
Phadampa (Guru), 177, 216
Pho Chu ("Father River"), 35
Postcollision phase, 15
Pranavananda (Swami), 204
Precollision period, 14
Pundits, 60 – 61, 70
Puranas ("Ancient Stories"), 6

Qin Shi Huangdi, 180

Rainbow circle, 165, 168, 170
Ralpachan, 56
Rasa, see Lhasa
Religions of the World, 154
Religious traditions, 152 – 186
    See also specific religions, e.g., Bon religion; Buddhism
Rennell, James (Major), 144
Richenzanhgpo, 123
Rimpoche (Guru), 266
Rivers, 38 – 148, 188 – 220
    Ganges, 136 – 148
    Indus, 80 – 119
    Karnali, 134 – 136
    Sutlej, 122 – 133
    Yarlung Tsangpo, 40 – 76
Roberts, James (Major), 248 – 249
Rock carvings, 113
Route of the White Clouds, The, 12
Routes, 28, 35, 51, 92, 216
    map of, 224
Roy, Rammohan (Raja), 158
Rug hooking, 271
Ruttledge, Hugh, 248

Sacred Books of the East, 154
Sakya-Pandita, 154
Sakye sect, 232
Sarasvati (Goddess of Learning), 154, 189, 204
Sarasvati river, 202
Sati, see Devi
Schlaginweit, Adolf, 250
Sella, Vittorio, 251
Semiprecious stones, 270
Senge Khambah ("Lion's Mouth"), see Indus River
Seven Years in Tibet, 232
Sherpas, 232, 236, 237, 240, 249 – 250
Shiva, 184, 186
Sikkim, 72, 168, 236, 266, 284
Skardu, 100
Smyth, Edmund, 40
Songtsengampo (King of Tibet), 43, 44, 56, 58, 178
Sources of the History of the Bon Religion, 188, 202
Subduction, 14
Sundarananda (Swami), 147
Survey of India, 144, 148, 240
Sutlej river, 122

Tagore, Rabindranath, 154
Tensing Norgay, 48, 248
Tethyan Ocean, 7, 10, 12
Thangtonggyalpo, 35, 158, 217 – 220, 246, 271
Tharu tribe, 136
Thisongdetsen, 56
Thondup, Paldan (Sikkim King), 72
Thothori (King), 56
Throne of the Gods, 188
Tibet, 15, 39, 40, 42, 43 – 44, 56, 160, 165, 175, 177, 216, 222, 266, 281 – 283
    economy, 282 – 283
    history, 282
    religion, population, language, 282
Tichy, Herbert, 188
Transhimalayas, 15 – 16
Treaty of Simla, 51
Tselde (King), 128
Tsongkhapa, 157, 160
Tucci, Giuseppe, 56, 168, 248

Vedas ("Sacred Knowledge"), 156
Vishwamitra, Kaushika, 156
Vivekananda (Swami), 157

Waddell, L. A., 7
Wang Fu-chou, 248
Wangchuck, Jigme Dorje (King), 77
Webb, 146, 148
Wengcheng (Chinese Princess), 44, 58, 222
Wien, Karl, 250
Witches' Sabbath, 168

Xuanzang, 226

Yaks, 33, 51, 268, 270
Yarlung Tsangpo, 40 – 76
Yeti, 254 – 260
Young India, 158
Younghusband, 70